And Then Ther

Emma Sutton

First Edition, 2017
And Then There Were Four / Emma Sutton
ISBN 978-0-9955822-2-4

Published by Red 500 Ltd, UK
www.red500.co.uk
www.nibblesandbubbles.co.uk

This is a true story.

My name is Emma and my husband's name is Andy.

Other names and details have been changed to protect the two people who made our family a riot of love, chaos and magic.

For my father:
You always helped me see the funny side of life.
I only wish you could have met them, for together you would've had the
world in stitches.

For Andy, Nibbles and Bubbles:
Without you, this book would be called *Still One*, and the story would be a
lot less interesting. I love you to Ikea and back.

Contents

Contents

1. Spies Like Us

We are on a stakeout. Ways in which this is like a stakeout:
1) We are two adults sitting in the front of this car, staring into space.
2) We are going out of our minds with the monotony of it.

Cop shows know what the viewer wants — pace, action, adventure. Not soul-sucking tedium. Which is why they cut to the stakeout only seconds before something interesting happens. We have twenty-three more minutes of this; not exactly addictive viewing. We check our phones, sigh, wriggle, open and close the glovebox, fiddle with the seat positions, then the wing mirrors, then the radio settings. And wriggle. A lot.

Ways in which this is not like a stakeout:
1) There's no fast food in the car — not a burger, doughnut, coffee or soda in sight. To be honest, my stomach is wound so tight I couldn't eat a single thing without barfing.
2) We can't see the house we're 'staking out'. You might think it's a rookie error, but it's a crucial part of the plan.
3) In the back of the car are two child seats. You don't get that much in cop shows.

Upon reviewing these lists: this is nothing like a stakeout. It's a tad cloak-and-dagger; we're hiding out of sight until the Handover, so perhaps it's more like a cold-war spy exchange, although we've no spy to give them in return. Who am I kidding? We are two adults waiting twenty-three — no, now just twenty-two — minutes for something momentous to happen.

Handover is at 10 a.m. on the dot.

And we've arrived somewhat early. (I mutter 'somewhat', my husband snorts 'ridiculously' — and as my fingers yearn to thrum impatiently on the dashboard, 'ridiculously' seems to fit the bill.) I'm always early, whereas my husband is more of an on-time (his words) or cutting-it-superfine-if-not-late (my words) kinda guy. But Today is not a day to cut it fine.

The silence between us is intense. Not intense like the silence between people spoiling for a fight; no, it's intense because of the emotions that seep out of our pores. Powerful, extreme emotions that arise from the overwhelming importance of Today. A day we will never forget.

My body tingles and I don't know what to say, or if I even dare say anything at all in case I break the magic spell we're under. I am giddy, excited, nervous, scared, and all I can do is jig my leg incessantly. I should be ready, after all the preparation we've done and courses we've attended and forms we've filled in. But I am not. I am not ready.

I can't silence a mantra that fills me with dread . . .

'What have *we* done?' For in blame, we stand together.

(Cut to the not-stakeout: it just got worth watching again.) Our social worker arrives. We're released from the endless checking of our phones, which we justify by telling ourselves that 10 a.m. could suddenly sneak up and surprise us. She parks near us and walks over. I wind down my window. She leans in. She goes over The Plan again; The Plan we've listened to and agreed to during multiple meetings already. I feel like the stupid kids being told how to line up for assembly for the umpteenth time.

No, we won't go in.

Yes, we will act normal.

Yes, we will stick to The Plan.

We intone the words robotically, because there's no way we are blowing this, not when we have come so far, invested so much already. It's just another hoop to jump through. Yet nothing about this day is normal. We *normally* go in. We *normally* say hello. We *normally* have a cuppa. I *normally* don't feel this freaked out. Today my stomach churns, my knees wobble and I don't know whether to laugh, cry or puke.

We nod and promise to act normal, and then return to squirming limbo.

2

As ten o'clock advances, my emotions shift into overdrive. I'm shaking and look like I have the DTs. I need a distraction, so I thumb onto Facebook: 'Just four minutes to go, eep'. I post and run. I dare not read the messages on my timeline, for I am one 'Good luck' away from a blubbering wreck.

10 a.m.

Handover.

This is it.

For twenty-bleurgh minutes we've been stuck in time that wouldn't move. Now it has. Hundreds of seconds have crawled by and we're finally at the finishing line. I can barely breathe and wonder if I'm about to wake up from an out-of-body experience.

A shiver of relief courses through my body as we coast our car down the hill and onto their drive. We get out of the car and the doors *clunk*, *clunk*. We plaster on fake smiles and act normal. The front door swings open. There are no words today (weird), just contorted expressions, which I dare not engage with. We smile at the children and gently take them and their overnight bags into our arms, on the doorstep (weird). We're neither in nor out of their house: in neutral territory (double weird with knobs on). I focus on my little girl (for right now, calling her my daughter makes me feel like a fraud) and carry her to our car without a backwards glance. We strap them in, chatting about the fun we are going to have at the play gym today. They seem happy, excited, oblivious to what Today means.

As I pull on my own seat belt, I let out a *fuwoo*. I can breathe again.

The deed is done and I want to drive out of here as fast as possible, to leave behind the tension and the anguish and the strangeness in a squeal of rubber.

'Ready?' asks Andy as he revs the engine. Everyone's strapped in and yes is at the back of my throat but it stops at my molars. I jolt alert. My spidey senses are tingling. Something's wrong. What can it be? What have we forgotten?

'STOP!' I yell, as my brain solves the puzzle. 'Where are Nibbles and Bubbles?' The engine fades.

We search frantically under car seats and the children. Then I get out, dash to the back of the car and rifle through their overnight bags in the boot. I swear silently and profusely as the truth hits: they are not here, and if they are not here, they have to be in the house. Back in the house. The Plan didn't plan for this.

Nibbles and Bubbles are cuddly toys, a rabbit and a dog, but saying they're just toys is like saying Today is just Thursday. They are the first things we ever gave to our children, furry vehicles of hope and love saturated with such meaning they are elevated to the status of gods. Our daughter has not let go of Nibbles and loves her obsessively. We cannot leave without them.

'I'll go,' offers my husband, and I shrug him off in my frustrated impatience — a decision I will later regret. I storm quickly back to the house, deviating dangerously from The Plan and silently fuming that today of all days, we get this wrong. I stride through the front door and come face-to-face with things I was never meant to see.

'Where are Nibbles and Bubbles?' I demand abruptly, as I enter the front room. Ken turns away, wipes his face with his hand and starts scanning for the toys, but I've already seen too much.

There is devastation here.

Mary is crumpled against the wall, sobbing relentlessly, her knees buckled with the weight of this separation. Her grief, just beneath the surface these past few weeks, broke the moment that door closed.

We are not rescuing these children. They were rescued months ago.

We are ripping them from a family who loves them deeply. From people who held them when they knew not how to be held and went rigid with fear. A family who nurtured them through sleepless nights, panic and tantrums. A family who cherished them and taught them how to love and be loved. Mary made us promise that one day she would see the children again, 'Even if you're lying', she said, because she couldn't bear to think Today would be the end. So we made the pact, in a vain attempt to lighten her grief and assuage our guilt. I turn away, find the toys and dash out, unable to do anything to help. For we are the cause of their grief. Our gain is their loss. In every way that this is a happy day for us, it is a sad day for them.

I pout childishly. Annoyed that my special day has been tainted.

I slam their door behind me and run back to the car, away from the scene I want to forget. I hold the toys aloft, triumphant, feeling anything but. Then my little girl sees her bunny and delight spreads across her face like a sunrise on a glorious morning. She grabs her bunny and hugs her to suffocation.

I've saved the day. Yay for me. (I don't feel like celebrating.)

My husband drives off and asks if I'm okay, although I suspect he knows the answer. I stare out of the window and mumble 'not really'. I am filled with a sorrow that I did not invite to this party. I shake my head and turn to marvel at the sheer cuteness of our new additions — tiny perfect humans. One mass of curls with a bunny and one mischievous boy sit in those child seats. The girl reminds us constantly of who we have become: 'You're *my* mummy, *you're* my mummy, you're my *mummy*.' They have no idea what has just happened or what Today really means, and of that I am glad.

Today we take these children home.

Tonight they will sleep (or not) in our house, in cots that were prepped months ago. Their family of two joins our family of two and we become four. It feels like we've reached the end at last; the end of our long battle to become parents.

THE END

And Then There Were Two

Twelve Years Earlier . . .

2. Belle of the Ball

I am torn — wanting to linger and bask in the gentle glow of this late summer's day but needing to go in, for what waits inside is even more enticing. I am a sunshine girl. I love the coat-free, sock-free abandon of warm days, so why am I going into the hall of this grand Victorian house long past its heyday, with its tired décor and its wooden floor that desperately needs a coat or two of varnish?

Because this place is a new friend.

But on my first visit, it was a slightly disturbing stranger. That was a few months ago, as the seasons were warming up and I thought that it was odd then for a sunshine girl to hide in a gloomy roomful of strangers.

It's my first night. I'm shaking with nerves, so I arrive ridiculously early, even before the organisers, which gives me time — before the faded velour curtains close out the dusty sunbeams — to soak up my unfamiliar surroundings. The hall seems lonely in its emptiness: a room that aches for people to bring it to life, to give it purpose. I want to hug its loneliness away, and in doing so, hug my own away too.

I hang my bag and coat on a chair and pace purposefully, as if I'm analysing things rather than merely nibbling at time. I amble around with tourist eyes, gaping at everything. After a few minutes, the couple running the evening arrive and smile pleasantly, but they're busy setting up the sound system, sticking up signs and organising the cash desk. I try not to get under their feet. I potter to the toilet, plagued by a nervous bladder that sends high-level alerts with a frequency normally associated with cystitis.

I would've loved to arrive with a friend to make this experience less daunting and more familiar. But I couldn't wait. I'm impulsive

9

and wanted to come dancing. So, a few days after finding this class, I'm here, on my own. As I'm a chemical engineer, my work colleagues are mainly geeky men, all fully resistant to my suggestion that they come along and have fun. I have gritted my teeth and boldly set off anyway, but I yearn for someone familiar to stick out his arm so I won't bolt for the exit.

Eventually everything's ready and I need to pay for my lesson. Ann introduces herself and welcomes me, monies are exchanged and the evening begins. As I turn away from the cash desk, I face the man behind me in the queue — let's call him Bob. He's an elderly man, not particularly tall, and hunched over with arthritis. He has stiff shoulders, and I'll quickly learn to duck, or bob, under his arms during a spin because the first time I dance with him I nearly knock myself out spinning right smack into his low arm with my face. For now, Bob is just an old man, and I notice something that stops me in mid-step. I stare then clamp my jaw shut.

Slowly, with rosy embarrassment, I point a tentative finger to the left side of his head. I whisper, 'Cotton bud,' with exaggerated mouthing. He raises his arm to where I'm pointing. 'There's a cotton bud sticking out of your ear,' I continue softly. It's bright blue, poking out horizontally from his left ear, and I wonder how many people he's bumped into between his bathroom and this venue. *Did he come on the bus?* I shake that thought away so laughter doesn't dilute the compassion I want my face to portray. More wrinkles join the deep crevasses on his face as he gropes for the bud and pulls it out. He looks almost as surprised as I do. I slink off. Surely nothing can be as weird as that?

People arrive, strip off their coats, swap shoes and then stand in straight lines on the dance floor, and I get caught up in it all. I'm too busy concentrating on my own body and what my arms and legs are doing to remember much of the details of my first contorted attempts to dance. I twirl and whirl and giggle at my mistakes and love every single minute of it. The male host, Rob, comes over for a dance near the end of the night. In his arms, I float gracefully across the floor, and the music and magic light up my face. He asks, 'Are you enjoying yourself?' Joy gushes out of my mouth. He knows, as I do, that I'm hooked; dance is my new crack.

I've come every week, bar my summer holiday, when I felt the pangs of withdrawal. The hall has developed a glow, as if my joy has mended its cracked paint. In this faded room I've felt a giddy, sober ecstasy — the sublime combination of music and movement, that heady rush of being truly and wonderfully alive.

On my first day back I noticed some new faces in the room, and one of them has been having a peculiar effect. I'm awkward and self-conscious, a teenager with a crush, flushed with anticipation that I hope doesn't reach my cheeks, for it may give the many single men in this room the wrong impression, and I don't want to fend anyone off tonight. Well, except him. I arrived early and I'm now standing in a row of women opposite a row of men; Ceroc is a partner dance. There are sometimes more men than women, sometimes more women than men, so the extras line up off the dance floor, waiting for their turn to join in. I take little notice of the man before me as I drape my fingers over his loose palm at waist height, listening as the teacher walks us through tonight's moves.

In Ceroc, the man is in charge; he leads the dance, he chooses the moves and his hands alone tell me where to go. A firm palm held vertically at waist height and I'm likely to be pushed away into a holdless, on-the-spot spin. A hand held over my head and I'm turned in a spin under his arm, sometimes led as I whirl. A hand offered behind his back and I travel behind him and around. It is my job to respond, to be guided and never to lead. It's a hard lesson to learn. If I anticipate what comes next, my body is rigid, inflexible and I twist my arm in a way that will twinge for hours afterwards. I'm not used to letting a man be in charge — I'm too much of a fiercely independent free-spirit for that (as I write myself the heroine's part). But in Ceroc, I've learnt to go with the flow, to leave what happens next in someone else's hands, in direct contrast to my job as an engineer, where it's all about predicting and calculating the future with certainty.

An experienced dancer can lead a relaxed novice to heaven, spinning her elegantly across the dance floor until she feels like Belle at the ball — floating on delight and wonder, moving at one with the rhythm and her partner. There are a lot of men here: some of them are young, some older, some bold, some shy. And some hold you a little too tight in their overly damp hands. Whilst I smile and dance and twirl at their slightest behest, they are not him.

I go through the moves, constantly searching above the heads of the crowd, scanning the room for the head I ache to see. He's not here; my heart sinks. As the men move on and we practise again, I notice a few more stragglers turning up and joining the queue.

Is it? Is it?

I strain to look . . . Yes! He's here! Joy of joys, and my little heart flutters. I'm as giddy as a teenage girl at a Duran Duran/Take That/Hanson concert (choose as appropriate, depending on your age). I start counting — how many women lie on the snake between him and me? Sixteen. How many places are they moving after each turn? It was two; now with more spares, it's three. Will the man I seek stand before me? Does sixteen divide by three? Do I even need to ask myself that question? My heart beats a fast tempo in my chest.

What is happening to me?

The object of my pounding heart is tall. He might as well be ten foot tall, for as tall as he is, I am not. I don't want a tall man, although it does make him easy to spot across a room. He is also bald. Now, I'm no longer in my twenties, but I am decades from my sixties, and I love raking my fingers through a thick head of hair. I have a sneaky feeling that he might be in IT. I don't know what tells me that, but after Husband No. 1 (a story for another time), that's pretty low on my list of 'must-haves'. Don't get me wrong, I'm not super fussy about the men in my life (my marriage and soon-after divorce of Husband No. 1 compelling evidence of my lack of fastidiousness or good judgement or something). And I'm nowhere near as finicky as my friend who once rejected a guy who made her howl with laughter because his spelling was atrocious. Spelling is at least obscured, whereas this man is a receding colossus for everyone to see. But despite his too-tall-too-bald-ness, there's something that happens when he holds my hand, when he dances with me. I can't explain it and I can't stop it happening either. And I'm not sure I want to.

It all began the first time he reached out for the starting hold. I draped my fingers over his curved open hand (it's called a hold, but it's more of a touch), and I felt something. Like a static shock from a polyester jumper taken off too quickly, but more pleasant. I shy away from such romantic terms as 'magnetic', if only because the scientist in me would tut heavily at the airy-fairyness of it all. Yet there's something that draws me to him like flies to one of those blue buzzing lights in a Greek restaurant, even though on paper he ticks none of the boxes.

When I dance with him, I feel . . . I feel . . . what?

I feel like a lady (no, Shania, not a woman). As if in that touch, I'm transported into a Victorian period drama, all bustle and lace and curtsies. Not powerless or feeble, but elegant, feminine, cherished, strong. There's something about the way he moves, something about his gentle giantness that makes me feel utterly safe and protected. I want to rush into his arms, have them wrap around me and hide within them forever, like I did in my blanket-and-chairs den as a child. I don't even know his name. But this longing ruins my appetite and stops my brain working at full capacity. I become a fumbling, mumbling moron. Maybe I am just coming down with the flu.

A few weeks later, I pluck up the courage to talk to him (it wasn't the flu), and I find out that he's called Andy and he does indeed work in IT. My heart sinks a little, but it's too late to matter, for I am one smitten kitten. Did I actually type that? Before you know it, I will have written his initials and mine in a heart on my notebook and covered it with kisses and flowers and perfume. My heart is hammering in my chest but I have to strike now; he's pulling on his coat.

'Would you like to go for a drink?' I stammer, the words falling out of my mouth in an inelegant tumble as I feign indifference.

'I'd like to, but I can't. I have washing to do,' he replies with a let-her-down-gently smile.

Washing?

To say I leave deflated would be wrong. I leave utterly confused. It's the worst excuse I've ever heard. Why couldn't he just get it over with and reject me outright with a no? At least then I'd know where I stand. Now I don't know what to think. Is 'washing' the new shorthand for 'being gay'? Should I make a fool of myself and ask again, or . . . or what?

I decide to wait and see what happens next week, and of course, he doesn't turn up. Argh! Is he avoiding me now? I've been living my weeks in a daze, waiting for these few hours every Monday evening. I leave empty, though filled with the magic of twirling.

A few weeks later still, my confusion has thawed, the anger at my rejection melted by my obsession. I change tactics, looking for another way to reel him into my web (mwah ha ha). Instead of asking him out for a drink, I ask if he'd like to join a group of us going to a Friday night dance at a big dance hall. He says he'd like to (yippee! . . . whoa, hang on, there's more to come) but it's his sister's birthday. *Oh for goodness' sake*, I think as I nod sagely, aiming to portray an 'it's okay, stuff happens' facial expression as my brain does a *bugger, bugger, bugger* dance.

I've never pursued anyone in my life. Is the fact that I am a divorcee making me stick around when I should give up? He's making this hard work and I'm not patient nor one for chipping away relentlessly in order to get what I want. I'm a want-it-get-it-take-it-home-tonight kind of gal. I think of giving up in my frustration, and yet I know I won't.

And then one night, four months after his first excuse, two months after I rejected the softly-softly approach and started flinging myself at him like a brazen hussy, I ask him back to mine and he says yes. *Oh well*, I think.

I stop.

Did he just say yes? Really?

I look into his face and it's definitely a yes face.

Oh My Giddy Aunt.

We spend a heady, pinch-me weekend together. We go for a walk around a wintry reservoir. There's snow on the trees and I feel like the lead in a chick flick it's so perfect. The snow is angelic, the food is a gastronomic delight, my hand fits in his like a kid's in an enormous goalie glove and the scenery on our walk is frame after frame of *Planet Earth*, to the point I repeat 'it's so pretty' so many times I embarrass myself (and he pokes fun and we both laugh at how predictable I am). I think, *Life just doesn't get any better than this*, because if I say it out loud I might frighten him off. I look on the world with undisguised wonder (let's hope he's too tall to notice), such that even that patch of damp plaster in my kitchen looks like a slightly lopsided heart.

I skip into work on Monday feeling light and wonderful, and my colleagues wink at each other in their knowingness. We turn on our computers and check our emails as we chat about our weekends and they fish for gossip. And mid-sentence, my wonderful-weekend story is brought to an abrupt halt. My phone rings and I pick it up, wondering just what manufacturing incident has happened that needs my urgent attention.

It's not a voice I expected to hear. How odd and surprising — it's my twin sister on the phone. She never rings me at work.

'Has Claire spoken to you?' she asks softly and tentatively. Hairs prickle on my neck.

'No. Why?' Even as I ask the question I know that this is no ordinary phone call.

'I'm sorry to have to tell you . . .' And I don't want to hear what comes next because her voice is burdened with sorrow.

My father is dead.

Life stops, like a freeze-frame. The conversation interrupted by her call will never be finished. I put the phone down and stare at my wall for a moment. My colleagues blather on unheard. Then as my emotions catch up, I run out of the office, tears pouring down my face so that I can barely see. I want to run away from this moment but I can't outrun my grief. I barrel into a friend and he steers me into a small room, where I sob uncontrollably and wish this moment were different. He pats my hand. Just as I welcome a new man into my life, I lose another. It's so unfair. *He'll never get to meet him*, I think, and wonder which him is which.

My worlds clash in tragic Shakespearean juxtaposition. Over the next week or so, the sublime, skipping ecstasy of new love is jumbled and contorted with overwhelming grief and loss. I dance giddily with Andy, barely able to believe my luck, my heart leaping at his touch and melting with his kiss; I share grief with my family, reading the 'in sympathy' cards that arrive and picking the songs to play at my dad's funeral. Poor Andy, thrust into one of the most draining emotional scenes of my life. Yet he's kind and patient, listening to my woes and my silences, never interrupting, never trying to stem my tears, just holding me until I don't need to be held anymore.

And as inauspicious as our beginning is, it forges us into the couple we become.

A few years later, Andy receives notice to move out of his flat. *Coincidentally*, he suggests that now might be the perfect time to move in together (thank you, Landlord). Not only do we decide to move in together, but we decide to buy a house together, which Andy tells me is a Big Deal. Buying a house turns out to be a real exploration of our different approaches to life — his thoughtful, considered, analyse-all-the-facts approach versus my I-love-this-let's-pay-full-price-and-move-in-now approach. After a great deal of pleading, I win and we buy a house that I fell in love with at first sight and it's a year before I even notice all the faults Andy pointed out.

It takes Andy a few years to recover from that Big Deal, and then one Twixtmas evening, we are lying in bed snuggled under the Christmas fairy lights that are so girlie I'm amazed he let them stay.

'Will you marry me?' he asks, in a tone that's all 'shall we turn off the lights?'

I sit upright. I rub my eyes. It takes me a moment to gather my wits and be sure that he really said what I think I heard him say as it's nearly midnight, way past snore o'clock.

'Yes,' I say hesitantly, not because I'm unsure about what to say, but because I'm still not one hundred percent certain that he actually just asked me. As I look deep into his eyes, the twinkles tell me that yes, he did just ask me to marry him.

'Yes, yes, yes, yes,' I blurt out, in case the stupid grin and giddy dance weren't clear enough.

We're going to get married. (About blooming time.)

And we've already decided that we both want children.

So, one family, coming up.

3. A Bellyful of Baby

She's about to ruin my day and it's nothing to do with the needle in her hand.

I'm at the surgery, waiting to be inoculated against bugs and bites. We're not just planning a wedding but also a month-long honeymoon of a lifetime. Australia was high on the list, being halfway around the world, but going to an ex-colony sounded too tame, too ordinary. After all, they even speak our language — ish. So we looked for exotic and chose the traditional honeymoon destination of Cambodia. Hence the jabs.

After our midnight engagement, we dillied and dallied for months, telling ourselves there was loads of time to get ready for the wedding, until there wasn't. Now we're in serious panic mode. I rang a tent hire company in June, three months before the wedding — not just any tent but a funky Bedouin tent, for I'm too much of a snob to settle for a plastic marquee. A few drapes, cushions and carpets are worth re-mortgaging our house.

'Which dates are you after?' the never-even-seen-a-Bedouin lady asks. I hear her skimming through a paper diary on her desk.

'September 25, for a day,' I reply.

'And which yar?' Her accent is plummy, and 'year' sounds sickeningly posh.

'This year,' I reply, with a tone that's all 'isn't that bleeding obvious?'

'This yar?' Her voice squeaks and I can hear her flicking rapidly back through a year of diary pages in shock and disbelief. Should I say that it's a shotgun wedding to make our inconsiderate lack of preparation more acceptable? Despite her snooty assertions that they're booked for yars ahead, they can miraculously, if not magnanimously, fit us in.

It's now a few weeks before our especially expensive day, which we're stretching over two days so we can mix a legal ceremony in the local registry office with our own humanist ceremony and invite more people (still a tiny fraction of Andy's hoard of aunts and uncles, never mind his cast-of-a-West-End-musical number of cousins) and quadruple the cost. Plans are finally coming together and I'm starting to imagine that it's just a hop, skip and bonk before we'll add children to the happy mix of our union. *After all, the minute that ring is on my finger, we can stop using protection and make a baby,* I think wistfully.

'What?' I wake from my daydream and listen intently. The nurse pulls the needle from my arm and repeats herself.

'As long as you don't start trying for a baby on your wedding night.'

Come again? I frown. *Isn't that the dream?* We get married, have wild, abandoned, unprotected sex in the days that follow and, hey presto, we come back with thousands of photographs we never sort out or print, some carved-by-locals Buddhas and a tiny clump of cells in my womb. Apparently not.

She's brought reality into this fantasy, uninvited. I wonder, would I have chosen malarial Asia had I realised the full consequences of exotica? She gives me a stark choice — we can either take measures to avoid getting malaria or we can start trying for a family. But not both.

'But we can start when we get home?' I ask, meaning the very second we walk through the bedroom door, if not in the hallway.

'Nope.'

We have to finish taking the tablets (for another two weeks after we get home) and then wait a few more weeks before we can start phase two of our 'married couple with children' plan.

Oh well, maybe it's not too bad. When the honeymoon memories are fresh, and just after our tans (and our friends' interest in yet another honeymoon anecdote) have worn off, we can make a bellyful of baby.

Once the chemicals are no longer coursing through our veins, we take up the challenge and dive feet-first (well not feet, as such) into making a baby. We're filled with naïve optimism about how easy it's going to be — after all, everyone I know has knocked them out as easily as toast, including my twin sister and my mum, so I'm bound to have the same fertile genes.

We're like giddy teenagers whose parents have gone on holiday and left them to look after the house. We want to make the most of this exciting opportunity to be naughty together. We're not sex maniacs, we're trying for a baby, which makes it not only okay but positively encouraged by the man upstairs. We find new and inventive ways to squeeze more opportunities into every week, and being someone who rises to a challenge (even though that's Andy's part in the bargain), I throw myself into the process with unfettered enthusiasm.

The next few months are a lot of fun: a riot of contorted facial expressions, tingles, curled toes and yeses. I spend time with an Eiffel tower of pillows under my bum, during which I am forbidden to cough or sneeze, in case I create a tidal wave away from my womb. As I yield to the blissful daze of post-coitus sleep, I smile smugly, thinking of where the strongest swimmers are going, and snuggle into my husband's chest.

I coyly welcome him home with a big smack on the lips, a none-too-subtle wink, a too-tight hug. Our spaghetti bolognese congeals. But even cold pasta can't dampen our mischievous wantonness. We sneak in quickies before work in the morning and miss our favourite shows. Our previously demure routine is thrown gloriously out of the window, and we enjoy a time of messing about with the novelty of having sex that can (whispered tones of reverence, please) make. a. baby. *giggles*

After several months, we can't help thinking it'd be a lot easier if we were a bit, if not a *lot* younger. Sex is far more tiring than either of us remembered, and we ache in places we'd forgotten even had muscles. We crawl out of bed hunched over like geriatrics. We fight to wake up from our orgasmic haze. Time just evaporates as our bodies grapple with these new demands. But we're buoyed by the possibility of becoming parents and the newness of all this romping; nothing is going to stop us from having some fantastic news to share. And we won't have to keep this up for long, will we?

As winter strikes, the house becomes colder and it takes more convincing to jump into a fridge-cold bed and do the dance of desire. We find reasons to put it off until later, and later tonight slides to later tomorrow to later this week and we start to get worn out by it all.

We'd started at a sprint when we should have prepared for a marathon.

4. Is There an App for That?

'How's it going?' ask our friends and family, keen for news. But we've nothing to say. My answer lies between a rock and an ice-cold bed. *If there were news I'd have blurted it out before you even drew breath. Since I haven't, there's either nothing to report or I am doing an incredible (and highly improbable) job of keeping a secret.*

Should I declare 'we've had sex every night for the last ninety days straight and my lady garden is starting to get sore, but no babies'? Or confess that after a few months, the novelty of all-you-can-bonk sex has started to wear off and I just want to curl up and sleep? Do I share my concerns about the stork? We've come to the startling revelation that the magic baby, who turns up the very first time you have unprotected sex and is brought by the optimism stork, is not going to arrive as quickly as we thought. Having done the maths of doubt, I've calculated that I might not be as fertile as either my mum or my twin sister since both were nearly a decade younger when they popped out children as easily as bursting bubble wrap. My fertility is declining as steeply as my interest in sex (didn't we have it *last* week?)

Every month, I begin hopeful, but each Rorschach of blood confirms my failure to breed. With each tampon I discard, I leave a bit of my hope with it in the bin, and doubt grows like thrush to replace it. But we keep going until all the romance, luxurious foreplay and sensual cuddling is squeezed out and we're left with a just-get-it-over-with-will-you? sperm injection. We drag ourselves upstairs to do the deed, slouched like teenagers being told to tidy their rooms, with a silent 'Do I have to?'

We need help.

We turn to the infinite wisdom and contradiction of Google. We stick to websites written by MD-type doctors and it seems we are prematurely concerned. Most couples need to wait *two years* before bothering their GP; in fact (the online doctors continue in a slightly patronising tone), the couples who seek help after just one year *would* have conceived the following year without any poking and prodding *if only* they hadn't been so darned impatient. *How can they possibly know that?* I wonder, but I leave my scepticism with my libido in the fridge. We've been trying for only a year so agree to keep going, hoping the extra year will do it.

We've already tried the saner pieces of advice that friends have slipped surreptitiously into conversation: we've stuffed pillows under me until my bottom is so high that I say hello to parts I haven't seen in years; I munch on vitamins and folic acid; and I don't jump up like a gymnast off the parallel bars the minute he finishes. But if we're going to keep at it for another year, we need to preserve what little sexual steam remains. Instead of bonking whenever and wherever we can, we need to be strategic and focus on days when the eggs are ready and waiting, which is only a few days a month and gives us the confidence we might even make it to the end of another year.

But which days to play Humpty Bumpty?

Filled with the conviction that bonking on the wrong days is all that's standing between us and a child, we buy a fertility thermometer. We're looking for a slight rise in temperature that occurs on ovulation, and confidently expect a temperature landscape of Holland, all flat, flat, flat, flat, oops *trip* flat, flat. Sorted. I take my temperature and jot the numbers down. After a few days, I don't need Excel to know that the figures aren't the straight-line-then-blip that we were expecting. I read the instructions and find out I've been rather blasé about this subtle and precise temperature stuff. I need to put the glass tube underneath my tongue at exactly the same time every single day, preferably whilst I'm still half asleep, and then wait two minutes without doing the pee dance or muttering complaints under my breath. Hmm. I spend several months waking at 7 a.m., *even at the blooming weekend*, to scribble numbers down whilst Andy snores until I poke him awake. My temperature snakes around the chart with the raggedness of the stock market after Lehman Brothers or Trump (or whatever the latest financial-disaster-then-recovery is). Months of data and not a single clear peak in sight. Why? Well (according to further research), it can be affected by not sleeping well (check), stress (who wouldn't be with that rigmarole every morning?), infections (uh-huh) or even wine — ah. When we first started trying for children, like a good mum-to-be I stopped drinking; I was full of enthusiasm, what did I need wine for? My enthusiasm has run out and I'm shoring it up with boxes of Rioja. I wasn't prepared to be teetotal for more than a few months, and we're now in month fifteen of what's proving to be a long haul.

After three more months of wiggly temperatures, we're still not pregnant.

With glee, I throw the fertility thermometer away and swap it for plastic pee sticks that test the first pee of the day, even if I sleep in until 9 a.m. at the weekend. (Woo flipping hoo.) This is the one, I can just feel it. I buy a hundred and begin peeing on them every morning, waiting for the strip to turn pink. And I wait . . .

Andy and I frown over the results, comparing today's with yesterday's, moving the stick under different light, searching for a faint stripe, asking, 'Do you think that's a yes?' One hundred not-sures later, we're less than impressed.

Another three months and we're still not pregnant.

Enter Plan D. Why didn't we geeks think of this sooner? Of course, there's an app for that. Andy and I spend sixty-nine pence each buying different apps that promise to tell us the best day to bonk. We enter the start and end dates of my menstruation and the apps send us notifications (flowers in my case) that nudge us with a 'do it now'. Surely this technological breakthrough will be the answer to our slightly tardy, if not on strike, stork.

I notice a little blood blot on my toilet paper.

Strange, I think.

I refer to the app that contains all my hopes and dreams and it tells me that I am mid-cycle.

Odd. It's not my period then.

As I stand up, I glance into the bowl.

My breath catches in my throat. My mouth dries to sand. My knees are rice pudding.

Surely not . . .

I peer closer, barely daring to confirm it. And there it is.

A tiny group of cells, nothing really, and yet everything too.

It's our dream — where Andy's sperm and my egg joined to create a new life.

It's miniscule and yet that little clump of flesh and blood contains our hope. *Our* flesh and blood. Then my brain rushes in and starts asking all sorts of awkward questions and I almost convince myself it's nothing and wonder if I'm just torturing myself and so I call out sorrowfully to Andy. As he comes into the bathroom, all I can do is to point mutely to the toilet bowl.

He looks closely.

'Is it?' I ask, voice quivering.

He turns and looks at me with love in his eyes and nods with kind softness.

That small group of cells could have been something — a baby, a life, a promise, a future, a boy or a girl, yet it couldn't hang on. It's the closest we have come to being pregnant; a baby who never made it past the first few days of life.

'What do we do?' I ask with a broken voice, and wonder if there is more to that question than flush or scoop. We decide that there's no point bundling it into tissues to show the doctor.

I can't bring myself to let go of the hope that those cells represent. I feel I'd be flushing away my dream, our dream of being a family. Silently Andy turns the lever and sends it away.

Am I grieving for this clump of cells? Or am I grieving instead for the slow, lingering death of our hope? Can I really keep going through this heartache and failure? Can I keep holding on to the fragile idea of being a family? Because we lost this baby before we even knew we had it, my emotions are all over the place, sorrow at their core. We leave the bathroom like silent mourners at the graveside.

It's hard to describe just how demoralising trying for years to start a family can be, as the sands trickle through your fertility hourglass and you start to wonder if there's any beach left. Despite how sad

I feel though, there is a grain of hope to take from this funeral. We did at least make a baby, so perhaps we can make another one. One that will hold on this time.

I'm going swimming and I'm late.

Waiting for the pool to open (of course I'm not late arriving at the pool, surely you know me better than that?), I stand in a surreal bubble of joy. Skipping might look crazy and get me shouted at by the lifeguards. An impervious sphere blinds me to everything that doesn't match my serene bliss. I dive in with the poise of Tom Daley and swim through the turquoise water of Hawaii. Swimmers who bump into me are wondrous dolphins gently nudging me with their noses. I carve through the water with the effortless grace of Ellie Simmonds (I wanted to say David Wilkie, but his moustache tickled my prose).

In the shower earlier this morning, the usual custard-and-Marmite combination of thoughts floated through my brain: *Why do egg yolks go grey if you boil them too hard? What makes towels stay fluffy forever? (Aunty Sally can do it, why can't I?) What is it about the molecular structure of glass and water that makes them transparent?* Followed by a huffier, *Why didn't Andy replace the shower gel when he used it up yesterday?* Amongst this smorgasbord of randomness, another question popped in to say hello. *Shouldn't I have had my period by now?*

I react nonchalantly, but a second thought joins in: *You're right, I should have had it by now.* I get out and I check the app — my period should've started days ago. *Oh . . . I'm late . . .*

The word *late* burns as fast as a fuse through my detachment and awakens something that has been hibernating inside me: hope.

My hope is stood on a beach. The weather's blustery and wild, the wind tousles my hair, the sand tickles my bare feet, a flapping coat billows behind me as I stride over the dunes to crest the hill and meet that enchanting moment when the world opens and the sea and horizon appear before me. Next to me, her hand in mine, is a girl, my little girl, her hair dancing in the breeze. I never see her face but I imagine her giggle as we skip and dance together. I feel light, joyful, happy. I have dreamt this scene many times, even forcing it to come when hope was slipping away.

As I snapped out of it, I remembered that last night I dreamt we had a little girl and called her Alice. *Well if that's not a sign, I don't know what is,* I think. Two microscopic crumbs of data, and they start to take on unimaginably potent form. I've waited for this moment for so long that I can barely believe it's here, outside my dream. Could this be the day that I wait with giddy anxiousness for Andy to come home and shock him with the news that we can stop all the second-rate sex?

Until that moment this morning, when my heart clung to it like a barnacle to a boat hull, I hadn't realised just how much my hope was riddled with spongiform holes. My body aches to have a life growing inside it. I want to choose colours for our nursery, start comparing the technical specs of prams and make a mood board from *Mamas & Papas* catalogues.

I hug my joy as I go for my lunchtime swim, wrapped in an effervescent glow of smugness. All the thermometers, pee sticks and app notifications have paid off. They were right, those doctors — if you keep trying for that second year, you will become pregnant. I take off my metaphorical hat to them. This changes everything. The monochrome monotony of infertility has gone on a colour run and returned smattered with paint.

I chat to the little bunch of cells growing inside me. I tell them how excited I am, how much I love them (oh how I love them), how long we've waited for them, how incredible their life is going to be. I start to imagine what they will look like — tall and slender like Andy, or rounded and soft like me? With each stroke, the certainty grows, until I can almost feel a tiny bulge in my belly. I caress my swimsuit where the baby is growing and wonder if the hormones are affecting me; I'm besotted already.

A glorious, isn't it lovely, isn't the receptionist friendly and happy, isn't this locker just the right size, don't those two-sizes-too-small silver Speedos on that portly middle-aged man make him look like a hunk, aren't the women chatting side by side with full make-up the perfect addition to the pool, isn't this dribble of ice-cold water invigorating, isn't life grand type moment of gorgeousness. Superlatives gradually run out and I say 'awesome' because my brain is so filled with dopamine that I can no longer think of anything other than unicorns, rainbows and Disney clichés. If I'm not careful, I'll go all *Umbrellas of Cherbourg* and start narrating my every move in song!

I leave the pool oozing with the confidence of Ursula Andress, hovering over the slippery tiles, every sensation gloriously heightened: my towel is softer than ever before, my skin caressed by its touch; the hairdryer sends shivers of pleasure down my spine. I will never forget this moment. It is everything I have been waiting for, and now (thank you, Universe, bless you, angels) it is here. I just want to savour this moment, to stand in the sunshine (it's sure to be shining somewhere in the world) and grin until my face aches. I feel utterly grateful and blessed and amazing and awesome and just WOW.

I drive home via the chemist's and buy not just one but a double test, for if Hollywood has taught me anything (other than how scared I should be in a multistorey car park at night), it's that I need to have dozens of positives piled strategically around the bathroom if Andy is to pick up the hint. I hug this moment to me — the start of a brand-new chapter in our lives. With the broadest grin on my face, I pee on the first stick as I plan which pram to buy. I *know*. Deep inside I know, but I want a stick to wave at Andy.

And as I raise it to my eyes, I'm giddy, excited to see that blue sign that will confirm the incredible I-can't-believe-it's-taken-so-long, at-last-the-wait-is-over news. Oh glorious day, finally you are here and you're forgiven for being so incredibly late.

I glance at the stick and my grin flattens.

Oh.

That's not right.

I must've read the instructions wrong. I wait a little bit longer in case I've peeked too soon. I glance back to the stick . . . and the pack . . . and the stick . . . and the pack and stick and pack, stick, pack, stick and my smile melts. I cling to denial like a toddler to Mr Blankie.

But . . .

What about my dream? What about Alice? What about the app?

And as I lay my evidence out, I see how flimsy and insubstantial it was.

I skip a few stages of Kübler-Ross and fast forward to depression.

For a few hours, our dream was pulled kicking and screaming back into my life, and now it's disappeared faster than partying teenagers when the cops turn up. *Stupid, hateful, lying app* (back to anger then). I want to destroy my phone for its hideous betrayal. Before Andy comes home, my period starts and the whole sorry story is over.

We are still not pregnant.

I start to wish I'd met Andy sooner, that he'd never had washing to do, that I'd never wasted so much time in the wasteland that was my first marriage, that I'd never taken the pill, that I'd eaten better, that wine wasn't quite so lovely, that I'd been at my ideal weight — and a million other things that may or may not have wrecked my chances of conceiving.

But we're not giving up yet, not until we exhaust every route. And neither are our friends.

As our reserves of hope dwindle dangerously low, our friends and family struggle with the helplessness of it all. They want to support us, but since they can't exactly come over, nudge us both upstairs wagging their fingers and exhorting 'And don't come down until your baby is made', or start cheerleading during the act itself, they resort to the next best thing: offering random and creative suggestions as to how we might improve our odds. The conversation always starts with 'A friend of ours . . .' And I think, *Goody, they've been sharing our inability to get pregnant in casual conversation with their son's friend's PE teacher and the lady at the sweetshop.*

'. . . was having trouble conceiving . . .' *Hmm. A one-person study is hardly scientifically valid.*

'. . . and they took a vacation . . .' *You can buy babies as well as cigs in duty-free?*

'. . . quit their job . . .' *Because infertile and unemployed is an irresistible combination.*

'. . . got a dog . . .' *WTF? I think the RSPCA would have things to say about that one. So not happening.*

Not once do I jump up, punch the air with both fists and say, 'Good God, woman, I wish we'd known this years ago! You mean we need to put his thingymaoozit up my flumpet?'

We've read books, studied pages of online advice and used pee sticks, thermometers and apps scientifically proven to help — to no avail. We've struggled through another six months of tactical sex injections with our desire account in serious overdraft. By month twenty-three, even two apps sending us flowers and hearts isn't enough to rouse us from our sexual listlessness.

Now we're reduced to websites spouting stuff about wishing wells, fairies and Area 59, just in case some combination of sage smudging, crystals in my pants, manuka honey smeared anticlockwise on our nipples, a position that even a yoga instructor would struggle to hold for more than ten seconds, a new moon in Venus and some foul-tasting hot twigs affecting to be drinkable is The Answer. Perhaps we should start dowsing to detect ovulation? What am I saying?

And we're still not pregnant.

We need help.

Proper, professional help. Someone with proper qualifications framed on the wall, someone who'll discover where the problem lies and solve it.

We go to the doctor.

Turns out, we should've gone sooner.

5. A Professional Diagnosis

'YES, WE'VE HAD PLENTY OF BLOOMIN' SEX.' That's what I want to shout.

We're sat with our GP squirming in awkwardness. He's asked a few questions and skirted around the key issues as we discuss our inability to get pregnant without anyone mentioning the words 'penis', 'vagina' or even 'sex'. It's like watching a movie that gets suddenly steamy while your grannie is next to you on the sofa. The room is replete with embarrassed silences, unfinished sentences and lack of eye contact. We were just hoping for a simple answer to our problems.

'Have you actually . . . ?' he asks, leaving the sentence hanging.

'Yes, we have, quite a lot in fact, for quite a long time,' I reply, biting my lip to avoid admitting that our frequency has hit rock bottom of late.

After more discomfort and more unfinished phrases, he refers us to the fertility unit and we close the door with a sigh of relief — surely nothing else will be that uncomfortable? We leave with a scrap of hope, presuming the experts will find something to fix so we can go our merry way with the distributor cap (or genital equivalent) properly aligned.

A few weeks later, we commence testing. I expect a barrage of tests using all the incredible equipment and knowledge of a modern medical society but am supremely disappointed to discover there are just three tests in total. And not only that, but the specialists peddle discomfort as effortlessly as our doctor — more weirdness, prodding and euphemisms. If we had a baby for every awkward silence, we could've populated the actors and their understudies for *The Waltons*. They check my blood for hormones, Andy has a chilling experience in a locked room and I have an ultrasound that was not the ultrasound I wanted to have.

After the too-few tests, we return to the clinic eager to discover the problem and its matching solution so we can finally have a child.

Andy's sperm is okay, we're told. Must be me then?

My hormones are okay. Not me then? My tubes and womb look normal.

Hmm. Curiouser and curiouser. None of the usual suspects. Whodunnit?

We wait expectantly for our specialist to put all the clues together and solve the mystery in true Agatha Christie style. The doctor lowers her voice in dramatic fashion and reveals the official diagnosis to her 'expectant' audience:

'You have unexplained infertility.'

What?

That's it?

I feel cheated. It's like reading a murder mystery and finding out it was twins. You can't do that to us. We posed a searching and important question to highly qualified medical specialists with the best equipment and diagnostic tools available, and all we get is a shoulder shrug and a 'dunno'?

'We could have offered you IVF,' she continues, 'if only you'd come sooner.'

If we'd come after one year of trying, I would have been thirty-nine, and therefore offered one free cycle of IVF on the NHS. But we took the advice on the NHS website and waited, so at forty, I'll have to pay for it myself. The doctor highly recommends IVF and impresses upon us the urgency of starting right away. She also suggests an ovulation stimulant called Clomid, but again stresses we should start IVF now. We leave to ponder our options.

Of course, no sooner do we hint at it than our friends and family tell us stories of those who had IVF and now have gorgeous babies. We search for clinics near us that have successfully got a woman my age pregnant (they are rare) and the baby to term using IVF (there aren't any). We widen the net, prepared to travel hundreds of miles if it comes to it. Still nothing. It's an expensive, intrusive lottery. And our chances are as slim as winning the national one (I don't even buy a ticket).

That just leaves Clomid. We can take it once, for six months, and it might help. We think about it, but we're not ready for that one shot. My work life is becoming increasingly unstable and volatile, and the stress I'm under could break the final arrow in our quiver.

A few months later, after weeks of tears at home and in the office, I decide life is too short to put up with a tyrant for a boss and quit. Feeling far less stressed, we return to the fertility clinic and ask to go on Clomid. Doctor Number Three nods, looks at our records and says that I need a fresh blood test, as the last one is now out of date. Oh. I'd hoped to leave with a prescription and a solution in hand. *It's just another hoop,* I think. No problem. So I wait for the right point in my cycle and go to hospital to give another tube of blood. When we return for the results a month later, we see Doctor Number Four.

I am filled with tingly energy. It makes me bounce as I struggle to keep it under wraps.

This is it. Our chance to have a child of our own.

The final plan in this long and trying journey, the chemical sticking plaster that will heal us both. Six months of popping pills and it will boost my eggs or something and then we'll make one that clings on, that stays in my womb and becomes our first beloved child. I'm excited, confident, looking forward to solving this problem and making a baby.

Andy holds my hand and I smile at him; I'm glad he's here.

We're almost there and I can feel a baby playing peekaboo just around the corner of a packet of pills.

I'm excited, hopeful, grinning.

The doctor looks at our notes, flicks through pages, flicks back again, indulges in some small talk, then logs onto her computer and revisits our file, types something, stares intently at the screen, checks and double-checks, and our hearts sink, for yes doesn't take this long.

Eventually she looks at us and her smile says it all. A 'poor you' lopsided smile of sympathy.

She tells us that my blood tests have changed and I'm no longer suitable for Clomid. I'm probably not even producing viable eggs anymore.

. . .

I am in shock.

I hear the noise of her words but my brain rejects it.

That's it?

How can that be it?

I want to argue with her and demand that something be done but (and my heart breaks) there's . . . nothing to be done.

It's over.

I had hung my hope on Clomid — our final chance to conceive a child of our own. That sliver of opportunity has died. She offers us counselling and waves a leaflet near me, but no leaflet will do when I wanted some pills. I shake my head.

I mumble a thank you as we scrape back our chairs and leave, heads bowed.

What now?

We walk in silent despair from the clinic for the last time. I feel numb. As grey as the pavement beneath my feet. I'm frightened to let the knowledge sink in, in case I collapse in raw grief. Grief for the child I'll never bear. Grief for the experience of feeling a child grow inside me, of it kicking my tummy, of being visibly with child and showing that growing bulge off to the world. Like a house of cards, all my dreams fall in a heap and I see that they're nothing more than dust.

I want to undo that news. To unravel the finality of it all. After two and a half years of clinging to hope, desperately trying to convince ourselves that it's just a little further, just around the next bend in the road, we've reached a dead end. All the times I kept the faith as the months wore on, all the times I went to bed dreaming of walking along the beach hand in hand with a little girl . . .

It's almost too much to bear.

We drive home quietly to mourn.

To lick our wounds and get ready for a different battle instead.

6. If We Can Cope with This

'Bye-ee,' I call out cheerily from the study, exhaling slowly as the door closes. I've been holding my breath for weeks. My elder sister, Claire, has been living with Andy and me for a few months. She came for a weekend just after Easter, and I soon realised that something was wrong — not just a little wrong, but badly and disastrously wrong. She lay listlessly on the sofa for hours on end, giving only monosyllabic grunts in response to our questions and concerns, and I remembered when I'd seen it before — the signs we'd missed last time she spiralled into depression. I didn't want her to fall into that deep dungeon of darkness again.

I invited her to stay with us, to get her back on her feet, and she did for a while. We remade our spare room into something comfortable. Then she went home to get some clothes and texted me to let me know she'd arrived safely just before disappearing. She didn't answer my texts or calls. I rang again and again, I texted until my thumbs hurt and my fear grew like moss on a damp wall. My messages became increasingly frantic: 'Please ring'; 'Just let me know you are okay'; 'I am worried about you'. Nightmarish visions plagued my thoughts. Where was she? Was she okay? I barely slept that night, sick with fear.

Thirty hours later, my phone pinged — she was in London. 'I thought I would come here and vanish. My head is so messed up.'

I cried with relief that she was alive and rang her. She picked up. To say it was an emotional phone call would be a serious understatement. She sounded lonely, desperate, scared of her own head.

Thank God for British rain, which made being a homeless runaway in the smoke far less appealing. I begged her to come back.

When she arrived broken on our doorstep, I hugged her as though she were a soldier returning from war, thinking that this time we'd caught it early; that with love and support she wouldn't fall as deep this time. But my optimism proved unfounded. Things have taken so many turns for the worse I've lost count.

We've been bruised with grief for the child we'll never have and also blindsided, struggling through the tangled wilderness of mental illness, hacking our way through one day after another in a whole new world.

But today I get my life back.

Claire is driving to my twin sister's house for a few nights, and the relief in my body and soul is profound. This is our first weekend off in months.

As the stress recedes, I realise I need to do something for me. It's been five months since the door closed on Clomid. When Andy and I were dating, we said that we wanted to have children, and if not ours then someone else's. We said it in an offhand manner, like saying that if you won the lottery you'd buy your local pub to save it from being turned into flats. But fate called our bluff.

We can't have children. It's a plural problem, our problem, our family that hangs in the balance. I write 'we', yet when I'm alone, it doesn't feel like 'we' at all, it feels like me. *I* cannot have children. Those words stick on my fingers as I type. When I share that truth with others, people wince and shy away from it, as if it's cancer. People feel embarrassed, helpless, and mostly turn away, unwilling to carry on a conversation burdened with such facts.

As Claire leaves, my brain has a powerful thought: *If I can cope with this, I can cope with anything. I can cope with adopting a child.* And I begin to believe it. Claire is worse than a child — unpredictable, strong, scary, mentally unstable; I can't send her to the naughty step when she opens vodka at 8 a.m. My shoulders rise; my back straightens.

The closing door still reverberates as I take The First Step. Stage One. I pick up the phone, ring an adoption agency and declare that we want to adopt. I speak to a social worker[1] who asks me questions for thirty minutes, and whilst in hindsight I can remember exactly where I sat (at my big leather-topped desk), the colour of the phone in my right hand (orange) and the weather outside (sun streaming through the trees), I haven't the faintest idea what was said. As I place the receiver down, I feel a new truth surging through me. That phone call was my battle cry: 'I am ready now, world' — ready to be someone's mummy.

I feel alive; the future is full of new possibilities. We have prepared the canvas on which we will create our new family portrait. I dust off the dream of walking hand in hand with a little girl along the beach.

Andy seems happy, in his usual understated manner, when I tell him. He'd been waiting for me to be ready to take the first step.

Then the weekend is over, Claire comes back and her illness takes me to places I'd rather not visit again.

We get a brochure and flyers about adoption in the post: there are forms to complete and 'information evening[2]' dates. I immediately book the first available date, which is, disappointingly, weeks

---

[1] **Social Worker:** Someone who makes impossible decisions before breakfast. They walk a tightrope over a minefield that at any time can blow up and result in headline news blaming them, regardless of how little funding they receive. For if a child is abused, we don't point fingers at the neighbours who heard the screams and turned the TV up, or even at the parents who turned a childhood into a nightmare. We blame social workers for not being psychic. During adoption, social workers have to be absolutely certain that they don't give a vulnerable child to someone who might do more harm than good. Nearest equivalent: Bear Grylls armed with just a paper clip in a jungle filled with predators.

[2] **Information Evening:** An evening packed to the brim with incomprehensible information. It's the first time you encounter social workers from the Looked After Children service. And they probably just want to go home after a long day of making impossible decisions before breakfast. These evenings burst the bubble of your dream of a newborn baby given up by a mythical single woman in the 1950s. Nearest equivalent: A trailer for a complicated thriller that messes with your head; at the end of it, you're not certain whether it was a trailer or an ad, nor whether you want to see the film.

away. With an antidote to the ever-deteriorating situation of my sister's mental health, I'm on a mission now. A tiny flicker of light in a room darker than night.

Where the heck is Andy?

It's June, and we're at (I'm at) the information evening, or Stage Two. The room holds a dozen couples all looking as if they want to disappear in a puff of smoke. I bounce like an excited puppy eager to make friends (without the bottom sniffing). For the first time in years of dealing with the taboo of infertility, I'm in a room with people who might understand.

The atmosphere is one of dampened tension. There's a revered hush that no one's willing to break. People talk in subdued tones to their partners. I scan the room wondering about these people, about what brings them to this moment. There's a surprising lack of diversity; mostly white heterosexual couples, not exactly representative of the local community. Based on the meagre evidence of their clothes, shoes and handbags, they're mostly middle class. Some older than us, some a bit younger.

Are the others making similar judgements about me? A single woman? A lesbian, perhaps? I look through the 'Be My Parent' papers, overacting a casualness I do not feel. I feel like Bridget Jones dressed inappropriately as the bunny girl at the garden party.

Andy promised to leave on time (I urged him to leave early, but he resisted, saying there was 'plenty of time', a phrase I intend to remind him of the minute he arrives). I check my watch: he's cutting it super-fine. I duck out with a few minutes to go and ring his mobile. No reply. *Gah! Where is he?* I want us to make the right impression, to prove just how organised and responsible (and hence suitable as potential parents) we are. Turning up late is not an option.

He's conspicuously absent when the evening starts.

The presenters introduce themselves and apologise in advance for the slides, and then talk us through slide after slide on the adoption process. We're bombarded with jargon: Panel, Matching, Prospective Adopter Reports, facts, Introductions, meetings, timetables and more facts. I don't get it, but at least they distract me from worrying if Andy has had an accident or something.

Twenty minutes later, he arrives in his motorcycle gear. He is drenched, helmet in hand, and apologises as he slinks in, the meeting nearly over. I'm both embarrassed and relieved. He holds my hand, smiles at me, and a sarcastic 'plenty of time' dies on my lips in uncharacteristic instant forgiveness.

There's more information, and I'm surprised to learn that the children who need adopting have been removed from families because of neglect. There are very few relinquished babies anymore; it's not the 1950s, where young women give up their children willing or unwillingly. This is 2013, where children are taken from their parents because they're neglected or abused. It is depressing. But this is not the main reason that I leave feeling disappointed.

I had high expectations of a 'how fantastic, you want to adopt children' style celebration with a *Braveheart* speech to inspire us for the battle ahead. A knickerbocker glory of delicious hope with a dream family as the cherry on top. But instead, I was confused and bored going through information that I'd read several times and still don't understand. I leave feeling thicker than clotted cream.

I need a hug.

At home, I get an extremely soggy one from my husband, and we compare thoughts. It's not just me; Andy too is disappointed. Are they trying to put us off, we wonder? Was the entire evening meant to be rather dismal to sift out those people who are not truly committed? We'd wanted uplifting and life affirming and we got abuse, alcohol and unfathomable abbreviations.

Still, we've sat through worse in our day jobs, so we shake ourselves off and fill out another set of forms, ones that tell the agency we want to go ahead to the next stage. It's the same information we've already given in triplicate, but we write it all down again and wait.

I want to shake the presenters awake and tell them: 'Don't forget the dream. Because in all those facts and figures, you forgot to sell me my dream.'

Stage Three: A social worker arrives at our house to interview us. More questions and paperwork, although at least this time she's the one doing all the writing. The word 'interview' has put me on edge. What are the right things to say? What are the wrong things to say? Is the idea to rule us in as potential parents or find reasons to reject us? Thank goodness Andy is here to hold my hand and fill in the blanks when I stumble over even basic information. The social worker seems nice enough, smiling and approachable. She asks about our history, background, jobs, house and probably some other stuff, but I remember her yellow-lined notepad and black bag more than what was said. I ache to see what she's written. After about an hour, she stands up, puts her pad away, shakes our hands and wishes us luck. I want to blurt out, 'Did we pass?'

Stage Four: A few weeks later more paperwork arrives. I get my pen out and soldier on, although I can't help but wonder how many less articulate souls perish at this endless form filling. We send it off and a few weeks later we get exciting news: we are invited to (and required to attend) a four-day training course in October. It is the first official training and as far as the agency is concerned, this is when the clock starts for real. I tell myself we passed.

After a traumatic six months, Claire's doing a convincing job of pretending to be better, particularly because we're too caught up in the adoption to look too hard at the evidence to the contrary. She's different, if not entirely fixed. Despite our reservations, she moves back to her house (at the other end of the country) in September. In the space of her absence, we find a predictability, a routine, time to think, to dream, to start preparing for what might come next. We've barely begun to breathe again when October arrives.

Stage Five: Intensive Training[3]. We get excited. Well, when I say we, I mean I. I get excited, because as you might have gathered,

---

[3] *Intensive Training:* Four days where your emotions are wrung through a mangle; you swing from wildly excited that you might get a family to scared shitless at the challenges ahead. It's packed with intense exercises designed to give you a whistle-stop qualification in child development and adoption, whilst mostly making you feel utterly inadequate and terribly unprepared.

Nearest equivalent: The nightmare when you find yourself in an exam room in your PJs then turn the paper over and realise you have three hours to answer questions on strains of bacteria that live in a snake's ear canal.

Andy's not one for the giddy displays of emotion that chart my every moment.

We arrive and meet our fellow hoping-to-adopters. Andy holds my hand, and his big warm touch tethers me to the ground emotionally as well as physically. Nods of recognition pass between us all, a silent acknowledgement of the experiences and hopes that bind us together. It feels good to be with people who can truly understand our journey to this moment, people who (we imagine) have been through similar misfortunes, disappointments and dashed hopes.

There are eight couples including us, and we talk to each other as we wait in the coffee room, sharing a little of who we are. When they call us in, we troop into the training room, where low chairs are arranged in an L shape. There are two presenters and two other people sat at the back of the room looking as if they don't want to be noticed, which is kind of odd.

We start by introducing ourselves and writing out name stickers. Then we are given index cards on which to write our hopes and fears about adopting.

I take a card and write down a fear: 'My child saying, "You're not my mum."' It's the sort of venomous thing that I might have yelled as a child — something I might have tossed like a bomb, aiming for destruction. But it would be a true statement for my child. After we scribble our thoughts down, we put the cards face up on the carpet in front of us. Gazes dart around, looking at the cards. And we smile as we recognise how similar they all are. Our hopes and fears create instant rapport.

During the breaks, we all share our histories. As we listen, Andy and I reflect on just how lucky we've been. We simply couldn't have children. We had none of the agony of trying for fifteen years to have a child (how did they keep going?), or of touching the joy of pregnancy only to lose the baby before it was born. There is pain in this room that binds us together; nothing is unsayable here.

We are not alone.

7. Things Not to Say: Part One

Shut up, shut up, shut UP, SHUT UP!

We're sat in the break room on Day Two when a social worker sidles over, says hello and sits down. He's one of those who scribbles away suspiciously at the back of the room. We've been told they're sitting in, but we suspect there's more to it.

'I hear you want to adopt two or three children?' he asks.

'Yes,' we respond, and I then trot out my stock response: Andy wanted to adopt three, but I was set on a maximum of two: 'Two hands, two children.' After Day One of the course, focused on the extra challenges of adopting, Andy hastily revised his idea and now concurs that two is more realistic.

'You're the only ones looking to adopt two,' he adds.

'Oh . . . really?'

I'm surprised — there are seven other couples on this course, and it never occurred to me that everyone else would be adopting only one child. We explain we've always wanted more than one child, so it seems logical to adopt two who are already a family. The social worker nods and we wonder what this conversation is really about. Maybe he'll impart some words of wisdom, share his experiences of successful sibling adoptions, pave the way for confidence in taking on two at a time.

'That's brave,' he says as he peels away.

We've heard this word so often I want to roll my eyes. Do people say that to a woman expecting twins? I'd ask my mum but *(a)* she wouldn't remember; and *(b)* she didn't know she was having twins until the midwife announced, 'Wait, there's another one.' Are people trying to put us off with a disguised 'run, run and hide' or 'that's just crazy talk'? Maybe it is crazy. Maybe I've seriously underestimated how hard it will be to add two more lives into our family overnight. But I don't want them to say 'brave'. I would rather they said 'exciting' or 'amazing'. And I want to hear 'brave' even less from a social worker who knows a thing or eight about adoption.

Why isn't anyone else adopting two children? What do they know that we don't? Aren't siblings difficult to place? Shouldn't the social workers be encouraging us? The more we hear 'brave', the more we wonder if we're biting off more than we can chew. Friends of ours who wanted to adopt two were told at Panel they could adopt only one at a time. So if the professionals don't think we can do it, they'll stop us, won't they? Surely it's not in anyone's interest for them to give us more than we can handle, is it? (There are more questions than answers on this introspective roundabout.)

Are we brave, or are we stupid? Do I have 'Foolhardy' tattooed on my forehead and is everyone else in on the joke? Can I really be a mummy to two children overnight?

And, breathe.

'Brave' is just a word. They don't really mean 'brave' as in tackling the *Guardian*'s cryptic crossword; they mean 'brave' as in wonderful, heart-warming; the sort of thing they give you an award for in a glittering TV programme brimming with C-list celebrities hoping to get vital column inches to revitalise their ailing careers, hosted by the lovely Davina. Like raising money for charity, saving a drowning boy, rescuing people from a burning —

OH. MY. GOD.

They sooooooo mean the scary kind of brave.

Shut up! Please don't say 'brave' to me anymore.

Say 'wonderful', say 'incredible', say 'exciting'.

Just Stop. Saying. Brave.

My hands are clamped over my ears. I'm not listening anymore. I am not brave. I am just adopting two children at once. Overnight. What am I doing? What are *we* doing?

And I think (not for the first time) how much easier things would be if I could've just got pregnant.

8. Chocks Away

We're closer than ever — and scared as hell. Apart from scaring the bejesus out of us, the training course has brought the idea of becoming parents to life. Andy and I have talked more in the last four days about what it means to be parents than we have in all the years of trying for a baby. It now feels real, tangible, just beyond the tips of our fingers.

But the gift is bittersweet.

To prepare us for the challenges ahead, the course is necessarily hard-hitting and eye-opening. The children we hope to adopt are not our nephews or nieces, not children of our family or friends. They have been neglected and removed from the only home they've known. They have experienced separation, loss, grief, upheaval and more. *Poor little lambs*, I think.

At the start of the course, I jumped into a warm, comforting pool, enveloped by the glow of belonging, but now I'm floundering in turbulent waters with a riptide. There are times when I feel totally inadequate and question my ability to be a mum to these vulnerable children.

Next on the course timetable is a quiz about child development. We hesitate, afraid to get things wrong, but we're encouraged to have a go with the predictable mantra: 'There are no wrong answers'. When Andy and I guess (we dither because we don't know) that it's okay to bathe a girl and boy together at age nine, the frowns and tuts around the room prove that we found a wrong answer. We have no idea.

On the final day, we meet a couple of adoptive parents and I am dying for a happily-ever-after story to lighten the emotional load of the past few days. They say how much they love their boy, how he's a dream come true, and yet their smiles never reach their eyes.

I search their faces and words for a glimmer of hope, but it's not there. My gut says they're faking it. They drizzle on my dreams.

As the course finishes, the social workers tell us what comes next.

There will be intensive meetings with our social worker, who has been assigned to start preparing a humongously long report (the longest job application in the world) called the Prospective Adopters Report, aka the Big Report[4] for our Adoption Panel[5]. We nod enthusiastically.

'Your meetings will start next week.'

Really? Really really? Really really really?

Mosquitoes in my stomach start buzzing and distracting me, such that I almost miss what the social workers say next. But it burrows into my brain even though I wasn't listening because it is A-Maze-Ing news.

We're given a date for our Panel.

A date for the decision of our lives.

A date when the man from Del Monte might say *sí*.

Go us.

Then I hear 'end of February'.

Are you kidding?

We all look at each other with eyebrows so high it looks like we shaved them off and drew them on again in the wrong place.

February?

---

[4] **Big Report (aka Prospective Adopters Report):** The longest job application in the world, covering your relationship, your childhood, your education, your health, your finances, your past boyfriends, the safety of your house and how you will cope once the children arrive. Pages and pages of information about your life (and a sprinkling of embellishment) laid bare for strangers to read.
Nearest equivalent: A rambling application for a new show called Bear Grylls Meets Blue Peter.

[5] **Adoption Panel:** An interview based on the Big Report. The adopters get a chance to answer questions from a large group of people. The Panel then decide whether the adopters are suitable, are not suitable or have work to do. They don't actually make the final decision, as that has to be ratified by the head honcho a week later, who can disagree.
Nearest equivalent: The Del Monte advert where a man in a Panama hat comes to an orange grove in South America, tastes the orange and then says yes and the workers rejoice (if we're lucky).

Did she say February?

That's just after Christmas!

Only five months away (I calculate on my fingers with an audible gasp).

We had thought it would take years. Apparently things have changed since the tabloids last printed outraged headlines about how long children wait to be adopted.

Could we really be approved as parents that soon?

But we're not there yet.

As far as Andy is concerned, what comes next is 'ten weeks of intense navel-gazing'.

We sit in strained silence, strangers on our own settee. Just eight days later and we're starting on the Big Report with our assigned social worker. It'll be over one hundred pages detailing all the reasons we'll be awesome parents, to be read by the experts and laypeople who comprise our Panel. When we stand before a roomful of people and are judged. When the mysterious They will toy with our fate in a chequered room where the perspective is all skew-whiff and I'm a mere two feet tall. When They peer over us like giants in the receding gloom. A dark and scary Wonderland. That image doesn't help my nerves.

Our social worker takes a sip from her tea as we struggle to get comfy. She asks questions and writes notes as we try to act like responsible parents-to-be and probably come across as serial killers hoping she won't notice the muffled screams coming from the basement. It's all rather forced, like trying to convince a minister to let you marry in his pretty village church even though you don't believe in God and the last time you went to church was when your mum dragged you there as a teenager one Christmas.

She seems somewhat confused and disorganised by the process, which is not filling us with confidence, but not everyone's a hyper-organised control freak like me, so I let it pass. I want to like her, to feel that she's our champion, a cheerleader on our side through this process. But I don't get that warm glow from her. Is she impartial or our advocate?

At Intensive Training, we'd been warned to expect the meetings to last several hours, so we hunker down and settle in for a long evening of in-depth questions and analysis. I've barely warmed to the lyrical sound of my own voice when she tidies her notes away. I covertly check the time (in case she notices and marks me down as impatient) and . . . *That's strange; it's only been forty-five minutes.*

'We were told these meetings would last a couple of hours,' I stammer.

'Oh, no,' she replies, in a tone that says the suggestion is madness. 'An hour is more than long enough.' With that and a click of her briefcase, she's gone.

Andy's also shocked. He's taken an entire afternoon off work. They did say it would be a couple of hours, didn't they? What's going on? Is she breaking us in gently or something?

The next day she emails us a string of questions: twenty-seven of them. Where have we lived and worked? Any significant changes in our circumstances? Death, divorce, redundancy, infertility.

Infertility?

I startle to see that word alongside events such as my sister's breakdown, my divorce and my father's death (and the preponderance of 'my' in that sentence shows that I'm the one who brings all the trauma to this yard). We trawl through our diaries to work out the chronology, and sum up our relationship and infertility in a few lines:

2002 (December) started dating

2007 (September) got married

2007 – 2010 tried for children naturally

2010 – 2011 sought infertility advice — declined IVF, offered Clomid, postponed due to stress at Emma's work

2011 (October) sought Clomid treatment, had to be retested to check suitability

2012 (January) told unsuitable for Clomid

2012 (May) inquired about adopting children

Three years of sex with pillows under my bottom, over a year being poked and prodded, and then six months on the adoption journey.

Thousands of words reduced to a few lines because there isn't any room to write any more.

Some of the questions are like therapy. *Question 2: Describe your mother and your relationship with her. Did the nature of your relationship with your mother change at all during your childhood?*

As I type, a dam opens up; experiences and feelings come pouring out on paper and I'm riding roughshod over my memories, the words flowing from my heart onto the paper — it's rather cathartic.

I write 11,468 words, or thirteen pages of close-typed text.

As I email the social worker my homework, I think smugly how thorough I've been. But at our next meeting, she is not as impressed as I'd hoped.

'Thanks. You've been very busy with these,' she mutters. 'It's too long,' she continues. 'Can you precis it and send it back?'

'Yes,' I say, in my good-girl tone.

Precis it? My masterpiece? My no-stone-unturned tome? Gah. She never said there was a word limit. Why didn't she tell me there was a word limit? How am I supposed to sum up all that rich history in just a few words? What does she want? Why does she keep moving the goalposts? This is so unfair! How much do I need to cut out? Perhaps I should just sum up my relationship with my mum with 'sometimes we got along and sometimes we didn't'. That would show her. I'm NOT going to shorten it, she can do it herself. Witch.

Of course I precis it. Of course I don't just write 'sometimes good, sometimes bad' because this is a game I'm playing to win.

Before we know it, it's the end of November and we're halfway through — six short meetings and hundreds of answered questions (I stopped writing lengthy dissertations) under our belts. And there's more to come. But we must do more than just type. We must also go shopping. And for the first time, we stumble across the Adoption Tightrope.

9. The Adoption Tightrope

We're on the Hunt, a shopping trip that has all the hallmarks of an expedition to Antarctica. It's required weeks of planning, brochures and online research (whilst being occasionally distracted by the latest smartphone reviews). Andy is revelling in it. Not me. I want to grumble 'you choose', but it's not like we're shopping for a new (how can we possibly need another?) cushion. We need a new car.

Andy has a laissez-faire attitude to push-along vehicles for our children summed up by a parody of a song from *Joseph and the Amazing Technicolor Dreamcoat*: 'Any Pram Will Do'. Little does he suspect that I've been poring over the technical specs of prams the way that he's been swotting up on cars.

Having been passengers in the moving anarchy of my twin sister and her three kids, we know we need a car that separates the kids from each other by the length of a piss-off punch, and them from us by the length of a well-aimed it's-not-fair kick. We need a boot that can fit tents, prams, food for a month, crates of wine, clothes, tools, a set of goalposts, kit for a football team and the ubiquitous bucket and spade as well as pockets and nets in every nook and cranny to hold other mysterious 'essentials'. No longer will we travel the length of this fair isle with just a phone charger and some crisps.

This is the fifth weekend in a row we've wandered around car showrooms, and my need to go to Dunelm Mill for a cushion we don't need is reaching fever pitch. Luckily, like aircraft circling Heathrow, we're about to land. We've finally sacked all the competition and narrowed our choice down to one. We stroll up to it and do the car dance: getting in and out of the front seats, testing the driving position, opening the glovebox and wondering if anyone puts gloves in them anymore and then converging on the boot to gape at All. That. Space. I start calculating how many twenty-inch mohair cushions it will hold. When Andy points out that the boot folds down and I can sit on it to put my boots on for a walk, I forget about mohair. *Oooh.* The car salesman ambles over, drawn like a moth to Andy's I'm-so-excited jig (not his most macho move).

'Are you buying a car?' he asks.

I roll my eyes and respond with deeply unnecessary sarcasm. 'No. The blue-and-yellow signage and complete lack of parking had me thinking this must be Ikea. Take me to your tea lights.' I don't say this out loud.

'Yes,' says Andy.

He asks what car we have now. I want to say 'a blue one', but I let Andy answer, even if the question is a badly disguised 'can you afford it?'

'Why are you changing your car?' asks the salesman, who is clearly confused as to why anyone would swap a BMW for a Peugeot.

'We need a family car,' I explain. His face lights up.

'How old are your kids?' he asks, without missing a beat.

Uh.

Andy and I look at each other. Then at the floor.

We stumble onto the Adoption Tightrope.

We're caught off guard. Rabbits in the headlights of his innocent inquiry.

What do we say?

Do we lie?

Do we say nothing?

It's a good question. A logical question. A question that anyone would ask in the same circumstances. A question I've asked myself in similar get-to-know-a-stranger small talk. And if he thought our hesitation is weird, things are about to get even more bizarre.

'We don't know,' I respond somewhat apologetically.

There is a loud silence in the space where the salesman's planned response ('What a lovely age') goes to die. We didn't anticipate his question, but he *really* didn't anticipate our answer. This is blindingly obvious from the disorientation that ruffles his unruffleable, heard-it-all demeanour. His face screws up and his gaze darts around.

We are balancing on the Adoption Tightrope.

How much do we say?

We've got used to playing our cards close to our chest, especially as things are still far from certain. And he is a stranger.

I consider a small lie, but that could create a tornado of forgettable lies over which to trip, a tangle of our own making. And then we'd have to start the Hunt again because we'd be too embarrassed to come back.

'We're adopting.'

Relief flashes across his face and his shoulders relax.

'Oh,' he says, 'that makes sense.'

We get to the other side of the tightrope intact. If feeling a little off balance.

10. What Am I Doing?

'What's wrong?' asks Andy when he comes home to find me snivelling into soggy tissues.

Earlier today I discovered I won't get any adoption pay. If I had a job, I'd get either maternity or adoption pay. As someone self-employed with a birth child, I'd qualify for maternity pay. But as I fall into the too-rare-to-bother-Parliament-with category of both self-employed and adopting, I get zilch. That legislative oversight leaves us five hundred pounds a month worse off. I was counting on that money to balance our budget.

I take arms against this discrimination and unfairness. I sign a petition, invite my family and friends to do the same, email my MP (who never responds) and fear that nothing will change because there aren't enough of us to matter. Without thousands of placarded protestors, how on earth will our voice ever get heard?

Now, my anger has subsided, and the fear beneath has risen to the surface. I tip over an emotional precipice I hadn't even noticed I was inching along.

What are we doing? How will we manage without that extra money? How will we make ends meet? Can we even afford to be parents?

And then because I'm already spiralling, other thoughts join the circus of doubt. *What am I doing? How on earth will I cope at home with kids on my own? I don't know if I can do this. I don't know . . . anything.*

The unknown is dark, scary and foreboding.

It's all too much, too fast, too overwhelming. A tear rolls down my face and before you can say 'adoption pay', my breathing is a fit of gasps and sobs. By the time Andy comes home I am a sniffling wreck.

'Is it Claire?' he asks.

I shake my head. (The look of relief on Andy's face tells me that, like me, he still worries about her.)

'M-m-m-money,' I finally blurt out, and Andy's face screws up in disbelief.

'Money?' he says in a tone that says 'I thought someone had died!'

He smiles kindly and listens patiently in the hope that I'll eventually make sense.

'Money [garbled] budgets.'

'I just don't know [unintelligible].'

'Sn ub ha wa adoption pay.'

Gulp, breathe, sniff, breathe, sniff.

'How *sob* will we cope?'

'I don't even know *sob* how much you earn.'

But money is simply fake tan plastered over my lily-white fears. I'm freaking out about becoming a mum. What if I don't know how to be a mum? What if they scream all night or pull my eyelashes out while in my arms and in my shock I drop them and they break? What if they put my phone in the washing machine (or worse, my iPad)? Or rack up an enormous porn bill by accidentally dialling a chat line and leaving my mobile connected when they toddle off, bored? Or cover themselves in honey like human flypaper and roll around the floor collecting dust bunnies and leaving a sticky trail that's impossible to remove? Or make mud pies from their own poo and the contents of the compost bin and spread dysentery? Or push the handbrake button and the car rolls down the hill into a petrol tanker that's next to one containing hazardous waste and causes a conflagration that kills hundreds of my neighbours? What if I don't like being a full-time mum and my clients all leave me and I don't know how much money we have and I feel trapped financially in a family that's driving me crazy?

I'm afraid of going ahead with it, and even more afraid of what will happen if I pull out. I am frightened of the future, and that terror is magnified because of all that 'brave' talk. I don't feel brave. I don't want to have to be brave. I know I can cook, wipe faces, organise, paint and sing and read books, but right now I'm scared witless by the knowledge that it's not going to be enough.

What if I am not enough? It's the question feeding all my fear.

'I don't know how to be a mum,' I tell him.

'I don't know if I can do this.'

'I don't know what it will be like to look after children twenty-four hours a day for six months or more.' As adopters one of us must be off work for the first six months to help the children settle in. After a short discussion, that person is going to be me.

'I am not ready.'

I have lost sight of the dream and all I can see are piranhas.

After my sobbing subsides and my breathing slows, I grapple for something solid, something I can control, something like cold, hard cash.

'I can't predict what life will be like,' I tell Andy, 'but there are a few things I can control — and that's things like budgets, planning, meals and so forth.'

And we start treading on tricky territory.

Traditionally in our relationship, money has been a trigger for debate, intense floor staring, finger pointing, accusations and counter-accusations, escalating volumes and swearing, sulky defensiveness followed by long silences leading to bad tempers and one of us walking out whilst shouting 'you never listen to me'. So we have eliminated such discomfort by avoiding it until Andy's credit card bill (no finger pointing here, ho hum) mysteriously grows like a triffid and his zero percent interest runs dry. Since I'm allergic to confrontation, we have arabesqued around the topic and kept our debts and spending on a for-our-own-eyes-only basis. We've been married for six years and I don't know how much he gets paid and that's worked fine — until now.

We'll be down to one income.

His mythical, secret, unquantified wage.

We're going to have to unstick our heads from the bliss of ignorance and sort this out.

After things (meaning I) have calmed down, we sit down and write out a budget. It's tight: we might just get through this, we might just make ends meet, providing that adding two children to the household doesn't impact our expenses by a penny. As I look at the spreadsheet, these nice tidy figures calm my fears, and my control freak goes for a nap, all tuckered out.

I still don't know how to look after kids or be a mum, but we'll sort that out later.

I blow my nose and make us some pasta.

11. Suspicious Minds

We're off to Comparison City tonight, over a meal at a local pub. We're meeting other couples from the Intensive Training to swap notes on our social workers (they told us not to, which is why we have to), whinge about the process and celebrate the fact that Panel is just around the corner.

We're now three-quarters of the way through the weekly meetings (pages and pages of questions answered) with our social worker, and she says she'll soon pull it all together into the Big Report, to meet our Panel date. Everything is going smoothly for once and we're in a buoyant mood.

The first thing we do at the pub, after hugging and air kissing, is share notes. And that's when the trouble begins.

'How did your home visit go? Can you believe the knife-rack request?'

Uh, home visit?

'She told us that we didn't say enough during the course. What did they say about you?'

Um, we haven't had that session yet.

'Did you tell them all Andy's worst behaviours in the dish-the-dirt sesh?'

The what now?

'How long are your meetings?' we ask, casually. They've all had two-hour ('Our record is three and a half hours') meetings. *Uh-oh.* We have the same Panel date as they do, but Andy and I are in a very different place ('different place' being a euphemism for paddles, creeks and shit). We haven't bought a cot, had a home visit, nor dished the dirt. We frown into our drinks.

We leave warmed by the camaraderie but chilled by a nagging suspicion. The same one we've had since our first overly short meeting with our social worker. We resolve to confront her about this at the next available opportunity.

We have a meeting next week, so we'll do it then. We're not going to let her fob us off anymore. No more half-hearted mumbled assurances that we will meet our deadline for Panel. We need to know. We can handle the truth.

We both agree that before she says anything, we'll ask about what else is left to do and how she plans to be ready on time — possibly referencing the other adopters but only if we have to. We are anxious to get some answers, and to have our fears allayed.

She's due at 4 p.m.

At 4 p.m. there's no sign of her. Perhaps she's caught in traffic, we say. It's happened before (yet last time she rang to let us know). She's a bit late, we say at 4.15. The meeting is nearly over, we grumble at 4.30. We tut and ring the adoption agency to find out what's going on. There's a delay while they go and find out, and then we get the message that she's off sick. *Nice of her to let us know. Andy took the afternoon off work for this.* We park our frustration and questions. They can wait until next week's meeting. After all, she told us she just needed to pull all the information together and write the Big Report over Christmas and we'd be good to go. Everything is still on track. Probably. Possibly. Hmmm.

She doesn't ring to arrange another meeting. *Odd. Is she still ill?* We vaguely hope she's okay whilst mostly being self-centred about the impact it is having on us. A week goes by. Nothing. We start to get concerned, for the plan doesn't leave much leeway for a couple of weeks off at this late stage, especially when we're clearly already somewhat behind. I ring the adoption agency asking politely when she might be in touch and wish I hadn't. Our social worker hasn't got a cold or flu; she's off *sick* sick — and she won't be coming back.

What?

No. No. No. No. No. No. Nobbing no!

'Gutted' doesn't cut it. After all this time, all the training and meetings and essays, when we thought there were just a few i's to dot and t's to cross, just inches from the finish line, we fall over our shoelaces and face-plant onto the track (the crowd gasps) and lie there, unable to get up.

Why is this happening to us? It's so unfair.

The agency tells us that we will be assigned a new social worker soon.

'Will we still be ready for our Panel in February?' I ask in a voice squeaky with desperation.

'We hope so.'

I sigh. A lot. I sigh in despair, in anguish, in impatience, in trepidation of the uncertainty of it all. I wonder if I broke our social worker with my lengthy dissertations. We suspiciously wonder at the timing of it all; she knew we were meeting up with our fellow adopters; she knew that she'd be found out. Coincidence? Who knows.

In the last few weeks before Christmas, there is no news.

Christmas comes and goes and? — No news.

The New Year? — No news.

And 'All I want for Christmas is a new social worker' becomes my refrain, sung through the gritted teeth of impatience. We're frustrated and powerless . . . Waiting . . . Tetchily.

The minute that Andy goes back to work, I'm on the phone to the adoption agency begging to know if they have any news. They don't have a new social worker for us, yet. Another version of 'no news' then.

When we were so close we could almost touch it, the end has run off with the milkman.

In early January, as we drive into town to do some shopping, I'm pondering our childlessness, the strangeness of this adoption process, these irritating delays: a tangle of confusion and grief and hope and frustration. And amongst a trail of similarly forgettable days, this one's about to be remembered. The sun's shining, and as we drive up a hill, over the canal, through some green traffic lights (this mundane location is ingrained in my mind) a thought enters, like the whisper of an angel, bypassing thinking and debate and then spinning my heart as it glances past en route to my soul.

I start. (I'm glad I'm not driving.)

I catch my breath.

Oh.

My eyes widen and water.

My heart recognises it immediately, like the voice of a beloved friend you haven't heard in years cutting through the chatter in a crowded room. My mind toys with it, rolls it around my brain as it works out how it connects with all the other stuff in there. And yet when it settles in its new home, it's clear it was meant to be there all along. There are moments when a tiny shift makes sense of your life and you experience a new reality. This is one of those.

And that truth that I did not conjure up, but that found me in the midst of anguish, reverberates like a huge gong of happiness, bringing new joy to my heart.

What if . . . ?

It's a simple idea. So simple you might not even recognise its majesty. So simple as to be blindingly obvious in a 'why haven't I thought of that before?' shrug. And yet, it is deeply moving and profound. *What if they're already here?*

Oh.

OMG.

What a magnificent, expansive, exhilarating thought! What if the children who need us most as their parents are already here? My mind jumps and creates an idea of children, not far from here, already here, already born, who will be our children but who came through a different route. An invisible thread is connecting me to some children who need me. This truth tells me gently that life is going to plan, if not the plan that we wrote for ourselves. I will be a parent, I will have children, I will be a mum, I will have a family.

My hope is reborn, and in that hope, my tears of grief for the child we never bore turn to tears of joy for the children who are already born.

The universe has other plans for me. Everything will be okay.

There's news!

It's mid-January and we're meeting Social Worker Number Two (SWN2), henceforth known as Pam. There's a month until our Panel, and if SWN1 was as ready as she said she was, with some dots and crosses and a following wind, we might still make it. I'm excited and slightly giddy because we are . . . nearly . . . there . . . Hallelujah! Yes, we've had a bit of a delay, but we've brushed ourselves off, tied our shoelaces and will now race to the finishing tape.

Pam arrives, sits down and is clearly different. Her voice, her posture, her attitude — all gutsier than the one we broke. We are cautious and on our best behaviour; our future family now lies in her hands.

'Will we meet our Panel date?' I ask, my fingers crossed so tightly they turn numb then white.

'No,' she states.

Scrub that hallelujah. Seems I was a bit hasty. But I admire her honesty — it's refreshing, given the lies we seem to have been peddled of late. My shoulders droop in frustration. We ask about the Big Report.

'Our first social worker said it was nearly finished,' I say in a whiny tone that even I find annoying.

'I haven't seen it,' she replies, shaking her head. 'Can you send me everything you have already done, please?' she asks. *Goody*, I think. *Back to square one.* We agree to send her everything.

'When do you think we might go to Panel?' I ask. I give her some options: 'A week, two weeks?' You could cut the desperation in my voice with a cake slice.

'I can't say. I really don't know.' I don't like this refreshing honesty anymore.

SWN1 sat on the sofa, asked us questions, took notes and emailed us homework. We expected much of the same from Pam, but she arrived carrying an unwieldy box with large lengths of plastic pipe and hints of colourful plastic poking out.

'I'm going to give you a task to do and watch how you solve it, to get to know you better,' she explains. I raise my eyebrows. Pam empties Noddy playhouse pieces onto the floor and asks us to build the house.

There are no instructions, but there's a picture on the box. How hard can it be? I spent years designing chemical plants and then improving them. And more recently, in my role as a corporate trainer, I devised and led these sorts of exercises (without the Noddy bit) to teach people about team dynamics, creativity and communication. I am so far within my comfort zone that I've fallen down the back of the sofa. Easy, lemons and squeezy spring to mind.

In a different situation (i.e., the rest of my life), I'd dive in, randomly push pieces of pipe together until I worked out that I'd gone wrong, pull it apart, mutter as I tried different options, open some wine, try something else, then something else, drink more wine; only when I had exhausted both myself, the wine and a stack of YouTube videos would I meekly (and somewhat slurringly) ask Andy to help. But not tonight. Oh no.

'Shall we lay out the pieces first to see what we have?' I say, in truly cooperative style. I let Andy lay out the pieces and ask him how I can help. I am never this egalitarian in real life; but tonight I'm playing the game called Adoption and whilst I'm not entirely clear on the rules, building under the influence is probably a bad move, so I decide to demonstrate how resilient, patient, thoughtful, prepared and parent-like we are. I leave my control freak outside (screaming into a padded box). Like a good girl, I've learnt how to play nicely when someone is watching (though I struggle to maintain the act indefinitely, and never after three glasses of wine).

I let Andy lead because he's more thoughtful and systematic than I am. He quickly realises that there is a piece missing. We remedy our mistake and within minutes we've assembled a credible, if not structurally sound, Noddy house without a single word of blame or any shouting. Quick, quiet, studious, effective and boring.

Parents 1. Noddy 0.

I am secretly hoping for some reaction, a smattering of applause maybe? But Pam just scribbles and her face betrays nothing. Is that good? *Come on, come on,* I think, *please give me a grade.* (I am so competitive it hurts.)

And whilst I am busy patting my own back, she says something that stops my brain in its aren't-I-brill? tracks.

'My job is to find some children for you' — nothing earth-shattering there — 'and I'm also looking for a family for two children, too.'

I get goosebumps, as if a warm blast of air has rippled over my neck.

It's not so much what she says but her tone, all secretive and happy and I-know-something-special-but-I'm-not-telling. Like the way your partner drops hints about your upcoming amazing birthday surprise (or he would, if he knew what was good for him, Andy).

Does, does, does (my brain is paddling furiously to catch up) . . .

Does she mean that these children would be a good Match for us?

What sort of children?

How old are they?

Boys, girls, twins, one of each?

Tell me more, something, anything — I need to know!

This snippet has me reeling. I'm as unsteady as a drunk lamb, and I want to scream or shout or just sob my heart out (or all three at once). She says she just has a 'feeling' about them.

A feeling?

What does that mean?

Her not–poker face is twinkling.

It's a good *feeling. She has a* good *feeling about this. A good feeling that they might be* the *ones.*

This is good news.

This is GREAT news.

These few teasing words are tantalising, a hint of a family to come.

I yearn to hear something, anything, more, but she refuses to divulge it, explaining that it's too soon. We have more work to do and she doesn't want us to focus too much on any individual cases, in case they cloud our judgement. I want to grab her and shake the truth out of her. This is torture. But I'm happier than I've been in ages — she has rekindled the hope she stole when she said we wouldn't make Panel.

The Noddy train has both a new driver and new hope in its engine.

12. Tuesday? See Monday

Why didn't you tell us this five months *ago?*

By now, we should've (and would've if only someone had mentioned it earlier) painted giraffes on the walls, chiselled the sharp corners off tables and turned our boiler down to tepid — to prove to the Panel that we have a child-friendly (but distinctly adult-unfriendly) home. It's exciting but confusing: we've no idea how many beds or bedrooms we need, or what age or gender our children might be.

We start by ensuring our children can't spray floor polish in their eyes or drink bleach by installing catches on kitchen cupboards and drawers. Sorted.

'Fancy a cup of tea?'

'Yes, please.'

'FFFF OW!'

'Are you okay?'

Frickin' rickin' stupid childproof catches. 'Just caught my fingers in the drawer again.'

We spend two painful weeks snagging our clothes and discovering that 'soft-close drawers' don't close softly when your fingers are trapped in them. We put plastic things into sockets to prevent electrocution (the social workers are unmoved by Andy's assertion that fingers in sockets aren't dangerous unless the fingers are made of metal). We play Monopoly with our lounge furniture, and the stove lands on 'Go Directly to Jail'. It's locked behind a grim brown grill that takes all the romance out of the flames. We light the fire one evening and find that it takes so long to unclip the bars (more pinched skin and swearing) and move the guard out of the way that it's easier (if considerably less romantic) to bang the central heating on full. Despite the faces I pull as we install these things (with the sing-along-you've-heard-it-before chorus, 'We never had this when I was a child/when I was a child/when I was a child/we never had this when I was a child and I turned out all right'), these acts are promises of the changes ahead, reminding us that a family is (on a good day) or might be (on a doubt-fuelled day) on its way.

We have to find the key to lock a window that in theory is designed to be fully opening. But in the ten years we've lived here, we've only managed to fully open it twice. Apparently the children we adopt will be sired by the *Mission: Impossible* team (theme music, if you please). In the time it takes me to go to the loo, they'll create an ingenious pulley system using my dressing gown tie to drag a heavy chair across the bedroom until it's beneath the windowsill, clamber onto the chair then onto the narrow sill, stand up and, whilst balancing with the agility of an Olympic gymnast on the beam, turn the handle to three o'clock (two or four o'clock and the escape is a bust). They'll ease the window into the tilt position without overbalancing and knocking themselves out. They've now just got to lean against the window, close it tightly and move the handle to six o'clock. As they move it silently to midday, the window opens like a safe in a bank heist movie. Now comes the tricky bit: they'll counterbalance the opening of the window with their own weight and then ride the opening window in a stunt borrowed from Buster Keaton before rounding the window's edge and landing back on the ledge, from which they can base jump out into the garden and complete their daring mission. This is what we need to protect them from, whilst also applauding their Ethan Hunt–like problem-solving abilities and Nadia Comaneci–like gymnastic abilities.

We find the key like dutiful submissives and lock the window to keep the children we don't have safe whilst suffering a stuffy bedroom at night.

Now onto the hazy bit — the kids' bedroom. We hope to adopt two children (don't even think 'brave'), one of whom will be a girl. She might be a baby (cot, mobile and monitor — check) or a four-year-old (um). We buy a cot bed; that's one bet hedged. Bedding is almost impossible, for everywhere I look it's unwaveringly blue or pink and it's like fingers down a blackboard because I want to raise children who break free of narrow stereotypes. *Why is there so little choice? Why aren't girls allowed to like dinosaurs and become explorers? Why aren't boys allowed to like orange and become . . . um . . . Donald Trump?* They're not even here yet and their bedding will inexorably tip them down a pink or blue slide into gender typecasting before they can even talk. I tell myself in no uncertain terms that I will upend these restrictive pigeonholes. I'll tell them these colours are not legally binding, and until the 1920s, pink was for boys and blue was for girls [deleted soliloquy cum rant]. Another dazzling bedtime story to rival *The Three Little Pigs*. I find some jungle-themed bedding and cling to it like a fretting adoptive-mum-to-be clings to her bottle of Prosecco.

When we proudly show Pam all we've done, hoping for a hint of approval, she just nods and asks for more. *More?* I shriek in my head. She asks me to prepare a risk assessment to prove that we have considered the lethal cocktail of hazards that can maim or kill a child with a single touch. Does she realise that as a chemical engineer I used to prepare health and safety assessments for manufacturing plants that ran to hundreds of pages? That I extensively considered toxic cocktails and events considerably more life-threatening than standing on an upturned plug? I can so manage this.

Wait till she sees this, I think as I spend an hour crawling around my house on my hands and knees, method-acting a toddler. I draw some important conclusions from this experience: *(a)* I'm not as young as I used to be; *(b)* the view is really boring down here — you can barely see the tele; and *(c)* the skirting could really do with a dust.

I create a table that microanalyses our entire home, concluding that it is indeed a deathtrap and how anyone lives in it without killing themselves on an hourly basis is beyond me. I list some actions to make it as safe as houses (oh, that simile won't work . . .), including one that states I need to invite some firefighters over to do a home assessment — well a girl's gotta do what a girl's gotta do, right?

Better put some slap on.

Now we've hidden the arsenic and axes out of reach, we get a house inspection by some pedant with a penchant for peddling panic. Pam and 'Ms JobsWorthy' look at our house in electron-microscopic detail, pointing out anything that might scratch, trip, cut, hurt or harm our imminent arrivals. They tout dire warnings about the possibility of children burning their fingers if they get them trapped behind the hot water pipe to a radiator. *When has that EVER happened?* I frown. I nod and yet decline to insulate two inches of warm copper whilst mumbling about radiators needing a supply of hot water because that is how they're designed to work.

During this Adoption Game, Andy and I have taken a conciliatory, if not obedient, approach. Until now. We're in the garden when the dispute begins. We have a split-level garden with a sheer drop of several feet onto paving, so we know (it's in my risk assessment) that we need a fence. The sticking point is not the fence/no fence debate.

'Six foot,' says Ms JobsW.

'No way!' Andy and I respond in shocked unison.

I look at my husband in astonishment. I hope they can't hear the expletives in my head.

'Why six foot? Surely the children are going to be about two-foot tall when they arrive.'

'Five foot?' the social team counters.

'What?' I hope that the sheer astonishment in my voice conveys that five foot is still ludicrous.

'Three foot!' Andy and I bargain.

Ms JobsW and Pam aren't convinced. JW says that the fence needs to stop strangers (or their birth family) reaching over and grabbing them. *Really? Tosh!* We yield a smidgen and offer them a four-foot fence, and as they prevaricate, Andy demonstrates with a tape measure just how tall and 'more than adequate' it would be to keep the children from escaping and save them from robbers and bandits. They finally give in.

Four feet it is.

'What are you going to do every day from the time Andy leaves the house to the time he gets back?' Pam asks at the end of our meeting (Ms JW has left).

My mouth opens and a strangled gurgle croaks out. I do a credible impression of a child caught drawing on the wall with Mum's best lipstick.

In all the years I've worked from home, Andy's never asked me to account for my time or provide a detailed breakdown of how much time I waste on Facebook. Providing he gets fed and I earn some dosh, he doesn't micromanage me, which is why we're still married. I've worked, walked, swum, danced, gone networking, blogged, stared at my computer hoping for inspiration, written business plans, mind-mapped my future, delivered training, workshops and coaching, failed to ring hot leads and dithered over my website content without ever having to justify myself to anyone. I like my life that way. A kind of free-flowing, take-every-day-as-it-comes life with a bit of dinner thrown in.

Until now, I'd glibly imagined that with a family my life would be much the same — with some extra skipping along the beach. But Pam is not so easily convinced and asks me to create a plan. I nod enthusiastically with a 'that sounds reasonable' expression on my face.

Now, sat at my computer with a blank timetable in front of me, I'm a teenager with an essay on nihilism and Nietzsche to write — and I'm not sure how to pronounce either of them, haven't done any research and am darn sure that winging it isn't going to work. What on earth *am* I going to do when Andy's at work? This is a lot more ominous than the cute jungle bedding would have me believe parenting will be like.

I ponder the endless hours and finally resort to asking the know-it-all that is the Internet. After a few minutes' research in amongst an hour's pointless pottering on Facebook, I have far too many ideas and no idea what to do with them. There are as many playgroups and toddler jamborees within a few minutes' drive of my house as there are gorgeous notebooks in my house. (My name's Emma and I'm a stationery addict.) I ask my friends to help (aka do my homework for me): 'Why on earth would you want to do that?' comments a friend, which I interpret as, 'Why are you creating a schedule?' when the subtext is actually, 'Why would anyone want to spend seven days a week with their kids?'

I tell them that I'll mercilessly plagiarise their ideas. Then I have more ideas than coloured pens (an addiction that plays nicely with my notebook one): baking, messy play, parks, stickers, feeding the ducks. My friends Rosie and Liz concur that having a plan was useful for those days (or weeks) when they were too sleep deprived to think. *Sleep deprived?* I shiver. I need a chunk of sleep the size of a Titanic-sinking iceberg each night to even function — eight hours of it, preferably uninterrupted. Sleep deprived? Let's brush that unlikely event under the carpet and get back to my beautiful, fictional timetable. I fill it with trips to the park, baking, dressing up, story time at the library, water baby classes, Stay and Play, movie night, family outings, long walks in the countryside. Not even a wink to reality.

One of my friends who has youngish kids can relate to this timetable. Bev says I need an asterisk against every option: *could change at a moment's notice, and some days we will sit in the house in PJs and just play. I think she means 'sit in our PJs and drink gin'.

I reply, 'My real plan is: Monday — wing it until exhausted then plonk them in front of tele and hand over to Andy the minute he walks in the door. Tuesday — see Monday.'

I laugh at our online banter, little knowing just how much I will be eating my words when push comes to shove comes to tantrums.

13. Things Not to Say: Part Two

If anyone asks if I'm adopting 'from abroad' one more freaking time . . .

The adoption process is unusual, at times incomprehensible, involves more essays than all my O and A levels put together, and every time I drop 'adoption' casually into conversation, I must then navigate the chat through the dark and stormy waters of ignorance. If you meet someone who's pregnant, there's a plethora of small-talk cul-de-sacs from which to choose: 'When's it due?' or 'That's definitely a boy/girl/flamingo.'

Since most people have never met someone who's adopting, they tend to fall headfirst down some conversational black hole, based on the little they know. But what *do* you say to someone who's adopting? Here's a handy guide.

Things to say

Where are you at in the process?

It's the adoption equivalent of 'When's it due?'

Are you adopting a boy or a girl?

This does somewhat presume that we're adopting only one child, but don't worry, we'll gleefully correct you if you're wrong.

Are you excited?

This focuses on a positive outcome; it's the polar opposite of 'brave'. I might fall weeping over your shoulders as I divulge how scared I am, but that can happen with pregnant women too.

Things NOT to say

Brave.

Enough said.

Are you adopting from abroad?

What? This is not some fashion statement for the paparazzi based on famous adopters. Nearly all UK adoptions are from within our own borders, for children here are crying out for families and homes too.

Good for you.

The words seem positive, but they're often imparted with a tone reserved for a nephew who has just announced that he's raising money to buy a snake to eat his annoying little sister. Patronising? Do you think so?

It's wonderful.

Now if you mean, 'How fantastic, you're finally getting the family you've wanted for so long and I can't wait to meet them,' then you get my thumbs-up. However, if you mean, 'What a wonderful thing you're doing for those children,' please stop. Yes, we are giving these children a much-needed home, but no, we aren't doing it *for them.* If we could have had our own, then we'd be blossoming and birthing. This is not some ecological ideology about the number of people on the planet, something noble and selfless. In our case, it's the only way to have a family, and your putting this altruistic notion over our true motivation makes us deeply uncomfortable.

What made you choose to adopt?

Really? Do you want to open those wounds right now outside Tesco? Have you really thought that through? You want a blow-by-impotent-blow account of our inability to conceive, blocked tubes, his empty blanks, a few miscarriages, some failed IVF treatment and more? This is not a road I suggest you go down. Full stop.

It's just like being pregnant.

(With thanks to my mum for the tirade that follows.) Adoption *is* like being pregnant in a few respects — we would still need to build a fence, and we get a child at the end. *If* we are approved, *if* we get Matched, *if* a child is available. But then the analogy falls flat (and just so you know, this list is far shorter than it was on the night I monologued over Andy's favourite TV show).

Here's why adoption is *unlike* being pregnant:

1. There are no visible indications of the major event about to happen in your life, so you can't get that cracked tooth finally

sorted on the NHS (but you don't have to worry about eating brie or accidentally petting a lamb either), no one gives you a seat on the train or the bus and no one gets excited on your behalf.

2. There are no physical side effects (well, apart from getting RSI from typing hundreds of pages of answers to the same question over and over and over again); you don't chunder into a bowl and hope that the puke on your top doesn't stop people going on about how pregnancy suits you and how you are glowing.

3. You don't have to buy special elasticated jeans and tops made entirely of Lycra, or oils to rub on stretch marks or special cushions to help you sleep, nor do your bosoms grow so that strange men start to look at you with a new leery drool. You basically get to keep your body in its pre-baby condition (bar the impact of cake and gin).

4. You don't have everyone predicting the sex of the baby or touching you like it's open season on your belly. There are no kicks to feel, and there is only endless paperwork to help you get excited or mentally prepared for what is going to happen.

5. There are no decent excuses to send your partner out for odd foodstuffs or a bar of chocolate in the middle of the night (definitely on the con side of this table).

6. There is no definite timescale regarding the child's arrival to help you prepare or help your boss know when you might leave work. It's more like being impregnated by alien — you wake up one morning to find that you're either five months pregnant or that your pregnancy will take two and a half years to come to fruition.

7. You don't end up with a newborn baby. The youngest children available for adoption are a year old, and the competition for them is intense. Personally I'm not all that set on a baby, but that may have something to do with my need for long, unbroken sleep.

8. You don't give birth, so you have no stories to share with expectant mums — no incredible it-changed-my-life remedies to help friends sleep in their final trimester, no advice about birthing pools, no horror stories (or otherwise) of the TENS machine or injections or gas or labour or what happened *whispered tones of horror* 'down there'.

9. You have to answer hundreds of questions covering everything from your first kiss to your A-level results to convince a committee that you're capable of loving and caring for children and that you'll never hit the papers and make social services look like they handed children to the Child Catcher from *Chitty Chitty Bang Bang*.

10. People come around and inspect your house to see if you have your knives in a gravely dangerous item called a knife block or dare to have hot water pipes warming your radiators.

11. You can drink gin without a single person frowning at you, tutting loudly (for that is the British way to show disgust at others within hearing distance) or condemning you verbally for the damage you might be doing to your baby (on the pro side).

It might not be like being pregnant, but I'm eating a lot more cake to cope with the weirdness of it all. When you're pregnant, you also don't get to choose the type of child you want. I joke to Andy that I want to tick a box that says 'Eats well and sleeps through the night', but these aren't the choices we're given.

In the last six months, our ideas about the children we want have evolved. We've gone from three children (Andy's vote) down to a 'brave' two. We want one to be a girl (to balance out my five nephews and not one niece), and we'd originally considered children up to the age of six, but this evening, Pam gives us some case studies that have us changing our minds.

'These examples have similarities to the children I mentioned earlier,' she hints.

Which ones? Which similarities? The cute stuff? Or the she-devil stuff? More torture. Sometimes I wish she would stop with this dangling of morsels. We ponder over the fictional sibling groups and scare ourselves a little — will we ever be ready to cope with the reality of adopting? Hence Evolution Two: we decide to adopt younger children so there's more time for them to settle in without school getting in the way. So, we are now set on two children, one a girl, aged between one and four years old. Those are the simple choices.

Pam gives us a table of options that has us poring over information on the Internet and talking long into the night as we search our souls.

On half a side of A4 paper is the hardest set of questions we'll ever answer. Against a list of statements, we have to pick one of three options: 'Would accept', 'Would not accept' or 'Would discuss'.

Tempted as we are to tick 'Would discuss' against all of them, that would make us look like spineless, unprepared nincompoops. We start with the easiest statement, 'Children who have suffered neglect', and tick 'Would accept' because we are adopting, and asking for one who hadn't would be like asking for a tiny purple-striped elephant that speaks Swahili.

We debate. We discuss. We question ourselves and our answers.

Would we accept a child whose parent had schizophrenia? Would we consider a child from parents with addictions? If so, which — drugs and/or alcohol? What about a child who had disabilities? One who had been sexually abused? The choices are agonising and will affect the shape of our future family.

For every 'Would not accept' I tangle with what the choice says about me and my willingness to love a child whatever his or her circumstances. I admire those with the courage to adopt children who have disabilities, but in our steep-staired three-storey house that's not really an option. It's hard to look at the list and not see a child's face behind every statement. My heart wants to accept them all, love them all, celebrate their abilities however far they are from the bell curve. Yet, some of these children are not for us.

And that leaves a hollow feeling inside me. I'm defeated by how hard life can be.

If we gave birth to children with these challenges we would have loved them, so why don't we want to adopt one? Maybe that 'brave' mantra has sapped our courage. Maybe I don't feel that at the end of this long process of disappointments I have the strength in me to fight for a child with special needs. Maybe because in my dream on the beach, the child beside me walks without a crutch.

We come face-to-face with our prejudices, shallowness and closed-mindedness. What does it say about me that I have chosen not to adopt a child with life-limiting abilities because that's not how I imagined our perfect family?

Ouch. I'm disgusted I even suggested that these children are not perfect. *hangs head in shame*

We make these difficult choices knowing who we are and what we are capable of, and console ourselves with the knowledge that we're one of the few couples adopting siblings.

Tonight has been an uncomfortable night.

14. Now I'm a Believer

'Can you read and return it tonight?' asks Pam, from our sofa.

It's early March and the Big Report is done (kind of, nearly, almost). It *will* be done, once we read it, sign it and return it to Pam by email so that she can submit it at the eleventh hour if we're to hit our Panel date in April. If she doesn't send it first thing tomorrow, we'll be delayed on the runway.

'Of course,' I agree enthusiastically (knowing that Andy can't). *How am I going to manage that? There are a lot of pages.* I am thinking and don't hear what she says next.

'[missed it, so no idea] Panel and Matching on the same date?'
Huh?
What did she just say?
I rewind.
Did she just drop the M-bomb?
'Can we?' I splutter, incredulous, as my brain invents the start of her sentence.

She wants us to go for Panel and Matching together? It's a whispered combination, as rare as a deserted Bournemouth beach on August Bank Holiday Monday. My giddyometer spins off the scale.

I nod vigorously, my eyes wide and my mouth too tacky to speak. As my brain starts processing, Pam gets up and leaves. When the door closes behind her, our thoughts tip out like a jumble of building blocks.

What? Matching? How are we going to read this tonight? Did she say Matching? It's hundreds of pages — is she crazy? Matching? That's real children. We're going to read it. We're not missing Panel. OMG, she said Matching!

The news mashes in our brains and out loud.

Then we read like our lives depend upon it.

A few days later, Pam's back for another meeting. Ta-da! The Big Report is done and submitted (no, Andy didn't read it all) and our Panel is in five weeks' time. I breathe a sigh of relief, and . . . *Pam's awfully smug today. Is that because she got the report submitted? Or . . . does she know something we don't? What could it be?* I am tingling in anticipation. I wait for her to break the tension.

'Are you ready to start Matching?' she asks, as if there's any doubt.

This is the Big Moment, when all the hoop jumping is over and we start to create our future family. Instead of paperwork and theory, this is about real children. Real. Children. Children who could one day sit on this sofa next to me, cuddling up and listening to a story. We'll be looking at names and faces of real lives and . . .

I hesitate a little.

Am I ready?

This is The Moment we've waited for. For years. I am filled with the enormity of This Moment.

Breathe.

We don't have to choose now. We can say no. This is just the first step. It might take months, I tell myself as I gulp some air. I want to snatch the information from her hand and pick a child now.

Yes. I am definitely, achingly ready.

No. I'm not ready.

The Moment has been building for so long that now it's finally in front of me, I'm scared to touch it, as if in reaching out, the spell will be broken and I'll wake up. Just over the crest of this moment is not the sandy beach of my dreams, where I walk hand in hand with my little girl, but something even better. I'm about to crest a different hill, and finally, before me, the possibility of a family will open up and appear.

This one is real. This one is now.

How will I know whom to choose? How can I be sure? What if I don't feel anything? What if we don't like the look of them? These children are not just for Christmas; they are for life. The Moment is finally here. I look over at Andy and we nod together. A broad grin of excitement spreads across my face.

'Yes,' I blurt out before I change my mind.

Pam takes some pieces of paper out of her case and I wriggle. She has three sets of siblings needing parents to show us today and gently reminds us that it's okay if the answer is none. I nod again, hurrying her along, knowing that I'll be gutted with 'none'.

What happens next is indelibly tattooed on my mind.

Imagine a sweeping camera shot. Music plays gently in the background to create a light tension and fill the determined silence of The Moment. The shot sweeps across the chairs, from Pam on my right, to me in the middle, to Andy on my left, tracking each piece of paper in succession. You cannot see the expressions on our faces, for the director doesn't want you to know what we think until we speak.

Pam passes me the first sheet of A4 paper. I look at the photo of a sibling pair (*Oh, a boy and a girl*, I think) and read the little bit of information about them, gulping it like a parched dancer at a rave. When I reach the last word, I turn the paper over and frown, hoping for more, a litre short of sated. There are just a few paragraphs — their names, their personalities (shy, thoughtful) and the fact that they like playing and going to the park. I'm not sure what I was expecting. It's hardly earth-shattering. I read it through twice, my eyes pinging back to the photo several times. I'm disappointed. There's nothing that screams 'oh no, these would be terrible', but neither does the photo shout 'pick me, pick me'. I pass the sheet in silence to my husband.

The next set is also one of each, slightly older, and there's a little bit more to go on. This time I get a 'not really' feeling, although I can't explain why. I start to lose confidence in The Moment, dreading that we might strike out. I read it through again but no sparks appear and I pass it to Andy as the tense silence continues.

Were those the children Pam hinted about at our first meeting? I wonder. I prepare myself for hashtag gutted. I take the third and final sheet. I read it twice, as I did the others, and hand it to my husband.

I study the rug intensely. *It probably needs a bit of a clean, that rug*, I think to distract myself.

I look down, not daring to catch anyone's eyes.

Hurry up, I urge.

I watch Andy finish reading in my peripheral vision. *Come on.*

Back to the rug that's seen better days.

The seconds stretch to ... minutes, at most. Finally Andy puts the third sheet down.

I breathe.

'What do you think?' inquires Pam.

. . .

It's a question I desperately want Andy's answer to.

I dare not speak.

I can't trust myself to go first because then there's no taking it back. What if I tell the truth in all its glorious simplicity and show my hand, and then Andy says the exact opposite?

I dare not speak.

I am naked and vulnerable and powerless. I say nothing, for the tiny croak that might come out could ruin everything. For the thing that I hoped would happen, but did not believe could happen, has in fact happened. An enchanting moment that I'll never forget. The first two sets of children seemed nice enough, but I felt nothing more than searing disappointment. But the third set. . .

As soon as I saw their pictures, all hell broke loose inside of me. A shiver passed down my spine. A flush spread up to my cheeks. I could barely suppress a grin. She's smiling with a twinkle in her eyes that says 'mischief', wearing a big floppy hat, and he's looking content, crawling on his belly in dungarees. My heart pounded. It was as if suddenly my whole life made sense, that this journey made sense, that *I* made sense, like the feeling I got when Andy held my hand to dance with me all those years ago. An inexplicable feeling that blinded me to everything but that sensation. I looked at their pictures and something clicked, as if I'd met them before. It was like God grabbed me and shouted 'THEM' inside my heart.

I can't explain it. I've fallen in love. There isn't a shred of doubt in my mind, heart or soul. I simply know.

These are my children.

I am fit to burst. My composure is starting to break; it's a good job I'm sitting down. The Moment is more than I'd ever hoped for, even sweeter for the cold indifference I felt towards the first two sets. But what if Andy feels different? What if he thinks the second set is the right one? What if he doesn't like any of them?

The moment stretches. I let my silence lie in the gaping void between her question and his answer. Devastation is just a word or two away and I can't even contemplate how this evening will implode if Andy's thoughts contradict my own powerful yearning.

In my hesitation, Andy talks first.

'The last ones.'

My breath rushes out.

[Director's note: An enormous gospel choir in purple and gold appears and starts belting out a hallelujah chorus in a sunbeam-filled church, their harmonies lifting the congregation's spirits as high as the crooked spire. A cloud of doves flies out into the sky past blossom-filled cherry trees, and huge bells ring in glorious celebration.]

I nod, vigorously, unwilling to let the love gush out of my mouth, afraid that my words can't do justice to how I feel.

'There was nothing wrong with the other two sets, but there was something about the third lot,' Andy explains. *Did he read my mind?* I nearly jump up and hug him and spin him around in a dance. I nod my head quietly.

'These are the children I mentioned,' reveals Pam. All four of us landed on her desk the same day, and when she saw our photos, she said she 'just knew'. All because SWN1 went off sick. Funny old world.

She asks if we mind that they like a lot of hugs and kisses. 'Not at all,' I say. *Bring it on*, I think. She tells us more about the children but I'm too deafened by the gospel choir and church bells.

'There's no rush. You don't have to decide right now,' she says, and I am seized with a ridiculous urge to shout, 'It's too late already! I've decided: I want these children and I want them now!' I ache to rush, but this is no decision to make on impulse. It's important to get it right. We say that we want to progress, and she says we need to confirm tomorrow.

After she leaves, I read through the meagre details again and again and again and again. As my heart stops pounding, I search for the hints that these children are wrong for us. This is one of the most important decisions of my life, and yet my heart chose in an instant. We have to be sure, but I've never been as sure of anything in my whole life. I read it twenty, thirty times. There are no warning sirens going off in my brain. I don't want a single doubt in my mind to taint the process ahead. I look and peer and search and I can't find clues that subtly tell me they're going to be a nightmare.

Andy and I talk for hours. This is our positive pregnancy test moment. We cry, we hug, we dance, we talk some more. We search for all the reasons why not and when we can't find a single shred of one, we both agree. We want them to join our family.

I cannot believe this feeling: my whole life has changed.

I text a friend: 'Sorry I haven't replied, been falling in love with possible kiddies instead.' She asks for more details and I respond, 'We're not supposed to say anything, but I am bursting.' I want to shout from the rooftops and tell the whole world about the fairy-tale ending that is just around the corner. It's still too early, like announcing you're pregnant before the first scan; there's still a great deal that can stop this Match.

But I know that tonight, I met my children.

After a night of giddy excitement and little sleep, we ring Pam and confirm that we want to go ahead. We want to be Matched with the third set of children.

'Are they still on the market?' I ask, desperate to know that another couple will not sneak in and steal them from us.

'They won't be offered to other adopters now,' is her reply. *Phew!* The thought of losing them is too much to bear.

Saying yes sets a whole new chain of events into action, like some autocatalytic reaction (four years at university, three researching my PhD all for that one reference). There's just over a month to Panel, and to be Matched on the same day we have to jump through a whole new set of hoops in record time — more meetings, a gradual divulgence of information regarding the children and their background and of course the obligatory paperwork to convince the Panel that we are the Perfect Match for these specific children.

And there is a tiny spanner in the works.

Pam is the *children's* social worker and *our* social worker.

She can't be both.

We need two independent social workers at the Matching Panel, one to represent the views and needs of the parents (i.e., us) and another to represent the needs of the children (i.e., not us). In the interests of impartiality and the process and all that stuff, it's time to bring on SWN3. And I can't help but hear Lady Bracknell from *The Importance of Being Earnest* saying, 'To lose one social worker may be regarded as a misfortune; to lose two seems like carelessness.'

We are now on to the understudy's understudy. A man this time, who has a heck of a job to do — in just a few weeks, he's got to read the Big Report (although he gets longer than we did) and start attending all the meetings with the foster family and so on.

Talk about hitting the ground running; it's more like jumping onto a treadmill spinning at top speed and hanging on for dear life.

15. The Adoption Triangle

Warts ahoy. We've seen their photos and have read about how lovely they are. It's time to complete the Adoption Triangle — birth parents, adoptive parents and children. We need to read about their birth family and why they were taken into care and put up for adoption.

We're sent the warts-and-not-much-else account of the children's birth family, used to convince a court to grant an adoption order. It makes sobering reading. It doesn't mention the love these parents have for these children, or describe happy times, or contain photos of birthdays or Christmases. As I read, I want to throw my arms around these children, hold them tight and whisper, 'I'll protect you.'

A few people are judgemental about people whose children are sent into care, as they wait for their Ocado delivery of blinis and Bombay Sapphire. They're outraged that we *allow* people who've already neglected one child to *continue* to give birth. Yet the unspoken alternative is sterilisation, a mere hop, skip and a jump away from eugenics, which didn't end well the last time we went down that rabbit hole (and may God forgive me for such trivialisation of the matter). 'It's scandalous', they continue, 'that these people should be allowed to churn out children like . . . that family, do you remember, Alastair? Oh dear God. On that flight back from Barbados last Christmas.' (They shudder.) They're indignant, outraged, ready to write a stern letter to the *Guardian*.

'And where would that leave me?' I ask.

'B . . . An . . . Wh . . .'

They step meekly down from their soapbox.

Don't get me wrong, I don't want children to be neglected and taken into care, but without this reality, I wouldn't have a chance of becoming a mum. It's not an easy truth to live with.

Their birth parents will become part of my life. If I judge them, how will I ever talk to my adopted children in a way that leaves them able to discover information about their birth parents for themselves? I am magnolia; I won't colour their view of their birth parents by overemphasising the little I know, or whitewashing the situation by disguising the truth, or adding a splash of disdain from the oh-so-exquisite luxury of my AGA-Smeg-MAC lifestyle.

They're not that different from you and me. We're all just one biting recession away from a life that quickly spins out of control. Like my sister. She had her own home, a good education and a career. Yet when mental illness hit . . .

Birth parents love their children. They fight for them, they cry over them, they grieve when they lose them and are bereft when they're told they can't have them back. Their lives are not the life that I've known, but they're doing the best they can in their circumstances. It seems a shame that I'll benefit from their misfortune. As a society, have we let these people down? Have we failed to save them from poverty, from drugs, from drink, from the darkness in their own minds? Have we cut, sliced and slashed budgets until there isn't enough support, advice and help? We say we want hospitals with no waiting lists, first-class schools for our children and hundreds of coppers and social workers to keep our society running smoothly, but when push comes to shove, we'd rather buy a wide screen tele to watch *Downton Abbey* and go skiing twice a year than volunteer more taxes to pay for them.

I've blubbed through enough episodes of *Long Lost Family* to know that birth parents never forget their children. Every birthday they experience their loss again as they wonder where their children are, and whom they are celebrating with. They speak of unbearable, unshareable secrets and a guilt that never leaves them.

Maybe I'm naïve, maybe I'm unrealistically optimistic, but I refuse to demonise their birth parents. I refuse to see them as inadequate, as anything other than people who are doing their best, even if their best falls short of what society decides is the standard of parenting that children deserve.

They are the people through which these children came into the world.

Children who may one day be my children, part of my family, our future.

They've made this dream possible.

And if only for that, I thank them with all my heart.

16. Their Story

Even though we know so little, it's possible to say too much.

Our family and friends are hungry for news. We finally have something to share, some good news, our own 'we're expecting'. And people want to know everything — the trouble is, there isn't much to say. We know so little.

How old are they? We can do that one.

What are their names? That one too.

Then conversation grinds to a premature halt. Everyone wracks their brains for a way to rekindle our exciting exchange.

What happened to them?

Ah . . .

The first time, Andy and I were caught out and told them some of what we know, for we wanted to have more to say, to keep the flow going, to stoke the fire of our own giddiness.

The second time, we felt ashamed, like we'd been caught licking the TV during cake week on *The Great British Bake Off*.

The shame bites, and we agree on a pact of silence.

Think about it. Do you really want to know what my children have experienced? How they were neglected? Do you want your first feelings towards them to be sympathy, horror, pity? Should your eyes search for wounds before you even notice their smiles? Do you really need to know if they've been starved, mistreated, abused or addicted to drugs before they were born? Would that not taint your opinion of them and create a self-fulfilling prophecy, limiting who they'll become? Will you be forever seeking evidence that substantiates what you know of their history? How will knowing how they were neglected help you to welcome them, to treat them with respect and dignity, to love them unreservedly?

Are you hoping for a glimpse of the gossip behind the headlines?

These are two young children who have experienced neglect. They've lost their family and everything they knew. They need love and compassion, and that will come more readily from a heart and mind empty of gothic stories.

If anyone asks, I tell them, as I tell you now, that it's *their* story, not ours. It's *their* history.

It happened before they met us, before they lived with the foster family. That story is for them, and them alone, to share, if and when they feel they want to. It's not left my mouth since.

When pressed, I state vaguely, 'It wasn't that bad.' And it doesn't matter if that's the truth or not.

You will not find their story in this book.

17. A Four-Sided Triangle

We're sitting straight and ultra-polite on our tea-with-the-vicar best behaviour — because today, we're being scrutinised by the children's foster carers at our home. It's like meeting your boyfriend's parents: you want to make a good impression, you want them to like you and you want their blessing. All of which makes this more daunting than is strictly necessary. This is our chance to swot up on the children so we can buy all the stuff we need. I've a long list of questions about what food they eat, what they drink from, their favourite stories, bath routine, bedtimes and more, even though I don't know what I need to know, or don't know what I don't know or some such Donald Rumsfeld-ness.

The foster carers are the heroes of this story. They welcomed two frightened children into their home and nurtured them through a traumatic event. They'll have a huge impact on our lives, especially during the two weeks of Handover (called Introductions[6]), and they've already made an unforgettable impact on the children we hope to adopt. Saying I'm nervous is like hinting that Everest is a bit of a hill.

They arrive with their social worker (we have so many I need a collective noun for them — a confoundment of social workers?) and sit down as we arrange ourselves around them. The foster carers are Ken and Mary, and they're a lot older than we thought they'd be. They sit stiff and rigid; the atmosphere tingles with the

---

[6] **Introductions:** A two-week vocational course on how to parent with gradual handover of responsibility from the foster family to the parents. This 'course' barely scratches the surface of the necessary skills, is unbelievably exhausting and leaves you feeling woefully unprepared.

Nearest equivalent: Learning to drive a ten-tonne army logistics lorry over enemy territory, dodging mortars, in just twenty-four hours.

static of our lives rubbing up against each other. We break the ice with the inevitable 'Cup of tea?'

Then Pam suggests they start by sharing their photos of the children.

'I didn't know which ones you'd want to see, so I brought them all,' says Mary apologetically. I am greedy to look at all of them, to round out the three we've already committed to memory. We see the photos of when they first arrived with the foster family, when he was just a baby. They tell us how rigid the girl was, how her whole body went stiff when they held her, how she didn't recognise her brother. And we admire how lovely they look now. As Mary tells the stories behind the photos, her tone explains everything: the love they feel for these children is palpable, powerful and peppered with grief. As she talks about how wonderful they are, Ken's eyes fill with tears. We've never considered how the foster parents might feel.

It's clear that they don't want to let them go, that they aren't ready for the separation that's looming. If they were ten years younger, they say, they would've adopted these children themselves. It is a statement saturated with regret.

I interrogate them, hoping to learn something to bury my fears — what do they like to eat, what time do they wake up and go to bed, what are their favourite things to do? I am a leech for facts, but I have no idea what the important information is in this random haystack. My questions grind to a halt, for Ken and Mary are becoming increasingly distressed. However supportive we are of what they have done, we are dripping water into a bucket with a massive hole in the bottom. There is nothing we can do to ease their pain. We are the cause of it; we are taking away these kids to whom they have dedicated over a year of their life. As we skip with excitement towards the end of this journey, we face the hurdle of their loss.

It's no Adoption Triangle — it's an Adoption Square.

They leave us with a DVD of the children and a shadow of grief on our hearts.

Andy and I watch the DVD to lighten the atmosphere. The tiny silver disc is a window into their world; it contains four short clips. In the first we see the boy toddling near a sofa, playing and making noises (*ba, ugh, wa*) as he goes. After a few seconds, he starts to get upset; the clip ends. It adds real depth to what we've read. He's evolved from a photo and words on a page to a grunting, moving, giggling boy. The next shot is longer; the boy and the girl are playing together. He's putting bracelets on his arms and she's taking them off him and hiding them beneath the seat of a plastic car. He takes them out, puts them back on his arms; she takes them and hides them again. She's in a party dress with a red tutu skirt and is a mass of curls and jewellery. He's in a smart shirt and nappy, and curiously has no trousers on. Then she notices the camera, goes up to the lens, stares down it and declares, 'It's my bobble,' in her high, squeaky voice.

Three words and our hearts melt.

Another clip: they're bouncing on a sofa, giggling their heads off, full of mischief and fun. She calls the cameraman 'Ken' and 'Daddy'. The final clip sees them crammed under a small glass table, toggling the lamp's switch on and off, smiling impishly at the cameraman.

How gorgeous? I can't stop myself grinning.

They are everything we dared to dream of, and more. The videos are brilliant, like someone stole a truckload of cute and tipped it over these two tiny people.

I play with the word 'perfect' on my tongue, rolling it around the inside of my mouth and then pinching myself in case this is all too much.

I imagine these children in our house, playing underneath a glass table we don't have, looking at me the way they look with undisguised love at the cameraman. Then they're bouncing on our sofa, giggling hilariously while I'm staring, caught up in the beauty and innocence of it all. I want to shower them with bracelets to hide all over the house, in every single nook and cranny. We'll move them in and walk hand in hand into the sunset and live happily ever after.

We watch the DVD as obsessively as we devoured the A4 sheet about them. Over and over. We notice (uh-oh) that she can open doors and wonder how that affects my risk assessment. And when Andy goes to work, I watch it some more, hugging my knees with joy.

These lovable, cute, apparently perfect children could be joining our family soon. Really soon. Like a few weeks soon. Well, a few weeks until we meet them then another two weeks till we bring them home for good. Giddy does nothing to express how I feel; I am floating on a cloud of hope. Am I dreaming or awake? Please Lord, do not wake me up from this moment.

And I fall in love all over again because I can't help myself.

18. Crackerjack Friends

As the pile teeters on my arms, I adjust my balance, like a child on the BBC TV kids' programme *Crackerjack*, trying to stop my tower of prizes tumbling to the ground.

I've had lunch with my friends David and Truda at their place, and I'm delighted to discover that they're almost as giddy as I am.

'Come with me,' says Truda mysteriously after lunch, and she does that finger-worm thing. I meekly follow, looking back to David in confusion. He just smiles. I shrug and go.

'You'll need some of these,' she says, rummaging through a kitchen drawer filled with unbreakable plates and cups in a kaleidoscope of colours. My face reads gobsmacked.

'Do you have plates?' she asks, and I shake my head, ashamed to admit that we've nothing more than fence panels and a cot bed. Truda cherry-picks items and piles them onto my outstretched arms, which soon resemble the Leaning Tower of Plastic, whilst I blink in confusion at how two tiny children can possibly need this much stuff. I follow her blindly around her house as she stacks more and more things on top. *I'm not sure I can carry any more.* Finally I tip my armload into a black bin bag. *Wow! How sweet. That's amazing.*

But Truda has barely warmed up, clearly on a decluttering roll. I win pillows, duvets, bath toys and the entire Gap clothing line for boys aged two to three. In the playroom my jaw scrapes the floor — it has more wooden swords than a National Trust gift shop, more Lego than the Lego movie and more toys than, well, a toy shop. I drive home on a high, not because of the bootful of goodies, but because I've spent time with people whose excitement is so infectious that I momentarily forgot how scared I am.

There's so much to do.

We need to build a fence — well, Andy does. He's offered to do it, in that I'm-a-man-so-bashing-and-burning-stuff-is-my-domain BS, even though he is to DIY what I am to nursing (without the fainting). A month of snow and ice-hard ground, coupled with his lack of fence-building expertise, has had Andy putting it off, but I'm not failing the Panel for lack of a fence. He won't admit that he's out of his depth, and after too much (to my mind) and not-quite-enough (or the fence would be up) nagging, I plead for help. Our friends (bless them) pitch in and put up our fence whilst Andy holds the hammer and I bring a steady stream of cups of tea.

We go to Mamas & Papas to buy a pram, scratch our heads at all the options, wonder which of these ridiculously complicated versions is right for our family, blanch at the prices and leave feeling confused and overwhelmed.

We buy a cot to add to the cot bed, so at least they both have somewhere to sleep, and then spend an evening putting it together with less grace and success than we had with the Noddy playhouse. And once our huffing is over, their room starts to look like a nursery. A prison of a nursery with blank walls, one chest of drawers and two slatted cells. Hmm.

We need to buy car seats, and in a shop with so many options my brain aches, I politely inquire which seats are suitable for children of their age. The assistant looks at me with a patronising glare and asks how heavy they are. I look blankly back at her and shake/shrug. We ask Pam to ask Mary to weigh them.

I research all the stuff we might need, get overwhelmed by the arguments on Netmums (parenting websites seem to encourage bickering; you read ninety-seven comments about nappy bins and are still none the wiser), ring my twin, Sarah, who says 'you don't need all that crap' and that I should buy just the essentials: bibs, a changing mat, stuff for the nursery walls in bright colours. As I frame wallpaper samples to brighten their room, my nesting instinct kicks in.

We go to another shop to buy a pram and wander around in a daze of stupidity. We don't really know if we need one (he can toddle), or if we want a push chair (what's the difference?), or a twin pram, or a pram with a boogie board (which involves a lot less disco dancing than the name would suggest) and they seem so heavy and unwieldy and even with our enormous boot how will I ever fit the wine in? Again, we leave feeling confused and overwhelmed.

I attend my last business networking event and then, with some trepidation, pack away my business like a children's TV presenter of yore putting a tortoise into a cardboard box filled with hay for the winter, except I know that I'll be poking and prodding this hibernating beast regularly so I don't lose my clients in a puff of baby powder. I'm excited about being a mum, but I love running my own business. I wonder how I will balance them but mutter something about there being plenty of hours in the day and where there's a will there's a way and some other optimistic nonsense.

As we traipse around Mamas & Papas again, I'm utterly speechless at the huge sums of money you can spend on a baby. How can a baby need a pram that costs thousands of pounds? This store makes me feel inadequate, as if the money I spend on my children is a direct measure of how much I love them, and I guess that's the point. I rail at marketing campaigns designed to brainwash us into thinking we're somehow incompetent if we don't spend thousands of pounds on car seats covered in custom-designed fabric (for them to puke over), embossed with their initials (despite the fact they can't read) and featuring Dolby surround sound lullaby players (to drive you bonkers on a long journey), heated seats with optional air conditioning for the summer heatwave (that lasts all of ten hours), a USB charger for their i(am-too-young-to-need-a)Phone, a drink holder, an ice dispenser, airbags, a pollen destroyer, an intercom, a clip for Mr Snuggles and God knows what else (we never needed it in my day).

I am tempted to splurge because my brain is soft on serotonin and my nesting instinct screams, 'Buy it all!' but money is tight. My business took a substantial hit whilst I was caring for Claire, and we're about to survive for six months (and not a month longer) on one salary, with no adoption pay. The most expensive indulgence in our house, after wine, is Assam tea, so after nearly choking on the cost of two car seats, we bow to our overdraft and buy two used seats. Yes, I said 'used' — despite the fact that everyone told us we *had* to buy new car seats, that second-hand was potentially endangering their lives. Did you tut at our irresponsible attitude to safety? We install the seats and everything clicks into place. Car? Check. Seats? Check. Beds? Two, check. Unimaginable quantities of stuff from Truda? Check. Pram? Still confused and overwhelmed (check). So, no.

Deep down, I feel a fraud doing a Hugh Grant in *About a Boy*, spilling crisps over the child seat and faking being a parent to win someone else's approval (in Hugh's case, to get laid). But those car seats make me feel proud.

We're that close I can almost taste the scent of children. (Which I naïvely imagine smells like baby lotion.)

19. A Sales Pitch to Toddlers

What on earth am I doing?

Andy's balancing at the bottom of a slide, arms and legs in the air. There are two cuddly toys at the top, and I'm taking a photo in a life that's being directed by Terry Gilliam (it doesn't make much sense anymore). A Python-esque cartoon foot squishing Andy could not make it much weirder than it already is. I don't belong here. My life is all out of shape; it's mine yet not mine, and I'm giddy and terrified and it's all so sudden, it's happening too fast, after years of not happening at all.

Let me take a breath and back up a bit. We're creating some marketing spin for our children-to-be. This is a chance for us to *(a)* help them get used to the idea that they will be getting a mummy and daddy; and *(b)* let them know those people will be us. It's also an opportunity to *(c)* mercilessly suck up to the foster parents, because we want them to think we are going to be incredible parents.

In these last few days before Panel (we are so close) we have to:
1) Create a scrapbook for the girl (photos and words)
2) Create a talking book for the boy (photos with audio recordings of our voices — ugh, am I the only one who hates how she sounds on tape?)
3) Shoot a short video of us
4) Buy each child a toy

The Panel will look at these books and toys, so we need them to provide irrefutable evidence that we're the Perfect Match for these children. And the minute the word 'perfect' enters my psyche, I know I'm in for an impossible task.

We also decide to buy a new front door. (Why now? Who knows.) We wait until the new door is installed before taking the photos and video of the house because we completely overestimate what toddlers will notice and inexplicably believe that they'll arrive at our house and declare in a confused manner, 'This can't be right — the door in the photos had a window in it, and this one doesn't. Jeeves, turn the car around; we're going home.' By doing so, we create a delay that ensures we have next to no time to cram it all in at the last minute (guess whose brilliant idea this was?). In the interim, we buy their toys: the very first magical gifts from us to our children — given before we meet them in person.

They're just toys. (How hard can it be?)

But they're not. They are expressions of hope, joy, a happy future together and more. Without being enormous (it's frowned on), they need to convey in fluffy form just how much we want to be the children's parents without creating competition (his is better than mine) or confusion (that's mine; no it's not). What if we buy a panda and they're scared of them? Which is the cutest teddy bear? My head spins.

We visit a local shop and discover some gorgeous toys. They're so luxurious and soft. I touch one, pick it up, bury my face in it, and as I snuggle into the deep downy softness, I know I want to buy them Jellycat toys (soo fluffy). We're nearly there. That evening, as I scroll through pages of Jellycat toys online, there is an unfeasibly long list of similarly sized toys to choose from. Andy mutters something about 'any of them will do' so I huff and declare his input no longer necessary. My eyes start to droop and my brain hurts as I weigh up the pros and cons of each choice, comparing and contrasting them until that Buy It Now button is burnt forever into my retina. We're running out of time. I choose a dog and a bunny and press Buy.

When the cuddly toys arrive a few days later, we start the photo and video shoots; everything must fit together into a seamless jigsaw of information (toy, Mummy, house with new door). It's like an audition tape for *Play School* and *Jackanory*. We go to the park and take photos of their toys on the slide, in our arms, on the swings. We feel awkward and out of place in the park — a place that we've never been to in seven years of living here. And we really hope that no one is watching. *Hilda, come and look at these strange people in the park. Should I call the police?*

For a week, I sleep with the cuddly dog and rabbit under my PJs to give them our scent. This will make us more familiar to them when we meet (in the smell dimension, at least). I stroke and squeeze their softness, hug them tightly, pour my hopes and dreams into them, tickle my skin with their soft fur, love them to suffocation, lose myself in their soft huggability. And one night, as I dream of a gorgeous man who is in love with me (oh George — I wish it were Clooney but it was Gorgeous George from *Amazing Spaces*, go figure), I go all mushy and flutter my eyelashes and he is leaning in for a kiss and just as I pucker up in expectation, a paw lands on my face, freaking the life out of me! I scream, punch the dog and rabbit away and wake with a jolt. I forgive them more easily than I do when my husband does the same thing (flopping his hand on my face, not puckering up for a kiss).

I print the photos and I use my creativity, washi tape and a loose relationship with the truth to create these books. I write that we love to splash in muddy puddles (because they love *Peppa Pig*). I do not say that Mummy is a neat freak and mostly stays away from puddles and would rather everyone wore a hazmat suit and not set a single muddy foot inside the house. I write that Daddy loves the slides, despite the fact that at six foot four his feet nearly touch the ground when he is sat at the top of it, and that even with his slim build, he gets stuck on most slides (as does Mummy).

I don't mention watching *Silent Witness* or *The Matrix*, or that Daddy reads business books about who-knows-what and that until a few weeks ago we'd never even heard of *Peppa Pig*. I don't say that we like to go to the cinema to see movies like *Avatar* and *Iron Man*, meet friends for a drink or a-few-too-many and then go for an entirely unnecessary curry that makes Andy's head sweat and lies undigested in our bellies until the morning. Or that our idea of heaven is a long lie-in at the weekends followed by a long stomp and Sunday lunch in the pub with a pint. I don't say that we eat fish fingers only once a year, on Valentine's Day (as a yah-boosucks to overcrowded, overpriced and underromantic restaurants), surrounded by daffodils (as an up yours to the predictable, extortionate, unscented red roses). I don't tell them how much Mummy needs a good night's uninterrupted sleep if you want her to be charming in the morning, but then neither did we confess that to the social workers.

We record voiceovers for the talking album, saying things like, 'I am your mummy' and 'This is your bedroom', and it is so strange and exciting. I'm not their mummy, I don't feel like a mummy; I feel like a charlatan, pretending to be a mummy to children I've never met.

These sales pitches are an echo of a future that's on its way. They start our metamorphosis into a family. We begin to see our house with children in it, our life with children in it. As strange as it is, we better start getting used to it.

Because that park is going to be the centre of our universe soon enough.

20. Nibbles and Bubbles

It's time to celebrate. PART-EEEE!

The Big Report is in.

The Panel date is in the diary.

We've chosen our children.

We've spun some words and photos to reel them and the Panel in.

It's been a long time getting to this place, so of course we're going to celebrate. Something small and discreet? Oh no. We're inviting everyone. It's a chance to say thank you to everyone who's helped; a swansong of hedonistic revelry before the reality of being parents kicks in; our last dance as a couple before our family becomes four.

We set a party date, even though we won't know for certain that we'll be approved and Matched. Pam frowns when she gets wind of the plan. We shouldn't jump the gun with a party, she tells us. Even if the Panel gives us a double yes (yes we can adopt, yes we can adopt these children), they're not the final decision makers. They only make a recommendation to the head honcho (HH). If this person agrees, a week later the Panel's decision is ratified. But only if this person agrees.

This makes for super-awkward party organisation. Let me take you through the calendar: Tuesday is Panel day. The following Tuesday, HH agrees or disagrees. If HH agrees, two days later (Thu) we meet the kids. We either have a weekend party after the Panel but before it's ratified, or a midweek one between HH (Tues) and meeting the kids (Thu). Now I don't know about you, but to me, corralling tens of people and their families with just twenty-four hours' notice to a Wednesday night party seems like a recipe for rattling around in an empty house and eating hors d'oeuvres for a fortnight.

We ignore our social workers' shaking heads and invite everyone around for a party on the Saturday after Panel. Yes, *dun dun duhhhh* — *before* it is officially ratified.

I get my iPad out, doodle a design for the invitations and call the party And Then There Were Four (a phrase inspired by Agatha Christie and A. A. Milne). We expect sixty guests (everyone's said yes), and we'd better give them something to line their stomachs. Nothing too lavish; I can't prepare my usual vats of chilli and lasagne for sixty given how much else there is to do. So I put my foot down (before Andy decides on an eight-course soirée) and agree on light bites (nibbles, really) with cheese. And yet the sides start to multiply faster than rabbits — there's crackers, celery (which no one will eat but it's mandatory), pickles by the vinegar load, damson cheese (what now?), cherry tomatoes, grapes . . . Suddenly even light nibbles gets complicated. And since we're celebrating, it's the perfect excuse for champagne, aka bubbles. The invitation says: 'Saturday from 3 p.m., for Nibbles and Bubbles'.

My bestie Allan texts a few days later: 'Megs asked if Nibbles and Bubbles are your children's names.' LOL! *Bonkers. Hang on, what if . . . ?*

Social media is a bit of a minefield for all parents, and even more so for adoptive parents; we've been warned not to put anything on social media, in case their birth family tries to find them. 'Nothing?' I squealed as my FB addiction got wind. Megs has provided an unexpected yet elegant solution — from that moment on, I call the children Nibbles and Bubbles online.

To make status updates and this book even more confusing, we also decide to use these names for their toys: Nibbles (the rabbit, of course) and Bubbles (the other one).

Now we just have one more hurdle to bumble over — Panel. We're waiting for the Del Monte men and women to say *sí*.

21. The Reckoning

I'm as giddy as a teenage girl at a Katy Perry concert. I need to run up a mountain and blast out 'The Hills Are Alive' to release the elastic band inside me that's wound too tight. Andy's driving and it's probably just as well, for my feet and legs are dancing. We've driven for about half an hour, to what feels like a secret location, in near silence. My insides are churning; I swing between wanting to be sick and wanting to slap myself.

We park and walk slowly towards the building because, of course, we're a tad early. We're present to every single detail and at the same time, not present. I take little notice of the sunshine poking through the trees, but the image is engraved forever in my memory.

Andy and I hold hands as we enter the rather dilapidated municipal building. Depending on what happens in the next hour or so, it will be described in the myths and legends that stem from today as either a gorgeous period estate or a hideous wreck. We sign in, sit down and wait for someone to escort us through the mysterious doors into the puzzle within.

It's six years since we married and started trying for a family. A year since I picked up the phone and took The First Step. Six months since we attended Intensive Training. We're here (at last), two months later than expected. One of the other couples from our training has already taken their little girl home; most of the rest have been approved (some with conditions) and are starting the Matching process. Not that it's a competition, but we'll leapfrog some if today goes to plan.

Pam comes down, says hello. We mutter stifled responses and follow her upstairs, twisting through the maze of corridors and fire doors that create bureaucratic ugliness in what used to be a stunning mansion. It's Victorian — all high ceilings, sash windows and fancy mouldings around the cornices, except in the cramped side room where we end up. It contains square frosted windows with metal security grills deep inside, a cheap coffee table and some boring brown office chairs (designed to suck the life out of you). There isn't even a hint of the Victorian splendour of the landing.

Pam gestures to a chair and then leaves. I perch on the edge of it. Then stand and pace in tiny circles in the room. Then visit the ladies to squeeze out a tiny pee. I want to drink something my mouth is so dry, but I don't want to be bursting for a wee when they call us in. I sit in rigid suspense.

I'm wearing the wrong life. Nothing feels right or fits right; it's like a suit you haven't worn for ages — when you put it on, it's shrunk and won't let you move smoothly. This is the most important day of my life and I don't know how to just be, how to let these emotions and experiences flow through me. So I fidget and sigh and struggle to contain it.

Then Pam and SWN3 arrive, and the room feels suddenly disturbingly full. Pam's here to represent the children's interests, but as the key worker on our case, she's also here to talk on our behalf, whilst SWN3 is an independent voice representing us when it comes to Matching. Pam is our hero. SWN3 is here mostly for show, like spare-wheel nuts you keep in the glovebox and never use.

Somewhere in the myriad of drab rooms sits a Panel of people who decide whether people meet the criteria to adopt. We're just one in a day of decisions that will be met with a whoop or a tear. We're about to enter a roomful of people who know a lot more about us than is comfortable for a first date — it would normally take me a decade of slurred late-nights to confess all that they've read in the Big Report: our hopes and dreams, stuff about our love life and exes, our finances, our school grades, the arguments we had with our parents as teenagers, our cholesterol levels, what our best friends think of us and more. Pages and pages of details that we hope demonstrate that despite our faults (we fessed up to a few), we can be trusted to take good care of a child.

Pam describes the process again, in simple words, which is good right now. She shows us the questions that the Panel will ask. It feels like a test. It is a test. Each person on the Panel will ask one, and the list includes queries about our finances, the work outstanding on the house, how soon I might go back to work and how we might cope if they attach to one of us more strongly than the other. Some of them appear to be stock questions, others are bespoke; they're things we've thought about, talked about and written about already. We rehearse our answers and the social workers nod happily.

Eventually we're invited into the room. We're a crocodile of nerves with our social workers at the tail. We enter (there's no chequered floor and the perspective seems fine), and I sit down with Andy on my left, with the social workers sandwiching us together. Our seats form the fourth side of a rectangle, and I notice that there are ten people in the room to impress. The chairwoman introduces herself and smiles, starting a ripple of smiles that don't help me relax. My stomach's so knotted I worry that I'm going to draw attention to myself in a way I don't want to.

Please don't let me fart.

I'm tempted to write that our future is in their hands. But it's not. Our future's been firmly in our hands since the beginning. We attended the training, made ourselves available for every meeting, read copious numbers of books, completed meticulous research, wrote answers to questions in great detail (sometimes too much detail), prepared a timetable, cried, danced, balanced our budget, made a Noddy house, read *coughs* and corrected the Big Report, got giddy over photos of two kids, cried again, painted the nursery, bought cots and jungle bedding, fretted over the perfect toys, slept with the toys, created books to introduce ourselves to the children, shot a silly video and lost a decade's worth of sleep. And now we sit here nervously waiting for The Reckoning.

These ten men and women are here to ascertain if we're suitable to be adoptive parents. They might say yes. They might say yes, but only one child at a time. They might say yes, but you have to lose weight. They might even say no. There's part of me that thinks they can't possibly say no, not after all the work we've done, not after all the hoops we've jumped through.

They ask their questions.

My emotions have got my tongue; even my thoughts feel drunk on emotion. Today Andy is the eloquent, chatty one.

Then it's my turn, because I'm asked when I might return to work. I say that it will depend, but not for at least a year (I am obliged to stay off for six months, and my plan is not a day more, but Pam suggested I say a year). I manage to sound coherent (I think). They ask us what will happen if one child attaches more strongly to one of us, and I say that we know that can happen and we'll take things gently and do what we can to help them attach to us both in time. They nod as we talk. Then the questions are over, and it is too soon, and I want to say more because I am not convinced by their faces and the pit in my stomach that I've said enough. We are thanked and asked to leave. We walk in a hazy blur back to the room, to sit in anxious silence. No one talks. Or maybe they do. After a while, the chairwoman comes back into the room.

Is that a twinkle in her eye, or a frown?

Her mouth opens and some words spill out and I think that she's smiling. She might as well be speaking in Latvian, for I haven't the foggiest what she says. I don't understand and my brain doesn't register what I'm supposed to feel. She stops speaking then turns and leaves. I turn to the social workers confused and ask, 'Does that mean we're approved?'

Their eyes are smiling, as if I've missed a big joke. I can't hear what they say but they are smiling and nodding and I know it's a glorious yes.

Yes.

That word fills my brain. And then it's joined by the most incredible display of fireworks, with Jean-Michel Jarre doing the music and lighting, and a huge crowd of happy people celebrating with flags and bunting and cakes and champagne, and I feel completely overwhelmed by how happy I am, and I have no words so fall back on a montage of clichéd images instead. It's like solving a problem on the chemical plant, drawing a cartoon that works perfectly the first time, and your husband surprising you with flowers all at once. With a good hair day thrown in. And finding you have lost a stone without even trying. And getting a big fat rebate from the tax man. And someone cleaning your car whilst you are at work. And being whistled at by a bricklayer who is quite nice-looking, actually. And receiving a handwritten letter from an old BFF reminding you of the mischief you both got up to in university and then laughing a little too hard and letting out a tiny pee.

We are approved to be adoptive parents.

And words and thoughts are swirling around me and I want to run from the room and shout to the world and dance in the rain and hug strangers in the street (even the smelly, unkempt ones) and give money to the homeless and spread the love inside me until the ripples reach the farthest corners of the world.

I can barely breathe and the emotion swells up and I cry. I hug Andy. I hug my social workers, even the one we barely know (who seems a little shocked, to be honest).

I have no words to describe how amazing I feel.

Now to prepare ourselves for part two: Matching. I calm down a little and prepare myself by going to the loo to have another drip of a wee.

While the Panel do whatever they are doing (my guess is tea and toilet), we're given another set of questions to read. We run through our answer to Question 1: Why do you want to adopt two children instead of one? Andy says, 'We always wanted a family, and by adopting two at a time, it's much quicker.' As soon as the word 'quicker' comes out of his mouth, the social workers' expressions turn to panic. Their faces scream 'don't say that' but they gently suggest that there might be a 'better way of putting it for the Panel'. Instead of stressing the convenience, we'll answer that there are sibling groups that need families and we wanted to be able to give them a home. It's the same information tarted up to be more Adoption-Panel friendly. The rest of our trial responses go without incident.

Just because they approved our becoming adoptive parents doesn't mean they'll approve the Match. This is the Big One. For this decision comes with two little faces, two gorgeous lives that we've begun to think of as our children. *What if they say no?* All the elation will evaporate faster than something very fast (I'm still not articulate). If they say yes to this, then in just over a week we will meet our children and start the process of Introductions.

We go in and sit down again, the seats still warm. Both more and less nervous than before.

'What will happen if you don't get Matched with Nibbles and Bubbles?' someone asks.

My face shows surprise mixed with horror, as if my brain cannot compute that option.

'We haven't even really considered it,' Andy says in response. 'Not because that couldn't happen, but because it was almost as if when I first saw them, I felt like they were our children.'

I catch my breath and look at him in swooning amazement. In all our years together he's *never* said anything as romantic as that. I gawp. Andy is eloquently sharing his feelings with complete strangers whilst I sit by in mute fear. I want to stop time, to freeze this second in my mind, to turn and admire his honesty with all my might and then wrap my arms around him in a romantic embrace. And a little bit of me is jealous — why doesn't he ever say things like that about *me*?

More questions, more answers.

We hand around the books we've prepared, showing them my craftiwork. Everyone nods encouragingly. Thank goodness they decide not to watch the DVD whilst we squirm. We show them the toys with the name tags that say 'My name is Nibbles/Bubbles, please look after me'. They won't touch them for fear of diluting our smell on their fur.

When we've said all we can, when we've shown them our hearts, our yearning, our desire to be the parents of these children, all the things we've made to help this process go through, when there's nothing more we can do to convince them, it's all over and we solemnly leave the room.

I am blind to the peeling paint, the brown chairs, the functional blandness of our surroundings. It is out of my hands, and before we know it (and far quicker than last time, if my memory is to be believed) the chairwoman comes back into the room, this time with a beaming smile, and says yes.

She smiles and shakes our hands and then tells us in more detail why the Panel voted yes to the Match, and I don't hear a word of it because my ears are ringing with the tinnitus caused by her yes. My heart has burst and tears are rolling down my cheeks and I just want to cry and cry and cry.

And I realise something that I've known all along: they could've asked me to strip naked and run onto a football pitch on national TV and I'd have done it if it meant that I would get to this moment. To be finally told that we get the job. To know, without a doubt, that we would be these children's mummy and daddy.

I am elated and spent all at once.

Nervous exhaustion combines with sheer joy to make me heady and giggly and incomprehensible. I don't remember how we get to the car, but I'm floating. I ring my mum and barely blub out the good news before I start crying and can't stop. I breathe a little, catch my breath and blub yes down the phone to my twin. On Facebook, I let the world know that they said yes and voraciously watch the stream of delighted responses. Andy drives to a local pub and I turn a box of tissues to papier mâché on the way. We celebrate with glasses of bubbly — I know, paying through the nose for actual champagne in a pub. Madness.

I alternately grin like a loon and cry.

Happy.

Joyous.

Euphoric.

This feeling is far more than any of these words or their synonyms can contain.

A magical unicorn, pot of gold at the end of a rainbow, four-leaf clover, lottery winning, cloudless blue sky (can you tell we live in the UK?) of a day. And if that isn't enough, in just a few days, we'll meet our children.

Wow! Wow! Treble wow!

22. The Void

It's as if the days between Panel and Introductions simply don't exist. There is no post-Panel, post-magical-honeymoon comedown, when you're stuffing laundry into the washing machine and feeling like it never happened. I'm still floating in a world of my own, buoyed by this knowledge inside, knowing that we've made it, we'll become parents, and we'll be meeting them soon.

Andy goes back to work and tells his boss that he'll be off for six weeks' paternity leave starting in eight days' time.

Friends hint that I should use this time to do 'all those things I won't be able to do when the children arrive'. And because they presume that we are clearly simpletons and haven't noticed the changes wrought on other lives when children arrive, they spell it out by adding: 'Having sex and staying up until the sun rises.'

I have just seven days (because I've already wasted one on social media) to do everything I might ever want to do for the next seventeen years.

And your time starts . . . Now!

But I don't want to stay up into the wee small hours or drink too much in the afternoon. I want to have great big adventures that involve going to the nearest international airport with just a credit card and my passport and asking for the first flight somewhere — not to run away, but to explore the world beyond my door in a fit of spontaneity, without even a book to read on the plane. That wild-abandon freedom-seeking mischief. I don't have enough time to tick things off my 'adventure list' — like walking Copper Canyon, staying at the Ice Hotel, learning to ski or climbing Sydney Harbour Bridge.

I try and create sleep credit, but even that doesn't work.

Pam rings to let us know that Bubbles (the girl) has barely put Nibbles (the bunny) down, and both of them love the toys and have even taken them to the park. She says they are responding really well to the books about us too. I have no idea what that means. I hope it means they are as excited as we are, and decide to assume that it does. I am excited and crying again.

I make some meals for the freezer. I finish off the children's bedroom, reorganise some empty drawers, prepare for the party. None of it seems big enough to fill the hours between The Yes! and The Oh!

And something strange happens.

A void appears in our house.

A silence that we never noticed before. An absence of two children whom we have not met and who until recently were nothing but a piece of paper and a DVD.

When Andy and I sit in our lounge and talk about what's coming next, we feel there's something missing — a lack. It's like being marooned on a deserted island in the middle of the ocean; the birds, insects, lizards, rats and pirates have scarpered, having sensed an incoming storm, leaving behind a disconcertingly unnatural soundlessness that chills your skin to goosebumps. We've never noticed the peace before, never noticed that the serenity in our house, when the TV and radio are turned off, is a badge of our childlessness.

A constant reminder of what is not in our lives . . . but is on its way.

As we near the end of our journey, the silence is deafening.

23. And Then There Were Four — The Party

Party time! My perfectionist side is having a field day. The ambience needs to be breathtaking: the crackers in the shape of the Tour Eiffel, the napkins incredible swans, the music the perfect mix of melody and lyrics, the sun shining, the room hustling and bustling and yet containing spare chairs when you want to sit down — and not a mundane (how was your journey?) conversation for miles around.

This party is my opportunity to express how excited I am to become a mum through the medium of snacks. I must ensure that everyone, from babies to septuagenarians, leaves saying, 'Darling, that was stupendous. I can honestly say that I've never been so entertained in all my life.' And these ridiculous expectations turn the hours before the party into a frenzy of fretting, racing around preparing food, moving furniture, arranging and rearranging where Andy should stand, washing up, hiding stuff in the dishwasher, grating, dicing, slicing, spiralising and more. I've created a gluten-free village (with neon signposts) in the kitchen, in the vague hope that my sister and I won't get poisoned by crumbs, though I'm resigned to the fact that after a few beers, no one's going to care two hoots about my dodgy digestion.

It's 10 a.m. and I'm already exhausted but there's so much to do I can't stop.

Andy suggests I sit down for a moment, but I shrug it off and rearrange the celery. He mostly stays out of the way, afraid to get under my feet or to help in case I snap when he destroys my Taj Mahal of crudités. Why do I do this to myself? I'd love to feel calm, floating above it all on a heady cloud of OMG. The invites say that the party will last 'until everyone goes to bed', and if I don't get a grip on my nerves, I'll be in bed before anyone arrives.

'It will be fine,' Andy says calmly as he gives me a hug, and I know that he means it. 'If we run out of anything, the shops are just around the corner.'

I'm scared to relax, as my emotions are bordering on certifiable today. I am tottering along a slippery emotional sword-edge that even waterproof mascara will not survive, such that no sane person would bet against my opening the door to guests looking like Kiss. The invitation also says: 'Celebrating our impending gorgeous arrivals, and other stuff that'll make Emma cry whilst Andy pretends not to be melting inside.'

After a few more hours' dashing around, putting chairs out then tripping over them and finding I can't open the cupboard I want to get into, moving the gluten-free zone until it's as far as possible from the bread (using a tape measure to be certain), lining up the drinks in alphabetical order, missing lunch entirely, having a flannel-wash to get rid of the glow that all this dashing about has created, getting changed and remembering to breathe, finally the doorbell rings and people start arriving and I get lost in a whirlwind of welcomes, rich hugs, presents and bottles of champagne, which I try to tessellate in the fridge. I keep moving bread away from the gluten-free area, shout hello as I run past people who arrived a while ago and whom I have yet to talk to, grab a cracker for myself and think, *I really need to eat something*, and toast our new additions with another glass of bubbly.

The presents are somewhat random — what do you give someone who is adopting? Our guests were warned not to bring toys for the children (to prevent their new home from being too different), so the selection's eclectic. Allan brings a bottle of champagne (yay) and a bottle of Calpol (eh?), saying, rather mysteriously, that I'll know why soon enough. We get a photo frame, a plant (that might not make it) and some toys for the garden. My brother Mark says that we've 'bagged tickets to the white-knuckle ride to oblivion', and I smile without really having a clue what he's talking about. I like Oblivion at Alton Towers, so I presume it's a good thing.

In the crowd of goodwill, someone's missing. *I wonder where Claire is?* I'm defending her gluten-free food like a knight defending a castle, and she's the only other person who needs it. She texted me when she set off this morning, and even with bad traffic, I think she should be here by now. I ring her mobile and it goes straight to voicemail. Several times. Hmmm. The door opens, and I'm caught up once more in the congratulations and celebrations and chaos of it all. I proudly give people 'tours' of the new nursery (it's a bedroom with two cots in it for Pete's sake). People humour me and pretend they're as interested in this whole transformation as I am (they aren't).

By 5 p.m. (woo hoo, I'm still awake) the house is crammed with adults and kids. They spill into the garden, as the weather's warm and fine. I spend most of my time climbing stairs and wandering between rooms whilst breathing in the heady feeling of celebration coming from every corner of our house and garden. The mood is positively buoyant and I'm feeling wonderful — the glorious centre of fabulous attention on this incredible day; a day to be in awe at everything that has happened and look forward to the adventure ahead, and I still haven't picked up on some furtive glances and the fact that not everyone's smiles are as broad as they might be.

I ask if anyone knows where Claire is and start to get worried. She should've been here hours ago, and out of the corner of my eye, I notice a look pass between my husband and my brother-in-law. Something is going on. There's a secret hiding in this room and I need to know what it is. I ask Andy where Claire is, and I get a look from him that isn't right. A kind of sympathy look. *Why is he looking at me like that?*

He takes me by the hand. I find myself led gently away from the hordes, and Sarah and her husband, Brian, join us in the hall. The crevice in my stomach widens until it is a gaping hollow — they don't need to say anything. I want to run away to avoid the car crash about to rip my party in two.

'Claire has been delayed.'

Okay, I think, hesitantly. *But that's not what your faces say . . .*

'She's been arrested.'

Arrested? WTF?

Suddenly my beautiful party, my floating on air, comes hurtling to the ground, and I crash into the pavement with wince-inducing speed. The air turns to ice and a shiver dances down my back. There's a roaring in my ears that nearly drowns out the rest of the story. Sarah and Brian continue; as they drove here, and less than a mile from our house, they noticed Claire's car. She'd been pulled over by the police, and when they breathalysed her, she was over the limit. Way over the limit.

No (softly), No (louder), No, NO! NO!

Not today.

I am a pinball machine, bouncing between thoughts and feelings.

Is she okay?

Is she hurt?

Fuck. Fuck! (And quite a lot more for good measure.)

How fucking dangerous.

Is she crazy?

She could've KILLED someone. (Thank fuck she didn't.)

'Was she drinking *all the way*, even on the motorway?' I demand to know.

All three of them shake their heads. They don't know, and even if they did, no one is about to pour lighter fluid on this fire. Andy, Sarah and Brian all look at me with compassion — they hid this secret from me, as it ate them up, for as long as they could so I could enjoy the party. And I love them for that.

I am livid at the senselessness of it. Andy and I have had our suspicions since she left us that perhaps she wasn't as fixed as she'd pretended to be.

How stupid I've been, how naïve.

Self-recrimination turns to pouting.

How could she?

Today of all days?

After six years, we can finally celebrate the fact that we're going to become parents. Our special, magical day and she (grr), she (ahhh), she flipping . . . she ruins it. She and her bloody selfish addiction and . . . and . . . and the sheer quantity of emotions overwhelms me. I weep softly.

I want to rage, to blame. To blame Claire for drinking, to blame the person who sold her the alcohol, to blame shops for selling alcohol so cheaply, to blame society for making it our drug of choice, to blame Russia for inventing vodka, to blame grain for being so darned fermentable, to blame booze for being so lusciously palatable (it should taste like a cocktail of TCP and those eye drops that make you gag), to blame everyone who had some part in this horrific event, when what really frightens me is the blame I deserve. For I've stuck my hands over my ears and ignored the hints and clues; I've blinkered my thoughts and remained focused on our process, on our adoption, on not knowing that things might be turning bad again. So that if they asked me at Panel I could say, hand on heart, that she was okay as far as we knew.

I have sacrificed my sister on the altar of adoption.

We knew the Panel might ask us questions about her, that it might be a sticking point, and we strove for plausible deniability. When the Panel asked (as we knew they would) what would happen if she became ill again, we said that it would have to be someone else's turn, even though we couldn't have named that 'someone else'.

All the ignored clues come back to haunt me — the accident she had in her car, the times she didn't answer her phone, the times she texted me undecipherable gobbledegook; the painful phone conversations when she actually picked up, during which she struggled to make sense, and hiccuped, and we didn't want to believe she was drunk. We appeased our consciences by saying 'she's a grown-up', 'she has to make her own choices', 'we cannot live her life for her', and 'unless she asks for help there is nothing we can do'.

But today, we cannot hide from the truth. It stands before us naked and shocking.

What a mess. (Here we see a fine example of British understatement.)

I breathe.

What will happen to her? I am worried about her. She is not fixed. She is still ill. What does this mean for her life and her future and do I even have the space in my brain to add that to the challenges to come?

I slump.

I don't know what to think or say or feel anymore.

(Even my thoughts fall silent.)

I look at the others with tears in my eyes and pull that 'I'm okay' lopsided smile that says 'I'm not really but I'm putting a brave face on it all'. I've been well and truly blindsided during the most enchanting celebration of my life.

I shake the tears from my face. I stand tall and proud and hug my husband as we share a look of despair. I go back to the party, shrugging off the sympathy of others because there is simply no more room for any more emotion in me. I will not allow her addiction to take this day from me. This is not her moment; this is mine and I want it back! But despite my best efforts, my heart is simply not in it the way it was before. I can't keep all this stuff inside, and blurt it out to friends in a sob of tears. They stroke my arm and murmur their sorries and offer support and help. But they can't undo the wound.

I feel numb.

My brain struggles to make sense of the highs and lows of this party.

And I go to bed in a rather different state than I'd expected this morning.

24. Flowers

What if they don't like me?

We're sat in the parked car, fidgeting, having arrived (you guessed it) ridiculously early for this Important Day. It is 9.15 a.m. and we have a vast expanse of forty-five minutes to kill. So. Much. Time. The Tuesday after our party, the head honcho ratified both decisions. It's now Thursday, the first day of Introductions. And I'm bricking it.

My stomach can't decide if the sharks or the butterflies are winning. I can't sit here fidgeting for that long, but what else can we do? 'Why not go for a drive?' I suggest. *What if we get lost?* And my brain decides to catastrophise — *what if we drive off the edge of the known universe into a not-on-the-map black hole from which even a GPS signal and Google Maps cannot rescue us?*

Or worse, what if we're late?

We drive just a few streets away (leaving a trail of map pins on our phones to help us find our way back). We sit. And fidget. And check our phones. And post on social media. And wait. Out of sight. We get out of the car and go for one of the most bland, pointless walks ever. Well, not entirely pointless, because there are now ten fewer minutes to burn.

Today we will meet our children.

Our children. They don't feel like our children at all. They aren't really our children, except they are, but then they're wards of the adoption agency, so they're not, but we'll be looking after them, so they are, and it's all quite confusing.

I can't stop thinking about the moment we'll see them for the first time.

What if all my dreams and hopes come crashing down around me and I think *I can't do this*? What if they're crying and whining

115

and awful? What if they ignore us? What if they don't like us? What if they run and scream and hide and refuse to come out? What if they hate us? Worse still, what if they like him and not me?

As excited as we are to finally have a family, we're anxious about two weeks of Introductions that stretch like an interminably long practical exam for which we are pathetically unprepared. We've been promoted to parents because of a CV (Big Report) that overestimated our capabilities, and I'm face-to-face with imposter syndrome. Within seconds they're going to realise that I am in no way equipped to be a mum. This is alien territory to us and the foster family; these are their first foster children and they've never been through Introductions before. We'll be taking these faltering steps together — four adults with their ankles tied together by two children and a confoundment of social workers in the most awkward five-legged stumble ever.

There's a meticulous two-week plan for these Introductions. Today we'll visit them for an hour, tomorrow it'll be two hours. As the time gradually lengthens, our responsibilities build. The first week is mostly at the foster family's house, so that the unfamiliar (i.e., Andy and I) is gradually introduced to their familiar routines and environment. The second week the children come to our house. Two weeks today, we take them home forever. It is called Introductions, but it's more like an invasion.

I have no idea what to expect.

We're wearing the exact outfits we wore in the photos for the books and videos they've been reading and watching, to help them recognise us. It seems silly now, but it made complete sense this morning as we got dressed. It's now 10 a.m. (turns out you *can* kill time — just worry incessantly) and we drive up to the house. Ken opens the door and welcomes us in with a twinkling smile.

'Take a seat in the lounge. I think they've something planned,' he says.

That sounds promising or ominous or something (the sharks and butterflies cannot agree). My heart is pounding, my mouth is dry. I perch nervously on the edge of the sofa, waiting for I don't know what; I'm a child waiting outside the headmaster's door.

The lounge door opens and in tumbles a huge bunch of flowers — a pink riot of colour and petals and leaves that's moving all of its own accord. Then I spy her. Beneath this colossal display, wobbling in her efforts to hold it, is a tiny girl with cascades of curls. The flowers drown her, yet she bravely carries them straight to me. She shyly hands them over and in her sing-song voice says four incredible words that I will never forget:

'Flowers for my mummy.'

She looks at me, and I break out a smile before my hand flies to my mouth in shock and surprise. A lifetime of tears well up in my eyes, and despite my promise that I would not cry, tears pour silently down my cheeks. It's far from the first impression I wanted to make.

Happy tears.

A tear for all the times that I went to bed despondent. A tear for all the times that my period came and I lost faith I'd ever be a mummy. A tear for all the times I wondered why I couldn't grow a child. A tear for a child who never made it past the first few cells and was flushed away. And a tear of utter relief that a child has finally said that word to me. The word I have wanted to hear and thought I might never hear. The word I do not own despite all the preparation.

Mummy.

The most amazing word in the whole dictionary. I thought it would take weeks or months for them to utter it, and it was the fourth word she said. Even better, she used 'my' before it, binding me to her in a relationship. I feel complete in a whole new way. I stutter a broken thank you, but she's already gone. She and her brother follow Ken back to the kitchen, where he's making tea.

Andy sits on the floor, and within minutes these two tiny children are crawling all over him, hugging him and talking to him, tugging at his shirt, smearing dirty fingerprints over his glasses, asking questions but not waiting for the answers, bringing him books to read and toys to play with. I sit back, dabbing my tears and drinking everything in. They take to Andy like pandas to bamboo, and I feel that his idea of sitting on the floor was far better than my bursting into tears.

I dry my face and take a deep breath: we have fifty-seven minutes left to start getting to know these miniature people who are our little boy and little girl. Our children. I still can't believe it.

As they crawl over Andy, I scrutinise them. The boy wears cute little dungarees and a stripy tee shirt underneath. He toddles in an unbalanced fashion, using furniture to stay upright. His hair is straight and dark. His dark eyes draw you in like tinted water in a posh Chelsea garden. The girl seems tiny, her arms and legs so slight she might snap in a too-tight hug. She bounces around with unceasing energy and enthusiasm, a teeny pink tornado of noise and hair. He is quieter, more thoughtful somehow, and there is something of Andy's gentleness about him, although the giant bit is yet to come.

Mary gets out the books we sent them, and Bubbles goes to work decorating hers with the stickers we included. She sticks them randomly all over it, and puts Peppa Pig right on my face in my favourite photo, and I grasp my wrist to stop myself moving it (until she's busy doing something else). She says things like, 'That's you, Mummy', 'That's my daddy', and to Nibbles, 'That's your bed'. Here am I struggling to rewrite my own identity and she's just getting on with it. Am I her mummy? She is confident and sure; I'm anything but.

Andy reads: 'Once upon a time . . .' And before the pigs have even left home, Bubbles slams the book closed and grabs something else. We shadow the children awkwardly. They want to go outside. 'Coat?' we suggest weakly, and Bubbles says a firm no, letting us know that she's in charge. I admire her independent streak whilst also wondering if this is the first sign that she's going to be a bit of a handful (the euphemistic term parents use for children who are uncontrollable nightmares). We go with their flow and try to keep up. On to the next play station: the garden. We've only been here a few minutes and this might just be the fifth thing we've done — it's like circuit training on fast forward.

As they play in the sandpit, I've no idea what to do. It's barely off the ground, so I try crouching (my thighs burn), then kneeling (oh for a padded cushion), then bending (oh my back); I feel pathetic as I wriggle with discomfort. I'm out of place, like screws left over when you assemble flat-pack furniture. I don't know how to play with toddlers. I know I need to play with them, to build our relationship, but mostly I want to run back to a comfy chair and watch from a distance. I take photos of this special day, but they keep moving and every click has a blurred face and I want an amazing picture to immortalise this incredible day but the moment I press the button they turn, or blink, or move because they don't care about my photo.

But I can't hide behind the camera forever, so I get stuck in and start making sandcastles beside them. 'Isn't that wonderful?' type murmurations drip from my lips, but I'm faking it. My perfectionist control freak thinks, *It's not wonderful. That sandcastle is all cracked and has fallen down and is missing that piece at the top.* I don't know how to admire the sandcastle of a toddler. I skipped their baby years and arrived at this point with literally no relevant skills and a steep learning curve ahead.

Bubbles and I make a big sandcastle together.

'That's enormous, Bubbles,' I say with genuine enthusiasm.

'That's not enormous — my daddy is enormous!' she says without missing a beat, and I laugh. I look over and Andy does, indeed, look gigantic. A tower of a man in the Lilliputian garden of a toddler. I smile with love for these two special people. I want to smother her in kisses and hugs and never let her go. This precious child, this innocent and energetic human being, is going to be my little girl and now she's called Andy her daddy!

They've watched our video every teatime for over a week, and there are photos of us plastered over the fridge. Bubbles is in no doubt as to just who her mummy and daddy are. In fact, Mary will tell us a few days later that from the first day we met them, Bubbles stopped calling her and Ken Mummy and Daddy. And today is not just about us. We aren't the only ones whose dreams have come true, for more than anything in the whole wide world, our little girl wants a mummy and a daddy. When I ask her a few months later why she wanted a mummy and daddy, she'll say with a broad smile, 'For hugs and kisses.' That I can do.

All too soon our time is up, and I struggle to stand from the muscle cramps. It's been a magical hour, everything I could have wanted and so much more. Bubbles cries as we say our goodbyes: 'Don't go,' she says, and my heart twangs. We hug and go because we can't stay however much she cries.

As we wave goodbye from the car, I feel a frisson, a tingle of pure life flow through me that almost erases the mocking memories of awkwardly acting the part of Mummy.

This was a day that I'll remember for the rest of my life — the day that I finally met my children.

25. We Need More Spoons

It's Friday, and as we arrive at the house, we spy two tiny grinning faces at the window, excited to see us again, and my heart leaps. We spend two hours with the children, rocking them on a green something or other (a crocodile? what? how is *that* a *horse?*) in the garden, reading a page here and there and following them around like we're the chicks and they are mother hen. It's play — playing at being parents, relearning the words to nursery rhymes that after forty years we can't remember and frowning at ones we've never heard of. *Wind the what up?* We search for the sing-song in our voices.

On paper, Introductions seems simple: over two weeks we attend an immersive vocational apprenticeship on the children's routine. One day we watch the foster parents do it and the next day we do it, gradually earning our Brownie badges in meals (lunch, then breakfast, then tea), naptimes, bedtime and baths. Six badges and we'll be good to go (*Really? That's all there is to parenting?* I'm not convinced).

Today is Day Three of the plan, Saturday, and those cuties at the window clamber over us the minute the door opens. They welcome us again and we start on Badge 1: Lunch. Andy and I hang around watching Mary, asking her endless questions and generally getting under her feet whilst she mushes up some food for Nibbles and makes a sandwich for Bubbles, keeping up a non-stop narrative as she goes. I'm cluttering up her kitchen, trying not to get breadcrumbs over me (gluten!). I feel superfluous, unhelpful and out of my depth (but not in a culinary sense).

Mary is fabulous.

She explains every step in great detail and patiently answers all my reams of questions (Andy says I have a special relationship with details, and time, and cleanliness). She explains the general plan, then sprinkles caveats on top: 'If this happens, then try this.' She gives me more than just tips on puddings — she boosts my confidence, telling me I'll be a brilliant mum, which is exactly what I need to hear and the direct opposite of how I'm feeling right now.

There's so much to learn that a simple meal becomes an epic saga of Tolkien duration. Nibbles has a few teeth so eats solids, but his meal is still mushed up. He's learning to feed himself, and insists on having a spoon in each hand, but can't do it alone, so someone has to shovel food in with yet another spoon whenever he opens his mouth. I do the maths: three spoons per course for every meal (main and pudding) equals six spoons every meal. Eighteen spoons a day? We only have three. Bubbles can be a bit fussy, says Mary, and because she might not eat her tea, she grazes throughout the day on fruit and sweeties (Mary's name for raisins, nice move). Mary warns me that she hides apple cores around the house. I blanch at the thought of mouldy apples behind the sofa.

We watch them eat/demolish their lunch, then yoghurt. And I reckon (as my eyes widen) that only a small fraction of this yoghurt goes into their stomachs. The rest is smeared around their faces and on the trays of their high chairs, on their toes, the floor, the ceiling . . . Horror flashes across my neat-freak face, and I'm instantly besotted with baby wipes (I later order a boot-load online).

I find myself in the kitchen a lot these first few days, using it as a refuge from the strangeness of the sandpit. Here, I have long conversations with Mary about everything I need to know. And then later I wonder why the children bond with Andy more than me.

After lunch we chase them round and round the washing line while they giggle and squawk. They're delighted when we catch them and throw them into the air (or while Andy does and I watch with my heart in my mouth, scared shitless that he'll drop them — because right now I'm treating them like my grandmother's treasured china).

On the way home, we pop to the shops and buy spoons.

Lots and lots of them.

The Great Escape (Day Four). Today we break free from the heavy gravity of their house and take one giant step for family-kind. We walk across the road to . . . a playground. It's less than fifty metres away, yet it feels like a Grand Adventure. And we quickly learn that popping out to the park is not the grab-your-coat-ready type jaunt we're used to.

Leaving the house is almost as painful as splitting a bill between a dozen people who aren't sufficiently good mates — because naming-no-names (Tracey) had a starter, main AND a pudding, and no one likes his Drunkship (Greg) enough to pay for his jug of margaritas when we Soberistas nursed lime and soda all night.

Coat and shoes? They're the last thing on the list but the only thing that springs to our naïve minds. First we need to check nappies, dissuade them from wearing wildly inappropriate clothing, ensure that they're neither hungry nor thirsty, find a pair of matching shoes (um, no, I don't think you can wear those glittery Cinderella slippers, it's very muddy), choose a coat (maybe not that one, it's soaking, no really, it's too wet to wear, you'll be freezing, let's find another one, shall we?), screw their feet into their shoes without their socks giving them a Chinese burn (can you uncurl your toes, sweetie?) and dissuade Bubbles from taking her umbrella. Half an hour later, we're finally ready — with the umbrella but not the Cinderella slippers — for the Arctic expedition that is out of the house, down the street, across the road and into the park.

It's a small square of ground with railings, some marginally-softer-than-concrete flooring, a roundabout and a slide, which despite the colourful paintwork seems rather pitiful in the drizzle. After a few dizzying circuits, they've had enough and we go for a little walk. A veritable entourage for two celebrity children: four adults and a dog. Bubbles holds Andy's hand and looks up at him — most people look up at him, but she nearly topples over bending backwards to see his face. Then she says: 'You're my daddy.'

Aw. Bless. How cute? I think.

'You're my daddy.'

Aw.

'You're my daddy.'

He is, sweetie.

'You're my daddy.'

Uh-huh.

'You're my daddy.'

Yeah, so we keep hearing.

It's as if she can't believe her own eyes. Over the course of a fifteen-minute walk she's a record stuck in the last groove. She even goes over to tug on Ken's hand and share the news: 'That's my daddy.'

It is a walk of naming things — a leaf, isn't that pretty? Oh look, a stick, a tree, careful, puddle, mind the poo! I hold her hand and talk to her and she looks up at me with these big eyes full of hope, love and joy, and her simple eager acceptance of what I am makes me want to try with all my heart and soul to learn to be their mummy, and not just an okay mummy: a perfect mummy from the get-go. The grin plastered on my face tries to hide just how frightened I am of the enormity of what we have done.

My body is tight; my nerves and muscles are tense.

She skips over a puddle (please don't fall in), unaware of how her carefree wobble creates hot flushes of fear. She looks behind her and I wince and duck as a branch nearly knocks her over. Every step, every wild stumble of her body makes me tense, ready to pounce, to rescue, to swing her out of the way of the unseen catastrophes just around the corner. My brain is a chorus of fear: *Mud! Puddle! Muddy puddle! Branch! Poo! Branch! More mud! Bush! Poo! This walk is a deathtrap.* The urge to wrap her up and never let her leave my sight is almost too much. Nibbles is younger so he's always holding someone's hand or being carried. He is safe, so I only fuss over her.

Andy and I have walked for miles pondering life, the universe, where we might go on holiday this year, what we might do if we won the lottery and whether we've seen enough of our parents (the answer is always a resounding no, and we vainly agree that we'll make more of an effort starting sometime). But walking and keeping an eye on two toddlers near a stream changes it from a switch-off experience to a heart-stopping balancing act. It's only some poo, mud and a stream, yet I might as well have been cajoling them around the flaming, smoking ridge of Vesuvius as it's erupting, my nerves are wound so tight. Their giggles and excitement bounce off me — I'm Gore-Texed with tension.

And then we are back home and as the door closes, this tension glides off me. Nothing bad happened, and we are all home again in one piece. Though Mummy is a quivering wreck.

26. Ninja Skittles

A new day, another badge. Not only have we left the house, but we're chaperone-less. Part of me wants to drive off with this family of ours and keep driving into a sunset (despite the fact the sun won't set for six hours). Ken and Mary gave us less than convincing directions to a big park. We origamied the pram into the boot and trust we can reconfigure it at the other end. It is a breath of fresh air to go out, just the four of us, like a real family.

'I spy with my little eye, something beginning with *S*,' I say, to make the journey more fun. Mistake No. 1: not using phonics (*sssss*).

'Car.'

'Daddy.'

'No.'

'Chip.'

'Poo.'

I'm confused for a second until I wise up to Mistake No. 2 (they don't know what a letter is), Mistake No. 3 (they can't spell) and Mistake No. 4 (they don't know how to play eye spy). And that all sums up Mistake No. 5 (my thinking I have a clue what I'm doing). I revert to pointing out things. 'Look, a cloud.' We park, wrestle with the pram then make it to the playground. We watch, totally smitten, camera (phone) snapping as they scramble over the bus and clamber into the train, all smiles and delight in the easy wonder of a child. I have the wide-eyed wonder of a brand-new-out-of-the-box parent, where every single thing they do or say amazes me. 'Look Andy, she climbed the steps,' I say, as if they've just performed a triple back somersault with a half twist to land perfectly arms raised, feet together, without a single wobble from the beam. This is the first time we've been somewhere where there are other parents, and I wonder if they can tell we're out of our depth. Can they detect our new-parent smell (sheer panic)?

We're miles from home, and I really wish we could walk past someone we know with Our Children, nodding and smiling knowingly, bursting insanely with pride. How mad is that? They've been alive for years without any help from me, and all I've done is pick them from two alternatives (go me!). People look at our children, at their good-natured giggles, and then tip their heads with an 'aw'. I overhear someone say that Bubbles is 'impossibly cute' and swell with impossible smugness.

We toddle down the hill to a shallow boating lake. Bubbles has one of my fingers in a tight grip, and that simple feeling of being needed, of being a rock to her stagger, is wonderful. And then she's off, running down the hill as I speed-walk a few steps behind to demonstrate that I'm not worried and I've got this covered. Bubbles approaches the water as I turn to see Andy pelting down the hill pushing the pram, shouting, 'Get her, Emma.' Andy? Is he okay? She *could* tip head first into the pond, and she probably wouldn't like getting wet, but really? I dash over, mostly for appearances, take her hand and pull her away from the danger that isn't really there so Andy can stop bearing down on us like a freight train whilst harrumphing at me.

After pottering around the more-dangerous-than-I-gave-it-credit-for lake, we amble to the café for coffee and ice creams. We want to make them happy, to spoil them, to shamelessly buy their adoration. I steer the pram with Nibbles and bump into every chair ('Sorry') in this tight ('Sorry') space. Andy queues to buy ice cream and Bubbles goes over to help. She sneaks up behind him, and as he turns to ask me something, he knocks her over. She wails and sobs, and Andy bends to hug her calm. As I potter over to help sort out the kids and ice creams, I knock Nibbles over — with pre-dictably upsetting results. Silently they sneak up behind us then we knock them down, as though they are Ninja Skittles. We've never had to watch out for tiny humans around our knees before. We feel stupid and clumsy and glad that the ice cream arrives quickly to distract them.

The cones look colossal in their doll-sized hands. And before you can say 'vanilla', the cones, their hands, arms, elbows, knees, jeans, clothes, faces and even their hair (at the back, for heaven's sake), never mind the pram, table and most of the café, are a mess of sticky, melted ice cream. I scrabble in my messenger bag, find one solitary, scrunched-up old tissue and sigh. I consider waving it in surrender, but instead I wipe their faces. Where's a bulging bag of wet wipes when you need it?

It takes ages for them to finish the cones (they don't trust Andy enough to let him help), and knowing that there's not a single chance they will eat their tea tonight, we stumble inexpertly out of the café, hitting slightly fewer tables than on the way in. Across from the café is a large stage — a bandstand, sheltered on one side. They want to run around on it. Nibbles potters in small circles, wobbling like Bambi on new legs, as Bubbles runs around and around holding her toy bunny, her ponytail swinging to the rhythm of her moves. She's cute in her double-denim outfit, he in his bulging Puffa jacket. Bubbles' footsteps resound on the wooden planks, and she's dizzyingly persistent in circling Nibbles. He can't keep up and doesn't seem to mind that she keeps changing direction. Andy joins in and starts chasing them; I shoot a video, and at one point she rushes over to me, smiling in a way that melts my insides as fast as their ice creams, begging me, 'Save me, Mummy.' I reach out and gleefully hide her under my coat and know that I'd do anything she asks.

The most amazing sound is the giggles of my son and daughter.

The most fantastic sensation is their tiny hands holding my finger tight on a walk around the park.

Their smiles light up my day in ways I find hard to describe.

Their unasked-for hug or kiss is the most precious thing on earth.

They have me wrapped around their tiny little fingers. Which is a good thing, as we're about to learn just why the social workers call Introductions 'the most exhausting two weeks of your life'.

We get back in the car and drive them back to their foster family.

'Goodbye, sweetie,' we say, and her face breaks into tears.

'Please don't leave me,' pleads Bubbles.

My heart is in tatters.

'We'll see you soon. It won't be long.'

She's so tiny and helpless, and I just want to kiss her sobs away until she smiles again. We wrench ourselves away quickly and painfully, like a sticking plaster.

Tomorrow we'll see them bright and far-too-early for breakfast.

27. Brownie Badge Fail

Streeeeetch. *Yawn.*

I feel great! Surprisingly well-rested.

Uh-oh.

As my brain boots up, I have that nagging suspicion that something is wro —

Bugger. I pry my eyes open rather too quickly for comfort as I scramble for my phone. It's 6.15 a.m. Six fifteen? Fffffkkkk.

We fall out of bed and shake the dreams off with our PJs.

'How did this happen?'

'We should have left by now!'

'The kids'll wake up soon!'

We're an hour late. We dash about trying to squeeze time into nothing, splashing through the quickest it'll-do showers, muttering to ourselves as we wonder what (or who) is to blame for the fact that we're sopping wet and starving: there's no time for breakfast. We drive as fast as we dare and pray that the children sleep in.

They don't.

'Where are you?' texts Mary, with ten miles to go. Late, I frump. 'Nearly there,' I reply.

When we get there, she'll tell us that as they waited, they listened to the children giggling and chatting on the baby monitor as they tiptoed around, hoping the kids wouldn't twig that someone was awake and ignoring them.

We pull up on the drive, rush out, race straight upstairs ('We're coming . . .') and fall into their room panting, bedraggled and discombobulated. Nappies before coffee is not Andy's preferred order of things. We 'shobel' (Bubbles' word for 'shovel') soggy wheat biscuits into them with that dazed middle-of-the-night-what-is-going-on? look about us.

In this process, there are moments of sheer bewildering joy. Just watching them as they eat or sleep or play is a lesson in living in this moment. I usually live in my mind, thinking, planning, reflecting. Children just are. The thing they loved to play with yesterday is discarded today. The book they adored this morning is 'ugh' this afternoon. They race around, leaving us smiling and exhausted as we struggle to keep up. I want to press a button that slows them down to normal speed; they live at a hundred miles an hour.

Andy's doing a marvellous job — the children have really taken to him, whilst I'm just part of the 'accept one parent, get one free' bargain. But over the last five days, I have picked up a thing or two, earned myself a few badges.

The Umpteen Shades of Brown Badge: I no longer gawp or gip or shrink at the contents of their nappies. I've never held them up only to have their nappies slide off (those Three Men and their Baby are utterly incompetent). And I now recognise that special John Wayne walk that they do when their nappies are fit to burst.

The Tuckered-Out Badge: I can chase them around the table, the garden, the park, the washing line until they're just getting started and I'm out of breath and pathetically unprepared for the energetic demands of parenting two children. Birth parents get to build their muscles gradually — I ache all over. My lifting-and-carrying-gorgeous-angels-muscles (not the technical term) aren't prepared for this workout; the heaviest thing I lifted until recently was a bottle of wine. That's two tuckered-out bodies fast asleep every night (Andy's and mine).

The Postman Jelly Badge: I can wrangle them into clothing each morning, which is as easy as posting wibbly-wobbly jelly through a letterbox — there, just wrestled a jelly arm into a sleeve (that's the leg? Oh, dearie me!). And there's another: I have the Diddums Badge, as I've mastered the art of dumbing down my language so that 'wibbly-wobbly' pops out without a shred of embarrassment.

The Gremlin Badge: I can detect the quicker-than-you-think decline in behaviour that sees the mild-mannered Nibbles transform into a crying, fighting, kicking and tantrumming machine. I then warm his milk (see Goldilocks Badge) and pass it (and the buck) to Andy to help him settle down for his ninety-minute morning nap. During this time, we play with Bubbles or take her shopping or read to her, and I notice how much easier this whole process would be if there were only one of them. So much easier, if less 'brave'.

The Be Prepared Badge: I can load up my pockets and bags with tissues and baby wipes so I'm always ready to swoop in on incredible explosions of snot (or ice cream) that erupt with the frequency and force of a geyser. When I told Pam to 'bring on' the hugs, I hadn't accounted for how often these hugs (or kisses) would communicate both love and contagions to which I have zero resistance. I really must buy some echinacea and vitamin C to reinforce my immune system against these walking, talking germ monsters. Good job they are so cute.

The Goldilocks Badge: I can warm milk in the microwave for bedtimes and naptimes, test it on my wrist (ow, too hot!) and then add cold milk to make it . . . No, too cold, warm it up a little more, not too much — until it's just right.

Hardly an impressive parental résumé yet until last week I'd never done any of it. And in preparing that list, in stolen moments where I had a second to think, the day is nearly over. I'm still hiding in the kitchen and avoiding the difficult stuff, but in a few days, the children will come to our house and Mary will no longer be by my side cheerleading and instilling me with confidence, so I'd better dig deep and start doing the tricky stuff too.

How hard can it be? (Andy's done it.)

I can do this.

Time to woman-up.

'I'll put him to bed,' I say with a bravado that I do not feel.

'Just yell if you need some help,' says Andy, providing much-needed moral support.

'We're just downstairs,' says Ken, in case I imagine they're all going to the pub the minute my foot hits the bottom step.

Mary goes through all the instructions in detail, and then I carry Nibbles upstairs, ready for my first real test as his mummy. Bedtime. I turn on the baby monitor and pull the blinds down a little way while murmuring to him about bedtime, and then I cradle him in my lap and put the bottle to his lips. Everything I have seen the foster carers do without a hitch. Everything Andy has done without a single whimper. Nibbles opens his lips and I crow a silent yes. He takes a little sip and then his face screws up; he stops drinking and starts crying. I rock him, coo at him, stroke his back, but he is having none of it. It turns into a screaming, bawling, I-hate-you kind of crying. I hold strong, cuddling him, and he quietens temporarily, but sips only a little more, then pulls away from the bottle. My heart sinks. It's too soon. He needs to drink until his eyes are drooping, until the whole bottle is finished. He's wide awake, but I can do this. I am not ready to give up.

I walk him around a little, rubbing his back as he gurgles. He takes a bit more milk, but he's nowhere near finishing, or sleeping. I try everything because I am not going to give up. He starts to cry again and is getting more and more upset. He spits the bottle out and bawls. Now I'm ready to give up.

I whisper 'help' into the monitor. Just hissing silence. Nothing. 'Help,' I say at normal volume as he starts to scream; nothing. I lose my patience. I open the bedroom door and shout quite loudly down the stairs. Still nothing. I shout again, louder, and again, and still nothing. By this time, I'm as upset as Nibbles. I barge downstairs, awash with frustration and despair and failure, feeling helpless and alone. And I interrupt them chatting about cars (or something) with the downstairs monitor turned off.

OFF? I am not a happy bunny. If I hadn't had a tired boy in my arms . . .

'You should've asked for help,' says Andy, before wilting under my laser-guided glare. Ken steps in and takes over, and I sit down and cry.

I've failed.

I take Nibbles' inability to settle as a personal affront, as a reflection on my abilities as a mummy, which is ridiculous, but I'm tired and emotionally drained. I'll never be ready, never be able to do this with the relaxed confidence that the foster carers seem to have. This role seems like a gigantic step out of my comfort zone and I cannot see how I'll ever learn everything I need to know in the few days that I have left.

Andy comes over and gives me a hug.

It is exactly what I need.

Well, actually, it's not — what I needed was for him to come up and rescue me when I *first* whispered into the monitor.

But this will have to do.

28. The Guilty Shoes

They are coming here. To our home. Here. To our home. *pointing down* Here. (Can you tell I'm excited?) It's Day Six and time to welcome the children to our (their) home. At the mid-ish-point meeting yesterday, with more social workers than screaming girls at a Vamps concert, we all agreed that Introductions were going well and that we're on track for taking the children home in eight days' time.

For six days we've driven excitedly and in an exhausted stupor to and from the foster family's house. Today we get to stay put and let them come to us. For the first day in what seems like ages, we don't have to get up at the crack of dawn. We get a lie-in. Bliss. We've tweaked a few things to duplicate the familiarity of their foster family's house — for example, we've copied the hand soap and laundry detergent to make it smell the same, but it seems creepy when I type it up. I wonder what they'll think of our place. But I know they won't be thinking, 'I wonder what their house is like?' on the drive over. They'll be far too busy dropping their toys and getting frustrated when they don't receive an immediate translation of random letters and vowels such as 'wan ga boom'.

But nothing is going to ruin this incredible day. I'm totally and utterly prepared for anything.

I look out the window.

Except for that.

Last night snow blanketed the country, and our meticulously organised Introductions timetable is as feeble as King Canute against frosted water. The main roads are clear, and Mary texts us to say they've set off but will arrive late (late?) because Nibbles was still napping. If they arrive late . . . My brain analyses the knock-on impact of this delay on the accumulator that is my plan. The worst

135

is that lunch will be late — and that's not good for little tummies with no reserves.

Is that them? I peer out of the window at the sound of a vehicle. *This must be them.* Car doors open and clunk closed (it's not).

Why aren't they here yet? I pace, because I'm too nervous to do anything else.

Eventually they arrive, and as they rush up the path, the children show no signs of noticing the new front door. This combination of our old and new lives is the clashing of amateur musicians jamming. They follow us into the lounge, and as my bottom touches the sofa . . .

'Can I see my bedroom?' asks Bubbles.

I hesitate.

'Yes,' I say with the reluctance of someone keen to get the schedule back on track but unwilling to have no be the first thing I say in her new home. I open the stairgate and the children climb up. I presume that it's best to stay behind them to catch them if they stumble, but then I have to wriggle past two toddlers who are surging towards the top gate like shoppers at a Black Friday sale. Please don't let it be me who falls down the stairs.

They seem excited about their bedroom; they want to get into their cots, and Bubbles is telling Nibbles, 'This is my bed. This is yours.' I lift them so they can bounce on their beds, and they start exploring the curtains, the drawers and more. Nothing captures her attention for long. As they pull books onto the floor, Andy and I glance at each other and nod in complicit agreement: tonight we'll move anything we don't want to forfeit out of reach.

'Mine,' says Bubbles as she points at her bed.

'Yes. It is,' I agree with a smile.

'Mine,' she says as she points to a picture on the wall.

How cute, I think, *she's settling in really well.*

But she doesn't stop there.

'Mine,' she says as she points to my iPad.

'Um.' I'm a child who doesn't know how to share. *It's not yours. I bought it. It's definitely mine.* She ignores my protestations and rapidly reassigns a variety of random items to her expanding collection. And when it comes to anything pink, that's definitely and incontrovertibly 'mine'. She continues stealing our things for herself and her brother (which is touchingly considerate), and once my ego's gone off in a sulk, she's hard to resist; she's as cute as a puppy with fluffy ears and big paws.

We eventually eat lunch. Well, when I say 'eat'. . .

Bubbles has crustless sandwiches (not for much longer) and Nibbles some whizzed-up veggies. Ken and Mary rave about my homemade gluten-free quiche, which I don't get to eat because I'm too busy spooning food into Nibbles then scraping it off his chin, chair, tray and bib. The tessellation of spoons around his bowl and mouth is an intricate dance of manoeuvre and counter-manoeuvre. Bubbles picks her sarnie apart and it's impossible to work out what she's eaten without reassembling the crumbs in a bread jigsaw.

After they've left, we go around the house moving things onto higher shelves, texting people to let them know we're still alive (just) and doing some laundry. As wonderful and emotional as every day is, I'm dead on my feet and ready to punch anything or anyone who gets between me and my bed right now.

Yet this is a turning point. We are standing tall, feeling smug, happy to be at base camp. The summit is clouded in fog, and we can't yet see just how steep the climb is going to get and how quickly. Which is probably just as well.

We're living in the land of the midnight sun, or nappy, or story-book, or something. As we reach the last days of Introductions, the children live at our house during the day, leaving only to sleep. An endless, perpetual, interminable, ceaseless, limitless, never-ending, eternal day as protracted as that prose, which stretches as long as that single strand of spaghetti Bubbles was trying unsuccessfully to suck into her mouth for ten long minutes until I cut all the strands up with scissors to get tea over in less than an hour. We're stumbling through it like zombie automatons, needing both of us to make half a brain's worth, because Introductions has turned into Guantanamo Bay.

We wake at 5.30 a.m. (who even knew that you could set an alarm for a time beginning with a five?), shower, breakfast and drive for forty-five minutes over to Ken and Mary's before the children wake at 7 a.m. The plan says to take the kids to ours in their PJs, but we all vetoed that on the basis that they both need something to eat first. So we spoon mush in the region of their mouths (trying at least to avoid their eyes), de-cornflake them, strap them into the car and take them to our house. There follows a day that involves snacks, nappies, bath, stories, lunch, tea, baby wipes, tidying, untidying, PJs, clothes, park, garden and drawing (not necessarily in any semblance of order) before we drive them droopily back to Ken and Mary's to put them to bed. And that's the weird thing. In the midst of it, the days seem to never end, but can I tell you what we did? No. It's like my brain is too busy to store any memories of those hours, apart from their endless cripplingness. Once the kids are settled in their cots, we exchange monosyllabic grunts with Ken and Mary before excusing ourselves and driving home. We get back around 9 p.m., unfed, too tired to even speak. And given that tomorrow starts at 5.30 a.m. again, we fall in exhaustion onto our pillows in the vain hope of recovering.

We begin transferring their belongings — and there is more than we could have possibly imagined. Bin bag by bin bag, we dismantle their life at one house and move it to our own.

We're under strict instructions to do it *without the children's noticing*. Which isn't as easy as it sounds since they trail us like Ninja (Skittle) shadows. One morning as Andy is feeding them breakfast, I'm creeping stealthily down the stairs with a bag of clothes and Bubbles appears at the bottom.

I stop, one leg in the air, aiming for a whistling nothing-to-see-here.

'What you doing?' she demands, like a parent catching a child smearing Sudocrem over the TV.

I stand still, hoping for invisible.

'Where you taking it?' she continues inquisitively.

'Aaaaa ...'

My brain goes blank.

'Uuuuu ...' I mumble. Just as I'm about to pluck something plausible out of my brain, she turns on her heel and wanders back to the kitchen, bored.

I chastise myself. *You could have said anything and she would have believed you!* Followed by *Phew! Thank goodness I wasn't carrying her pink piano.*

I put the bag in the boot and go back inside to find Mary in their bedroom packing up dresses and skirts. There are tears in her eyes, the half-empty wardrobe a prelude to the coming emptiness in their house. As she pulls items off hangers, she tells me stories of their time together. I don't know what to say. I stand beside her and help her put these precious memories into bags. She keeps talking about what she's packed and what outfits they own and I listen silently, knowing that she has to talk to keep herself from falling apart. Could I do it? Could I let go of children I'd loved and hugged, bathed and fed, giggled and played with for a year? I don't know, because the truth is that I've never loved a child with that level of intimacy and intensity.

When Andy and I open the bags at home, we're shocked. Bubbles and Nibbles are endowed with a needs-its-own-walk-in-wardrobe amount of clothing that has me gasping. *Where are we going to put it all?* Bubbles has eight coats and twelve pairs of shoes, and they each have a jaw-dropping array of trousers, tops, jeans, dresses, party clothes and more. The four drawers that we've set aside will barely hold their PJs, but we haven't the space, budget or time to buy anything else. I really want to go to bed but instead stay up sorting out clothes, picking out my favourites and bagging the rest for charity. I shudder at a shell suit and cannot convince myself that triple denim is a good look for a toddler (or for anyone since the 1980s), but there are so many lovely items there isn't room for.

The children have become increasingly confused these last few days. At Ken and Mary's house, Bubbles frowns, looks around and asks, 'Where's my piano?' The next day, she notices one at our house and proudly informs us, 'I've got one like that!' We say we know and that in fact it is her piano, but she refuses to accept this news.

The beginning was a fairy tale; these last few days are more foreboding. Bubbles is disorientated and looks like she's woken up in a strange hotel room, unable to work out where she is. One day we take her to the foster family in her PJs and she falls asleep in the car. When we arrive, she cuddles into Andy's shoulder and he carries her to bed all smiles. The next night, she wakes as the car pulls into their drive, looks terrified, and kicks, screams and bawls as Andy tries to carry her inside without dropping her. Only Ken's familiar embrace and soothing voice will do, and she clings to him like a baby monkey separated from its mummy. It's unpredictable and distressing for everyone concerned — we've all had tears these last few days.

It's the final day of Introductions, the final day we return them to Ken and Mary to sleep; tomorrow we bring them home forever. The last day of exhausting treks along the motorway and getting up at silly o'clock then home at weary o'clock. We're nearly at journey's end.

It's afternoon, and we've been playing in our lounge. Things have been going very nicely if I say so myself. But as I come downstairs after a quick pee (and a stolen peek at my phone), there's an eerie tension in the air. Something is not right — it's too quiet. I turn into the kitchen and am shocked into mannequin mode.

Andy's balancing Bubbles precariously over the sink.

When he notices me, he snaps, 'Look after Nibbles,' but not before I see the blood pouring out of Bubbles' nose, mouth and head. I turn away before my vision goes all yellow, my legs wobble and I faint helpfully into a crumbled heap on the floor. As I steady myself, I think *honestly* in that resigned eye-rolling manner that my mum favoured through most of my childhood, but I accidentally say it out loud, which Andy doesn't exactly appreciate. *I leave you alone for a few seconds.* This phrase stays silent in my head.

Andy sits Bubbles beside the sink and continues to de-bloodify her face to find out what, if anything, is broken, split or worse.

'What happened?' I ask gently, though at least an octave too high.

Andy garbles something, in a bit of a huff, but after a few more delicate questions (with no hint of blame), I discover that Bubbles was running on our smooth wooden floor in her rather slippery (favourite) slippers and fell face first. She has a small straight cut between her eyebrows, which is bleeding extravagantly, but most of the blood in the sink is from biting her lips and a spontaneous nose bleed from the impact, which makes it look much worse than it is. Which is good, because it had Hammer Horror all over it a minute ago.

Andy is the perfect choice when it comes to dealing with such an emergency, not only because he doesn't faint, but also because he's a trained first aider. Bubbles starts screaming as he presses hard to stem the blood. He tries a standard plaster, and several screwed-up plasters later, as the cut's still bleeding, he cleans it again (more crying) and presses to help it stop (yowling). Seven Steri-Strips later the wound is closed and no longer bleeding. Now her face is cleaner, I come closer tentatively, looking at the gash from between my fingers until I'm confident I'll stay upright. I am no natural nurse.

Andy has already thrown her favourite slippers in the bin, which isn't exactly helping Bubbles calm down. She begins that juddering sobbing, and snot and tears create a new stream down her face.

'Do you think she needs s-t-i-c, I mean s-t-i-t-h (*argh, silent FFS*), s-t-i-t-c-h-e-s?' (This spelling bee lark is no easy matter when I'm feeling queasy.)

It's not a clear-cut decision. We swing wildly from a covering-all-bases 'she needs a tetanus injection, machines that go *ping* and a trauma specialist flown in from the big town' to the rather laissez-faire 'we'll have to wait for hours in A&E as the kids go bananas only to have the doctor replace our Steri-Strips with clean ones' and everything in between. We throw in a pick-and-mix of barely medical nonsense gleaned from a few episodes of *House*. I remember having my head stitched when I was about five, and the lollipop reward did nothing to erase the memory of excruciating pain; I wouldn't wish that experience on anyone.

Thank goodness she didn't fall face first on the stone floor of the kitchen — she might have cracked her skull wide open! Except the floor in the kitchen isn't slippy, so she wouldn't have (oh shut up brain, you're not helping). Suddenly our whole house feels like a rusty deathtrap just waiting to spring shut on their flimsy bodies. We can't avoid telling the social workers and her foster family; they'll notice a forehead of Steri-Strips. I text Mary to let her know that Bubbles has had a little fall, suitably downplaying the incident with the trips-off-the-thumb 'it looks worse than it is'. I want to confess to flush the sin off my skin. We calm down, decide on a plan and then head off in the car in double-quick (didn't even check their nappies) speed.

We're not going to hospital. We're heading somewhere far more important. Clarks shoe store. The best quality children's shoes in town. They measure her feet and we inspect every possible shoe to find the most non-slip, non-trip, non-Steri-Strip-inducing sole they have: in pink. We finally agree on some gorgeous pink sparkly Velcro-fastening rubber-soled shoes.

Twenty-six-pounds worth of tiny shoe. I almost gasp at the expense, trotting out how it's unbelievable that something so small could possibly cost so much (I bet the staff have a bingo card for just such mumblings). But this is a needs-must situation. And we need to feel better, so twenty-six pounds is nothing compared to the shame we're shouldering.

We leave with a tiny bag of tiny shoes and a smile on Bubbles' broken face. Her new indoor shoes more than make up for Daddy's putting her beloved slippers in the bin. I go home to amend my risk assessment and shower the guilt off.

The crisis is over.

It's been an exhausting end to our last day of Introductions.

The shoes become known as the 'guilty shoes'.

29. Their First Sleep

We are on a stakeout (see Chapter 1: Spies Like Us).

We drive away from Ken and Mary's.

'The lady horse goes trot, trot, trot,' sings Bubbles to her bunny, bouncing it on her knees. After the weirdness of The Handover and The Rescue of their toys (which led to barging in on The Grief), we begin the magical first day as their forever family. Bubbles' happiness beams through the clouds, brightening our mood.

We take them to an indoor play gym. For those of you who've never set foot in a play gym (it's a first for us today — in the olden days when I was young, it was a few toys in the church hall), these are specially designed environments with ball pools, slides, steps, winding passages, padded plastic things to climb over and nets to walk through all enveloped in a mirage of wipe-clean padded plastic in colours to make you wince and your hangover ten times worse and that probably hasn't been wiped clean since it was installed. Just hope you never scramble around the ball pool for a missing sock — this pool is a lucky dip of dust, unidentifiable food scraps, dolls' arms and snot that'll have you clicking Buy It Now on your phone to get a replacement sock rather than picking out another icky non-sock. It's a place where adults can ignore their kids, knowing they can't escape, while their kids race around screaming and wearing themselves out; a few hours' peace and quiet with occasional interruptions to settle disputes, wipe snot or tears from faces and take trips to the loo.

Nibbles' and Bubbles' faces light up as we enter. Giggling, they throw off their shoes and dash through the gate as we sign them in. Andy and I each grab a caffeinated drink and sit as near as possible to keep our watchful eyes on the children.

'Did you bring nappies?' we ask each other hopefully. 'Oh.' I wonder how long we'll get away with our new-to-this blundering. In this drunken haze of novelty and sleep deprivation, everything they do is a miracle.

'Look at him balancing on that net.' I grin madly.

'Isn't he brave?' I whisper.

I realise that no one else is even paying attention to their kids; they're here to sip mediocre coffee and read the paper in a room where screams and shouts reverberate incessantly off the hard walls like bullets from a machine gun, drilling into your ears.

'Aw, listen to her giggle, how lovely.' I wonder how I picked her sweet sound from the cacophony. We have the wide-eyed wonder of new parents riding a caffeine buzz. We're entranced by their every move, and marvel at their movements, their laughter and how they interact with each other, other children and the equipment. We act like Nemo's dad, all suspicious and jittery when we can't see them.

'Where is he? Oh, there he is. Is that one of ours crying?' More head bobbing. 'No,' *phew*, 'it's someone else's.'

I sigh with contentment.

When one of them gets stuck, we both kick off our shoes with a bit of a 'who'll get there first?' heroic dash to their rescue. And we discover just how difficult it is to contort our bodies through the gaps and holes. By the time I've slithered and inched my way through the labyrinthine spaces, they're either not there anymore (and are bawling their eyes out by the table I've just left) or are screaming with joy down the slide.

We're 100 percent parents. We've graduated with considerably less pomp and clapping than experienced at previous graduations. We get to look after them all day and then put them to bed in the cots that have been waiting months for them to arrive. We're glad to give up the twice-daily hike along the motorway and getting up at is-this-an-actual-time? o'clock. We imagine all the extra time we'll have in bed (to sleep). Bubbles and Nibbles sleep straight through every night, so Mary said (although Ken looked as if he was going to disagree before thinking better of it).

Despite their not wanting to leave the play gym, the rest of the day goes brilliantly. Nibbles naps, they eat (and destroy) their lunch and we spend the afternoon playing. After tea, we watch a little TV as they zone out, and they're both in bed and asleep by 7.30 p.m. #result

We must've tired them out, we conclude on little evidence except our own exhaustion.

In a haze of new parenthood — part tiredness, part joy, part bewilderment — we sit in our lounge and count our blessings. This is the moment we dreamt of for all those years. Upstairs lie two sleeping angels. Our children. OUR children. We finally have a family of our own. We might not have envisaged the daily visits by the social workers, or the paperwork, or the Panel interviews, but we wanted a family and we now have one. And everything in our lives feels brighter, shinier — as if it's had a new coat of paint. The world looks different today, because I am different today. All the doubts I had about me, all the fears about never being a mum, they're all erased with one giant stroke of children.

Maybe it's because I am tired, but I can't quite believe it. I can't even let myself fully feel the joy of having finally made it, because if I do, I might burst into tears and not be able to stop as all those bottled-up feelings fizz out of me like cava from a bottle that's been shaken.

Today has made all the rest of it worthwhile.

Today we've won the ultimate prize.

Today we've become parents to two amazing children.

And in this one moment, all the heartache, the disappointments, the hurdles and hoops we jumped through seem a long time ago, our scars miraculously healed by today.

The moment my head sinks into the feathers of my pillow, the blissful silence is broken. The cries start gently and escalate rapidly to deep distress. Poor Nibbles.

I open his door and tiptoe in. I rub his back and make soothing noises. I let him grip my hand. He's still not happy. I make sure he has dummies to juggle, but that doesn't seem to be it either. He barely registers I'm there. I warm a little milk and hope it might lull him back to sleep. He drinks some but is still wide awake and unhappy. That's me out of ideas.

Andy offers to help and I let him. He cuddles him and mutters soothing noises and he quietens a little, but then starts again.

Mary didn't really cover this possibility because they always 'sleep like a dream'. Ha. She told me innumerable times that I could ring her at any time day or night if we needed her, but phoning her now seems to be *(a)* giving up too soon; *(b)* irrelevant, because the things that are upsetting him are the things that are different; and *(c)* like rubbing salt into an ulcer. Whatever is hurting or upsetting him, he can't tell us.

Andy takes the still-crying Nibbles for a tiny bobbing walk downstairs and warms some milk. And as they go back upstairs, something happens. Nibbles stops crying. Halfway up the stairs, where there's nothing to see and it's a little darker, Nibbles finds some peace. I get up and find Andy sat on a step in the dark holding Nibbles against his chest. After forty-five minutes of distress this little boy has finally let sleep drag him back under.

The next day we will ponder why it was mid-stairs that he found his peace. Was it because there was nothing on the stairs to remind him of the strangeness of his new life? Did he wake up and not recognise anything?

I'm beginning to know how he feels.

30. The Best Seats in the House

Day Two of being a full-time family. Bubbles and Nibbles are beacons of light and joy shining their love into our house with their constant attention. They look deep into our eyes and shadow our every step like dancers learning new choreography. We murmur about how cute it is, about how lovely they are. We get a lifetime of hugs and kisses and think *How sweet* when they cling to our legs like lemurs, all wrapped tight and really tricky to shake off. We are surprised by their tenacity, smile sweetly through our tiredness and gape at how much they love us and want to be with us. We say 'aww' for hours, until the novelty wears off and we just want to pop to the kitchen to get a drink without two cumbersome burdens clamped to our calves.

At Ken and Mary's, the children wandered in and out of the house and garden, playing on their own, ignoring their foster carers unless they needed drink, food, a referee or a ladder in human form to get something they couldn't reach. But this is different. Try as we might, we can't shake them off easily, and this level of attention is hard to adjust to. Whilst they are both engrossed in listening to Andy read a story, I sneak off to the toilet for *(a)* obvious reasons; but also *(b)* because I want a snippet of me-time. I sit down on the loo and, as I turn, come face-to-face with my children, their faces alight with expectation.

'Wee or poo?' inquires Bubbles, and I've barely opened my mouth to reply when I'm interrupted.

'How big is it?'

I'm lost for words.

'That's wee,' declares Bubbles.

I'm surprised, because I half expected it to crawl back inside and wait for them to leave.

'She's weeing.'

giggles

'I heard it plop.'

They look at each other wide-eyed and grinning.

'What colour is it? Can I watch it come out?' she asks without a shred of embarrassment whilst I colour like a pale office worker on a hot sunny lunchtime.

No one mentioned this. No one said that before the children came to live with us I should have been luxuriating in peeing without an audience.

The following day, as the kids play with Andy, I poke my head around the door and mention that I'm off for a shower (aka don't run the taps for at least ten minutes).

'Can I come?' asks Bubbles. I go all Natalie Imbruglia (I'm torn). Again, I just want a few minutes of me-time, but I feel guilty refusing so reluctantly agree. I squirm with discomfort, invaded by her beady eyes and insatiable curiosity.

'Why have you got hair *there*, Mummy?'

As I wash my hair and skin, I start a running commentary — 'Now I'm washing my arms all the way from my fingers to my underarms' — hoping that a narrative will make this whole 'child watching Mummy shower' experience less weird than it is. It doesn't.

But something does happen. I become present in the moment. Instead of letting my mind wander, I pay attention to the experience of the water and the washing and I wonder how often I've let life wash over me without truly noticing simple actions like standing under hot running water and letting it drench my hair and skin. My children see the world with an innocence and curiosity that refreshes my tired view of these ordinary things.

A few weeks later, I buy a step with two treads to help Bubbles practise getting on and off the toilet without falling in. Unexpectedly, this makes room for them both to watch me on the loo: they mercilessly exploit it as an improved viewing platform: the best seats in the house (for a performance with limited appeal). I optimistically presume that the appeal will wane soon, but soon is a long time coming. It's the changes to ordinary aspects of life that astound me the most these first few days.

I've decided that we're going to eat together as a family at the table — a place that has been the preserve of a bowl of fluffy, slightly blue satsumas, a bunch of brown speckled bananas and unopened mail. I had planned to be a 'flour on the nose, chocolate on the apron' style mummy who patiently helped her children prepare jam tarts. But in just two days, mealtimes have become a bit of a battleground. I'm totally unprepared for how difficult it is to move food from a dish into their mouths. Bottomless reserves of stamina (which I don't have) are required.

As I watch Nibbles eat, I realise that for toddlers, eating is as complex as string theory. First, he has to use the muscles in his fingers and palm to grip the spoon tightly enough that it doesn't slip out ('I'll get it') while he's conducting his invisible orchestra. *The spoon is in his hand!* I make a tiny yelp of congratulations. Then he adjusts his wrist and fingers to tip the spoon at the right angle to enter the plastic bowl containing his sweet-potato mush. The spoon is looking good, the angle is right (*come on, you can do this*), but what's this? Oh no, he's too fast and can't stop in time! His entire fist has bellyflopped into the mush, and after extracting it with a pop, he panics. He hates dirty hands; whether it's mud, sand or ice cream, stuff on his hands means screaming until someone wipes them clean. I use five wipes. His hand is now so clean he could perform surgery, his meal is reduced by about one-third and he hasn't eaten a single mouthful. 'Come on, Nibbles,' I chant, with the zeal of a football fan. The spoon's approaching, the angle looks good and his tongue is out he's concentrating so hard. As he opens his mouth in anticipation, I shovel some food in.

He's nearly there. The spoon . . . is . . . in (whoop whoop), and his hand stays clear of the penalty area. Surely we're nearly done? Barely started. He scoops food onto the spoon again, but what's this? The bowl starts to run away, and since he's still conducting with his other hand, he's now chasing the bowl around the tray like a dog chasing its tail. It's nearing the edge and I shrink at the thought of what might happen and (phew) it's stopped by the lip of the tray. (At tea it will tip onto the floor creating a food Pollock.) He's jiggled a blob onto his spoon and now needs to get the spoon out of the gloop and to his face. Steady now. That mush is sticky stuff, but if he applies too much force, he'll create a trebuchet of food that seeks out any clean item of clothing I might be wearing (for it will unnervingly avoid anything else). Steady. The spoon is coming out with mush on and it's ... it's ... it's clear. (Is this going to take much longer?) Brake! He needs to counterbalance the weight of the food on the spoon but slow down, as air resistance is far lower than mush resistance. Now's the really tricky bit. Nibbles has to turn the spoon and stab it into a mouth he knows is there but cannot see, however much he squirms. I could amuse myself by sketching out the equations of the mechanics of this ballet (who am I kidding? university was a very long time ago), but this display is exasperating. I can eat my food, wash up and cook another meal in the time it takes Nibbles to get just a few mouthfuls in as he dissolves in a hunger meltdown of heroic proportions. Sometimes it's hilarious, but mostly it's like watching paint dry whilst repeatedly and desperately encouraging it to 'dry a bit blooming quicker, please'.

Within days we have hundreds of pictures of them 'eating'.

Today Andy's washing up as the children dither over their food. I'm drying up and putting things away. He turns around to check if they've finished yet. Then he shouts a warning, and I look too. Nibbles is almost stood up in his high chair, straining against his straps. It appears to be a valiant escape attempt, although his face looks a bit strained and there are rivulets of tears pouring down his face. He has an expression I can't place — is it a huge poo? Food that's too spicy? Panic, even?

'What's wrong?' we ask in unison.

We get no reply.

Odd.

No words come out. Not even a no (his favourite word).

He continues to writhe silently, as if he's fighting to get away from something; either that or he's expressing himself through the medium of interpretive dance, it's hard to tell. It's just so out of character. His silent tears are unusual. He's not making a single noise of any ki —

Alarms suddenly ring like sirens in our brains. We realise at the same time. Colour drains from our faces. Bile rises in panic.

He's choking.

Nibbles.

Is.

CHOKING!

Andy morphs into SuperDad mode, twanging off his washing-up gloves, loosening the high-chair straps (why are they so difficult to undo?) and rushing Nibbles over to the sink as Nibbles thrashes about helplessly.

'Stop it, Daddy!' demands Bubbles, trying to protect her brother from such rough manhandling. I stand and gawp, transfixed, hand over my mouth, feeling helpless, hoping and praying. I can barely breathe. Andy slaps Nibbles on the back. Nothing. Slap. Nothing. Slap. Ditto. I nearly throw up from the fear churning inside. I look away, then back, then away.

'Stop hitting him, Daddy! You're hurting him!' yells Bubbles, who is livid. I explain that Daddy is saving Nibbles' life but she is not listening. Andy wrestles Nibbles to a new position and bashes his back again.

And then I hear a sound as welcome as the first cry of a baby fresh from the womb. Nibbles is screaming his head off. He lets us know in no uncertain terms that we will not be getting a good review for this gastronomic endeavour. And we don't care, for those delightfully piercing screams mean one thing: the food is dislodged. He can breathe again.

I nearly crumple in sheer relief. I look to the ceiling and mouth a silent thank you to whoever may be listening. I sit down and stroke Bubbles' arms as I calmly tell her again what Daddy was doing. Andy hugs Nibbles and wipes away the tears that have created two columns of cleanness on his food-strewn face.

Visibly shaken, Andy and I hold him and hug him while the *what ifs* spiral around in our heads. What if we hadn't noticed? What if one of us had been on the toilet? What if he'd choked to death on a grape?

Would I have ever forgiven myself? I promise in future to prepare food of doll's-house scale so that lunchtime cannot kill them.

And after the adrenalin wears off (immediately for Andy, about a week later for me), we whitewash the situation by thanking our lucky stars and looking on the bright side. At least they're not decapitating Fireman Sam or chewing the hands off Barbie such that we're peering into and rooting through their every expulsion to make sure the body parts come out again.

'What's that on my foot?' Andy wondered this morning in the shower. Peering closer, he discovered it was poo. As he tells me this, I laugh. For a small boy who doesn't eat that much, an unfeasible quantity of gunk comes out Nibbles' rear end. Last night it exploded beyond the confines of his nappy, and when I went to get him out of his cot this morning, I retched, held my nose closed and called the Centre for Disease Control and Prevention (I have it on speed dial) demanding they helicopter in and *hut-hut-hut* down wires with powerful hoses and pop-up isolation tents to mount a full-scale decontamination. But they said that if I rang again they would report me to the police, so we managed a DIY version with a bucket of bleach, a bagful of baby wipes and the constitution of oxen.

I reflect on how my morning routine has changed. Before Children (BC), I had the luxury of time to fritter straightening or curling my hair, putting on make-up and choosing from a wardrobe bulging with clothes that were clean, ironed and impractical. Now, After Children, my 'vanity' routine consists of a super-speedy shower, chucking on the jeans and sweatshirt I wore yesterday and checking in the mirror for splodges of nappy-chocolate that might cause dysentery. None? Good to go. Andy and I have both succumbed to a sickness, possibly due to our somewhat cavalier attitude to nappies and their contents. After discovering how much nastier it is to change nappies when your stomach is ready to erupt out of every orifice, we resolved to treat nappies as if they are toxic in the extreme. Such that a tiny smear will become toxicity incarnate and morph into a supervillain aptly named The Emetic Turdster.

I've had enough. *stomps foot*

I don't want my house to smell of eau de nappies any more. Changing them is bad enough, but then there's that smell that lingers, ready to assault you just when you're sneaking a rare-as-a-clean-bib kiss with your husband. You look around, sure that the kids are busy, smile, sidle over and just as you're about to plant your smackers on his luscious lips . . . *Ugh. Gag!* And the urge dies as fast as public interest in whoever was on the last series of Big Brother (who?). I'm going to light some scented candles to create that vanilla with a hint of burnt wick smell. The sort of odour that regularly wafted around this house BC.

Candles? Check. Matches? Oh. There're not there. Oh yeah, we had to hide them. Hmm. Where did we hide them?

sounds of drawers and cupboards opening in rapid succession

'Andy, where did we put the matches?'

muffled response

'Okay, where did *I* put them then? Oh, come on, they must be somewhere. Where would be a good place to hide them?' Nope. Nope. Argh.

'Bubbles, sweetie, have you seen the matches? Me neither.' Darnblastandbuggerit. 'You didn't hear that, did you?'

My house smells like a Victorian slum on a hot summer's day and some Ms JobsWorthy has made me hide the one thing that can eliminate the odour: the match I need to light a scented candle.

hits head with hand and posts on Facebook to vent her frustration

31. Blisters

We are off out. Not on an adventure (at least not in the BC sense), but to the supermarket, so we can fill our shelves and cupboards with foods that the children might eat rather than just destroy/chuck at the ceiling. Bubbles refuses to even sniff milk or cheese, so to boost her calcium, we'll be buying all manner of calcium-richness, like chocolate milk (I hang my head in nutritional shame), to tempt her. It's not the exotic mix of samphire, quinoa and kimchi that as middle-class gastronomes we aspire to, but right now we're just aiming to make mealtimes a teensy bit simpler by postponing our highfalutin ideas of eating sushi together or even having a varied diet.

After completing an exhaustive pre-leaving-the-house checklist (filled nappies in the house are one thing; in the confines of a family vehicle they are enough to have us driving along with our heads stuck out of the window gasping for fresh air), we're ready to shop. We drive off and are barely in second gear when . . .

'Are we going to Ken and Mary's?' asks Bubbles. For nearly a week, every time we were in the car, we were shuttling her between the two houses, so it's a logical question.

'We're going shopping,' I say with fake excitement in my voice, shirking the underlying question.

'Can we go to Ken and Mary's?' she asks innocently, clearly not willing to be distracted from her quest for the truth.

I look helplessly at Andy, who shakes his head and shrugs. I don't know what to say. Sadness ripples through me. She has told us how much she misses them, and I try to imagine how strange this is for her. Maybe all adopted children feel like this but only the older ones can express what's in their heads and hearts. No one prepared us for this. I feel like I've been caught licking the lid of the cooking sherry during Dry January[7].

I gulp.

I try a deep breath.

'Can we go there today?' she continues.

'Not today,' responds Andy, in what will become our stock response. Her face crumples and my heart sinks and I want to hug her, but all I can reach is her foot, so I stroke it.

'Ooh, look a car,' we say to distract her, our voices overflowing with exaggerated surprise.

'Later we'll go to the park!' Blatantly tempting her with something else.

They aren't allowed to see their foster family until they're securely attached to us; otherwise, the adoption might break down (or 'disrupt'). The truth is that we don't know if they'll ever see Ken and Mary again (the social workers are divided), but right now, the answer's a clear no.

'I want to go back now,' says Bubbles.

And my tears rise to the surface faster than when I hear 'I do' in a romcom.

What am I not giving her (that they did)?

What's missing in our family (that they had)?

What am I doing wrong (where do I start)?

Of course she wants to be with them; it's what she's used to, what she knows. The novelty is over, and she just wants to return to the comforting womb of familiarity. However much we try to replicate their old life, we're different. These are the blisters that her new life is giving her, that *we* are giving her. We're not Ken and Mary. And these differences rub, and cause her pain.

I need to pull myself together and be grown-up about it all. But I feel like the last lonely child waiting to be picked by the team captains for games in school. Is Nibbles feeling the same? Does he want

---

[7] **Dry January:** A noble cause that serves to make the coldest, darkest, wettest, most destitute month of the year even less joyless than it already blooming is because an entire month of penitence is clearly what we deserve for brazenly celebrating Christmas with a bit of food and drink.

to go back too? We know he's finding it difficult. There are times when he is truly inconsolable. Sometimes a long hug can calm him down; sometimes a hug from his sister makes things okay; and when nothing else works, we bring out the *Who Drives This?* book to distract him. We don't always know what we need to fix, or even if we can fix it, and we wonder if it's the adoption, or something entirely different. We sigh and drive off, a little sadder than before.

This new life is causing blisters for all of us.

Family walks. Fresh air, exercise, beautiful views. What could be better? Andy and I love walking; it's been part of our weekend routine since we first started dating, through wind and drizzle, snow and fog. And now it's something we're going to do as a family. Andy and I will walk along holding hands whilst the kids run ahead, giggling as they pick up leaves and chase squirrels.

Today we're starting with a tiny walk to the park around the corner from our house (you can almost do it in slippers). The park of the photo-shoot oddness. We set off into the sunshine, leaving the pram behind. It's only a hop, skip and a toddle away and . . . Woah! Bubbles hits the pavement with a thump and I nearly trip over her.

'Too tired,' she declares. 'Wanna go home.'

'Um.' I look around self-consciously, wondering what to do. It's as far to go home as it is to go to the park, and I'm not giving in this soon. I raise my eyebrows and look at my husband. He's stooped so Nibbles can grip his finger in a vice, and is making even slower progress than I am.

'It's just a little further,' I say encouragingly. I stand and wait. After a few seconds, she's made her point or rested enough, and she gets up and carries on. Bubbles stops twice more before arriving at the park (to the sort of cheers reserved for charity ultra-marathon runners who decide two marathons in a row is too easy so do them in a pantomime horse outfit in desert heat just before they become not-another motivational speaker). Andy lifts Nibbles, puts him down so he can toddle for a few steps and then picks him up again. Oh for the pram. I'd estimated it'd take about five minutes to get here (it takes me two), but it's clear that I used the wrong thumb in that calculation. The reality? Twenty minutes. Twenty of the most frustratingly slow minutes of my life to get to the park. Bubbles limps around the corner but is instantly revived by the sight of the swings. The children spend ages running around, climbing up the rungs onto the slide and asking to be pushed on the swings. And we get home almost intact, having learnt a valuable lesson.

The next time, we're prepared. In the way that mountaineers prepare to climb Kilimanjaro. We've packed ice picks, emergency flares, whistles, layers and layers of clothing, sun hats, sun lotion, nappies, foil blankets in case of hypothermia, wet wipes, dry socks, Kendal Mint Cake and that expedition essential — pemmican.

We can't rely on the pram because Mother Nature doesn't create pram-friendly paths over the hills and dales. But since all Nibbles can do is toddle about five metres, we need an off-road, off-the-ground option. Some friends have lent us a back carrier, which is cumbersome, but with Nibbles off the ground, I'll get my thumb back and we'll be racing along at half-speed.

It's Sunday and I'm frazzled. I need some fresh air (not that nappy odour). I need to see the sky in its infinite variety (versus yet another reading of the *Bear Hunt*). I need to walk at a pace (not a crawl) without a stairgate to impede my progress. I need to feel light and free rather than chained and bound to the kids and their rhythm. I want do-it-with-my-eyes-closed versus mind-numbing-emotion-draining-complexity. All I want is a little walk so I can feel that it's all going to be okay (if not right now, then one day). Nothing strenuous, nothing muddy, just an easy potter along the canal.

We arrive and park the car. The drizzle has got heavier, but like it, I'm determined to persist. This is important. This is the dream, our life as a family. I'm tired. I'm fed up. I need a few minutes of peaceful walking to escape into my mind and puzzle everything out to the rhythm of my feet so that I can return home feeling as if something has been righted. I *need* this.

Andy and I put on our waterproof coats then our sturdy boots. Bubbles is swaddled in her warmest coat and her wellies, eager to go. She pulls my arm like a dog on a lead. We just need to get Nibbles into the back carrier. It's not the easiest jumbling of limbs and straps and balance to get him into the carrier and onto Andy's back, but then he is in and up and we can start this longed-for stomp. Nibbles doesn't look exactly delighted, but I assume he'll get used to it quickly. Who wouldn't want to be carried? Surely it's better than walking? We're still in sight of the car and out of sight of the canal when he starts to cry. I hold his hand, smile and use the old distraction one-two.

'Look, a bird, Nibbles,' followed by, 'Wow! Did you see that?' whilst pointing vaguely ahead in the direction of the canal. I can see the water glistening through the trees just ahead, and yet the distance suddenly warps and stretches and I sag a little. We're only halfway from the car to the canal when he starts to bawl. By the time we actually get to the start of our walk at the canal, his displeasure has hit screaming pitch (right into Andy's ear). Tears squirt from his eyes like high-pressure jets and no amount of 'look at the duck' distraction is going to stop him from expressing how much he loathes the carrier. Andy kneels down and lifts Nibbles out of the carrier, and as he stops crying, I nearly start. My hope evaporates as fast as rain on hot tarmac. Andy gives him a big hug and Nibbles is happier already, though I'm now sulking. We toddle a few metres alongside the canal, turn a corner and complete the smallest circular walk known to man.

Despite my craving for fresh air and exercise, for a soupçon of my old life, I'm not going to find it here today. Bubbles picks up some cherry blossom and hands it to me, but even its elegant beauty and hint of Japanese aesthetics cannot lift the despair in my heart. I'm tired and weary and I just wanted a slice of me back (*Is that too much to ask?* I whine internally). And back in the car, we discover just why you shouldn't let kids bring cherry blossom into a vehicle.

Nibbles and Bubbles are delighted to be going home. I peer gloomily out of the misty car window at the life I'm missing out on. This walk was a symbol of freedom, of independence, of autonomy, an antidote to the restrictions and constraints of being a parent, which I'm finding hard to cope with. I had hung my hopes on it, and they lie confettied at my feet like the cherry blossom.

The 'going for walks together' part of my dream broke today.

Will anything ever be simple again?

Are we aiming too high too soon? Or is this just a case of premature perambulation (without a perambulator)?

Time, perhaps, to go back to the drawing board, to set our sights on more achievable goals.

Like getting through the day in one piece.

32. And. And. And.

I'm going to burst into tears. And when I do, I won't be able to stop. I'm *tired*.

Not a *little bit* tired from, say, one night's interrupted sleep — then I'd be peeky, but a hug, a splash of caffeine and a giggle and I'd be good to go.

Not *quite tired* from fevered sleep — then I might be a few planks shy of a full load and my IQ would have dropped fifty points, but after some breakfast, paracetamol and a hair waving, pogo-ing boogie to the 1980s classic tune *Echo Beach* and I'd look and act normal enough.

No, this morning, I'm not quite here, as if I haven't materialised fully after transport from the USS *Enterprise*. My body's operating essential stuff on autopilot, but I have the emotional stability of my daughter in the afternoon (a little bit like TNT). I've never felt so tired, and I simply don't know what to do because the higher-reasoning bits of my brain are on strike.

My body is a cannonball of exhaustion, as if someone turned gravity up overnight, curling my spine into a ball and making my eyelids too heavy to open. The tiredness is deep in my marrow; no shower will slough this off my skin. I hanker for a den, a hiding place in which to growl and frown and hide my grumpiness from the world until I fall into blissful sleep, away from everyone and everything.

Yesterday when I told Bubbles I needed a magical cure for tiredness, Bubbles turned to her brother and said, 'It's a pig.' Random. But this morning, I snap at her for getting under my feet, forgetting how cute the pig thing was. Andy murmurs something about being nicer (so she'll love me as much as she loves him), but his tone is tinder to my short, highly flammable fuse.

I am doing my *sniff* best. and. this is and. and. so hard. and. and. and. I'm sooooo-oh-oh tired.

And. and. and. and. and. why. and. and. does Andy. and. and. and. have to be so and. and. and. mean? I am at my and. and. and. lowest this morning and. and. and. and. being criticised for doing my best at being and. and. and. a D-list mummy is not and. and. and. helping. What happened to and. and. and. promising to stand together, never and. and. and. criticising each other?

His words have detonated the dynamite.

I cry in the shower to get that shower-fresh yet blotchy-faced look that all new mums crave. My tears join the highlighter I dab fruitlessly under my eyes to hide the grey shadows of doom. I go downstairs on my bottom because my legs are weak and I used all my energy to wrestle the stupid, I-hate-you stairgate open. I've not even got the energy to blow the whistle of the Bottom Bottom Choo Choo train that I drive with the kids when we go down the stairs on our bottoms (to make up for not carrying them down).

Silent tears pour down my cheeks as I spoon muesli into my mouth, a sight that has my kids staring at me then Andy, me then Andy, until he gently suggests (with the unspoken 'get a grip') that maybe I might want to eat my breakfast in the lounge because I'm upsetting the children.

I am upsetting them? and. and. and. *What about you upsetting me?* I snivel into my yoghurt. and. and. and. I don't know how to get a grip. Today, in a minimalist approach to parenting, my mission is to keep low, avoid any danger and swoop on the first chance for a nap.

In becoming a mum overnight, the most difficult bit is not giving up my weekend lie-ins, or wiping cascades of slime from their noses, or placing my family heirlooms out of reach, or enduring the faint whiffs that invade every corner of my house (I'm sure there's a poo hidden somewhere, but can I find it?), or the endlessness of meals and laundry; it's not even being watched on the loo.

No, the biggest challenge has been accepting that I'm not as good at being a mum as I wanted to be. I'm not the (fictional) mum who never shouts at her kids and never feeds them spaghetti hoops, who never finds poo in her handbag and never cries in the shower before breakfast. All that trying and hoping and wishing created the false belief that when the dream finally came true, I would become WonderMum. I'm intelligent, super-organised, artistic, creative and good at cooking, and I got promoted a lot at work. I thought these elements would create the most jaw-dropping example of motherhood known to womankind. Am I the first to fall into this trap?

It turns out that my PhD in chemical engineering is no preparation for this role. In fact, it's been spectacularly useless thus far. I'm tired all the time and this tired version of me is less brilliant, less resourceful and far snappier than the BC fully slept one. I want to skip to the park or create flour bombs in my kitchen as we gleefully make concoctions that are second-cousins-once-removed to cakes. I want to sing, bash drums, dress up and enjoy all those things I wrote on my timetable. Instead I am weary. Impatient. Controlling. I shout. I get really frustrated. The mess they create drives me over an edge that I haven't felt since sharing a house with nine housemates at uni who had a 'it's not that bad, you can still see the floor/sink/plug' approach to cleanliness. I set myself a ludicrous goal of becoming the textbook mum to two children overnight.

Now I know why people kept calling us 'brave'.

My brain doesn't work, my body is on strike and. and. and. and. I just want some sleep. Today I hit the wall. I want to plonk them in front of the TV and crawl back under my duvet for a week and dream of waking up feeling like I give a shit.

But within this dark blight of sleep-deprived unhappiness there's a shard of celebration.

It's Wednesday.

That means we've been together for a whole week. (A week? Is that all?) Time to pat ourselves on the back: we're all still alive.

Today, I truly acknowledge that being a parent is much harder than I imagined, that I have fewer skills and less patience than I expected, and that when I am drained, just keeping them alive is a heroic achievement of unbelievable complexity that blows my PhD out of the water.

To all the parents out there, I salute you and your bravery.

I don't know how you and. and. and. do it.

and. and. and. you are amazing.

And Mum, I have even less idea and. and. and. how you looked after four children under five and. and. and. without a washing machine or central heating or and. and. and. a car and using terry nappies and. and. and. knitting clothes for us and. and. and. stuff that makes me shudder and. and. and. I love you, Mum.

and. and. and.

(pass the tissues)

33. Banana Thieves

Shopping is the new black. We're in Asda, the children firmly strapped into the trolley to avoid any hide-and-seek panic. As we push them down the aisles, we sidle past parents who are having a shouting match with their kids.

'What is going on?' I ask Andy with Roger Moore eyebrows.

'Where did everyone come from?' Andy replies. He's been watching too much *Question Time* and is now unable to answer a question with anything other than an irrelevant counter-question. Who does he think he is? The leader of the opposition? I look around; this supermarket is heaving, packed to the brim with parents and their screaming, bawling children.

Our eyebrows search for our hairlines (they've a long way to go on Andy's scalp) in synchronised realisation.

'It's Saturday!' we cry.

What the heck are we doing in Asda on a Saturday morning?

In the tiredness and strangeness of these last few days, I've lost track of things like my name, my hubby's name (henceforth he shall be known only as Daddy) and what day it is. We contemplate ditching the trolley, turning around and returning to the relative safety of our home, but the fridge is bare of milk and cucumber. We shrug and carry on, letting the cacophony wash over us as we smugly compare our little angels to the whirling dervishes of other parents. Nibbles and Bubbles are in hug mode — she's smothering him in slightly more kisses and hugs than he cares for, but he's taking it well as he slides as far away as possible within the confines of the trolley.

'Can I hold it?' they ask, as I pick something off the shelf, and they duly hug it and kiss it, 'Daddy's raisins', treasuring it until something more interesting turns up (when they drop it faster than the population drops its flighty allegiance to England during international tournaments when we invariably get knocked out and people remember their great-great-great-auntie who's Spanish). It's only taken a few trips for me to wise up to the fact that bananas (milkshake, anyone?) and milk (excuse me, someone has spilt some milk in aisle seventeen) and bags of spaghetti (who's for a game of pick-up sticks on the supermarket floor?) fail the catapult-in-to-the-trolley test. And don't get me started on what they can do to a dozen eggs.

Nibbles is holding a big block of cheese, which passes the 'can they hold it?' test by being non-breakable, non-crushable, non-bruiseable. As I search for the right type of yoghurt amongst a bewildering array of choices, I hear a little voice.

'Mummy . . . (something), Nibbles (garble) . . .' I grab a yoghurt and put it directly into the trolley (catapult catastrophe averted).

'Yes, sweetie. What is it?' I inquire, expecting an allegation of poking or biting.

'Cheese, Mummy. He's eaten the cheese.' Her frown intensifies her accusations.

'Don't be silly,' I start to say as I take the cheese from him, certain that fully wrapped cheese is safe from —

I laugh.

Nibbles has left a perfect set of teeth indentations in the cheese (straight through the wrapping). I roll my eyes (what next?).

'Oh, Nibbles, please don't eat the cheese,' I implore.

I miss the warning signs.

A few aisles later, tempers start to flare and behaviour starts to deteriorate faster than drunken festival goers when the beer runs dry, and I am trying my best to keep their spirits up with a cocktail of cheerleading, cajoling and threatening but it all falls on fallow ground and I am losing the will to live and I am not even out of the chilled cabinets. I search for Andy in the hope that he can help, but he's elbow deep in margarine.

For no apparent reason, I check the time.

It's only 11 a.m. How time flie —

ELEVEN O'CLOCK?

'How did you let this happen?' I ask Andy, randomly apportioning blame his way. Not only are we shopping in Asda (a cathedral of poor parenting) on a Saturday (its congregation swelling to they-must-be-filming-*Songs-of-Praise* amounts), but we've dropped a huge ball. Did you spot it? As a Bad-Parent Detective, did you notice our mistake? I'm pushing my children around the food-filled aisles of a supermarket when their stomachs are achingly empty. Of course, being toddlers, they don't say, 'Mummy dearest, would you be so good as to give me something nutritious to eat, as I believe that these rumblings in my stomach region indicate that my blood-sugar level is veering dangerously low.' Instead they express them-selves in the only ways they know — by fighting and biting and shouting and pinching and behaving like cheese-eating monsters. Monsters of my making. It is sixty minutes after snack time. I panic and do the unthinkable. I become a banana thief.

I don't steal it (because being arrested is not going to make today better); I find a pre-priced pack, break two off and give them one each. When I worked on the checkouts in Sainsbury's way back when Heaven 17 and ABC were first in the charts, I never understood the half-eaten packets of food on the conveyor belt. I'd wonder, *Why can't they wait to leave the shop to eat them?* with haughty ignorance. Now I understand. An eerie calm descends and I sigh with relief.

They finish eating in record time — I think Nibbles inhaled his banana in just three huge sucks. Then he wails. Crisis not averted. The Asda Meltdown is clearly destined for historical significance. Now I'm drawing the stares of the others as I fall painfully off my superiority stool.

I make soothing sounds to prove to anyone watching, judg-ing, that I'm a good parent. But nothing is going to solve their blood-sugar catastrophe. I suck it up: all the faces, all the expressions, all the inaudible and audible tutting, all the shame-slinging. There are those who empathise with me, who send me 'poor you' looks with kind smiles. There are those who smile in relief that today it's not their kids. And there are those who love to yap on about how I should raise children, despite the closest they've come to parenting is cooing into an empty pram outside the post office.

Shut up with your 'helpful hints'.

You don't know me.

You don't know my children.

Take your 'I watched one episode of *Super Nanny* so I know how you *should* handle this' smugness and go shop in M&S with your extra pennies. Being a parent is hard enough in your own home, but when you're in public and people are watching, it's even harder. Children are gloriously spontaneous and wonderfully unpredictable, and sometimes a thing like forgetting their snack makes your day implode. Shopping with toddlers is summed up by this equation: the quantity of the booze you buy in those final aisles equals the cantankerousness of your children in the previous twenty-three aisles. Today I bought three bottles of red wine, one bottle of cava and a litre of gin (and was so fed up I forgot the tonic, gah): a record amount.

After the most mortifying trip to Asda ever, I create secret stashes of emergency food in the car, in my handbag, in my pockets and in my desk (shh, that one's chocolate mummy medicine). I stop short of burying a food capsule in the park near our house.

But it's not just the children who are going hungry. In the last few weeks, both Andy and I have lost weight — nearly a stone in my case. Don't worry, it's weight I can easily afford to lose (I keep trying to leave it on buses and in railway stations but to no avail).

It could be that racing around after children takes more energy than my life BC. Every evening after tea they implore me to chase them around the kitchen table, for a meal provides toddlers with an energy boost akin to rocket booster fuel. The trouble is, my get-up-and-go got up and went at about 3 p.m. I once managed twenty straight minutes of running before I begged to have a break.

It could be that I never seem to find the time to eat. Four o'clock? I'm not hungry then — well, not for a full meal anyway. There's enough going on just getting food into them without try-ing to juggle my own coagulating tea as well. Hence we've fallen into a habit of feeding the kids early, promising 'we'll get some-thing later' only to realise that when 'later' comes we are too tired to prepare anything and have nothing but crackers and cucumber in the house anyway. Last night we ate a normal adult meal but only because it was in the freezer. I joked on Facebook that 'any casseroles left at the door would be very gratefully received'. This was a sarcastic nod to SWN1, who asked us what support our friends and family might provide once we'd adopted. As someone who's fiercely independent and hence allergic to asking for help, I asked for clarification.

'What do you mean by support?'

'Looking after the children for an hour, doing some shopping or dropping a casserole at the door,' she explained.

'Doing what?' A casserole at the door? *How very 1970s,* I thought, picturing it in a flowery Pyrex dish.

Tonight, my phone pings as I am clearing up the kitchen, where a food bomb appears to have exploded.

Odd.

Odd as in no one rings anymore. No one texts. My only communication with the outside world is Facebook, and if it weren't for the fact I can still get Wi-Fi, I'd start to believe I'd fallen into a parallel universe where all my friends were killed in a freak accident that coincided with the children's arriving. Did I miss MI5 sending me deep undercover to spy on a nappy-smuggling ring and hence warning all my mates to avoid contact for fear of blowing my cover?

My eyebrows shoot under my fringe as I read Liz's text.

'Parcel on your doorstep for tired parents Xxx.'

I run to and open the front door. *Come back!* I wave forlornly as she drives off and I feel sad, because I need someone to talk to who isn't a toddler or Andy. I want a conversation that's more than no, ye — no, stop that, later, maybe, no, yes, I said stop that! And I'm still wishing she'd stopped for a chat when I look down and discover a treasure better than company.

Near my feet is an incredible gift.

'Ohhhh.' I swoon.

On a plate, wrapped in cling film, is a cake.

A cake I can barely see because my eyes fill with tears that flow silently down my cheeks and ting on the cling film. As I reach down and pick it up, I am . . . (lost for words).

It's beautiful. Incredible. Touching. (For the rest of this list, see thesaurus.com.)

Not just any cake. A home-baked lemon-drizzle cake. With the recipe tucked under, so I know it's gluten-free and made for me. Hip hip hooray for Liz.

My mouth waters at the sight of it. I carry it into the house like a butler carrying the Queen's calling card on a silver dish. I stand tall for the first time in ages. I want to hug the plate to my chest, this thoughtful kindness wrapped in cling film.

And I realise that I'm very, very tired and very, very hungry.

'It's a cake,' I murmur as I return to the kitchen in a dazed but not confused state.

'Cake? For us?' the children ask in hopeful chorus.

'No,' I admit without a shred of guilt, 'this cake is not for you.'

This cake will be devoured after you've gone to bed, savoured on a pretty plate with a cake fork, and I will treat every delectable morsel like the gluten-free ambrosia that it is. Sent from my own angel.

I thought I was invisible, but this cake proves I'm not.

I'm not forgotten, alone in this house with my new children.

Liz has reached into our life, via our doorstep, and baked a cake just for me . . . well, us. And in a few days' time, on Andy's first day back at work, and my first day on my own, she'll leave another doorstep donation: a massive pot of stew that keeps us fed for days and days.

These are gifts of immense proportions, gifts that I will never forget.

Words are not enough.

34. How to Make Her Love Me

My brain has turned to mashed potato: it's stodgy, sticky and not good at complex algebra. It's Nibbles' naptime so I'm really hoping for a nap to reset my brain back to clumsy mode. I turn to Andy to ask if that's okay, but his face betrays a cunning plan.

He's been thinking. Uh-oh. I can't remember the last time I managed to rub two neurons together, but he has, and I know his answer's no. I ask anyway.

'Can I grab a quick nap, please — pretty please?'

He tips and shakes his head.

Andy is acutely aware of something I'm trying to forget. It's not long before he goes *whimper* back to work. He'll *abandon* me to look after *our* children all on *my* own (said through pouting lips and queasy stomach). Bubbles and Nibbles have attached strongly to him. They love and adore him, but they need to love me, too.

'Why don't you take Bubbles to the park?' he suggests.

'But —'

'If you can get Bubbles to love you, he'll copy her,' he continues. Bubbles is the ringleader. If we can make her love me, we get a convince-one-get-one-free attachment.

'She loves the swings.' His evidence and strategy is compelling and logical and watertight and I hate it because I know he's right. I don't want him to be right. I want to go to bed, to rest, to sleep, to catch a break. But I can't. Getting her to love me matters even more than rest right now.

'Okay,' I say, although my tone says otherwise.

'Bubbles?' I say as I walk over to her, plastering on sing-song optimism. 'Shall we go to the park together, just you and me, for mummy-daughter time?' Her eyes light up and she nods ferociously.

At Panel, when we casually answered their question about what would happen if the children attached more strongly to one of us than the other, it was easy to say we'd just 'work it out'. But the reality is harder to swallow.

Here's a typical morning: I wake in a bit of a daze and waddle half-asleep into the kids' bedroom. Nibbles is singing to himself and alternately chatting with Bubbles in strange burbles and pseudo-words. Bubbles looks at the doorway, searching the shadows for an outline and then . . . goes batshit crazy. Her face screws up, tears squirt from her eyes and she screams as she thrashes about yelling, 'Daddy, Daddy, DADDY!' I've tried everything to get past this, cuddling her, kissing her, blowing raspberries, twiggling her toes to 'This Little Piggy', singing 'morning' in a cheery voice, but she is determined to reject me. Yet the second Andy's face appears in the doorway, evil Hyde disappears and Jekyll smiles broadly, giggles and reaches out to him. And in this transformation she throws my porcelain heart on the floor and it smashes into pieces.

Today was the fourth morning of this abuse and I slunk away, head bowed. I sat on my bed and wept silently. I'm tired, my emotional stability is as rocky as a boxing film starring Sly Stallone, my brain doesn't work and *I don't know what to do*. The first few weeks she seemed to prefer Andy, but then she started ignoring me as if I were transparent, and now she screams at me until I turn on my heel and race away from her.

What's wrong with me?

Why won't she love me?

Love me? She doesn't even like me, and if this morning is anything to go by, she hates me with a vehemence that's frightening. My little girl hates me. It's little solace that after breakfast, she'll warm up a little, because this morning ritual is like chewing razor blades.

Hence we're off to the park. For unadulterated, uninterrupted mummy-and-daughter time. We go through the pre-park checklist and then bounce off finger-in-tiny-hand. She keeps looking up at me with those big eyes of hers and smiling, and I know I'm doing the right thing, in the hope of dampening (if not extinguishing) the fire of her morning rejection.

When we get there, there's only one thing on her mind.

'Swing, Mummy? Can I go on the swing?' she asks. I need to be the best mummy in the world, so of course I say yes and lift her in. I push her gently as she giggles and grins and loves every minute of it.

'Higher, Mummy,' she asks, hooked on the exhilaration and recklessness of going so high she nearly bumps out at the top.

'Hmm,' I say, acting coy. 'How are you going to pay for it?' She frowns a little and offers me her palm containing an invisible coin. I shake my head.

'I think a kiss is the right price,' I propose. She leans forward and gives me a peck. 'That's not enough. I thought you wanted to swing higher? You'll need a bigger kiss than that.' I am playing hard to get and praying this strategy doesn't backfire.

I pull her close and she gives me a massive kiss. And the exchange rate is set; as the swings die in the arms of inertia, she buys momentum with a pucker and a slobber. I push her as hard as I can, listening to her whoops of joy, and then as the swings slow down she asks me beautifully, and we kiss and swing some more. She giggles and laughs. I blow raspberries at her until she copies me and sends globs of saliva into my face. I tickle her through the seat, playing a game of poke the tiger, and I lose myself in the simple joy of this moment and the incredible girl before me. We swing, kiss, swing, kiss, swing, giggle, raspberry, tickle, kiss, swing and laugh until my arms twinge and we swing and kiss and giggle and sing and I don't stop however much my biceps hurt because this is our shot. Crunch time. And I'm not going home until she is mine.

I check my phone in case Andy has texted to say Nibbles is awake and OMG I've been swinging her for over an hour (no wonder my arms are cursing this scheme).

Yet by the end of this hour, something is different.

Is it her? Or me?

Who could spend an hour with a girl so in love with life, so in love with the swings, who just wants to giggle and have fun, and not be touched by her simple joy? I stopped thinking about this morning and how she screamed me out of her bedroom. She's so full of love, my little girl, and today she shared it with me, meted out in kisses that flutter on my face like fairy wings. We walk home sated, more refreshed than I would've been from the snatched sleep (but don't tell Andy). Her tiny hand grabs my finger tight as we half-walk, half-skip home in the sunshine. She picks a daisy and gives it to me and I know that Mummy done good.

This was the tipping point — the moment that I became as beloved as Andy. Our relationship was forged on the chains of a swing, exploiting the principle of leverage. A small input in just the right place has had a huge output in love and friendship and attachment.

She never screamed me out of her bedroom again (well, she did, but she screamed Andy out too).

35. A Stranger Stalks the Kids

We're leaving the house and not even going to the supermarket.

#result #littlethings

We are going on a picnic.

We've created a few memories to treasure (versus memories to delete) recently: We took the children on their first bus ride, and Nibbles almost bounced out of his seat as he excitedly chanted 'Bus? Bus, buuUus, busbusbusbus, bus, buuUuuUuus, busbusbus,' spreading smiles like happy flu to all the jaded passengers, including me. And we surprised the children with a paddling pool in the back garden after their nap — we had to boil the kettle to warm up the water ('It's freezing, Mummy'), and the fuss they made when a leaf blew in was stupendous ('Mummy, Mummy, Mummy, Mummy, MUMMY!'), but they loved sailing boats and dive-bombing balls.

Buoyed by these snippets of delight, we're off for a picnic in the sun.

#majorlogisticaloperation

After meticulous research (which took longer than the picnic will), I've selected an ideal location: close to a car park with a short, flat (aka trip-free) walk to the picnic area, which is suitably off the beaten track to be free from noisy families and their scraggy mutts. Not only that, but it has my favourite thing — a beach. Okay, not an actual beach. It's a sandy edge to a lapping reservoir, but since the coast is one headache of a long drive away, I'll take any lapping water and sloping edge I can get.

Food is the number one priority because they love food and it's fast becoming our most effective bribe. I pack their favourites (crisps and bread) along with a decent proportion of vitamins in the form of chunks of cucumber, cherry tomatoes and pre-sliced apple held together with an elastic band to stop it turning brown (search: parenting hacks).

173

We pack everything we might conceivably and inconceivably need, from sunglasses to wellies, nappies and mosquito repellent (oh for those carefree days of drinking from a puddle when you forgot a drink and went for a long hike). Since the canal-walk-that-wasn't, we've made a big fuss over the child carrier, converting it into a real treat. Now they fight over who gets to be as tall as the giant previously known as Andy.

We drive to the car park closest to the beach. Nibbles gets into the back carrier without a hitch and grins when he's hoisted aloft. Bubbles holds my finger tightly, and with smiles all around off we go. The children couldn't care two hoots about the stream or the view but are super giddy about the picnic and ask, 'Is it picnic time yet?' the minute we close the car doors.

As I amble along, the tension glides out of my body, carried away on the cool breeze that reminds me that summer's not yet here. The sun shines in a deep blue sky, glinting through the lush green trees. Bubbles picks up sticks and reaches to give them to Nibbles; I pass them up. I hold my breath — there is nothing wrong, no one is crying, everyone is smiling, everything is okay and I touch our happily ever after. Everyone's had a good night's sleep and this day is *whispers* perfect. Life is (dare I even say it?) wonderful. It's a month since we first met them, and with four weeks under our belts, we're starting to find our feet a bit and gel as an ensemble. It's the sort of moment I'd imagined we'd string together day after day, like pretty sparkling fairy lights; the reality has been a frustratingly disappointing tangle where half the bulbs are blown and it takes ages to unravel and you wonder if it wouldn't be easier to just buy new ones.

We put down the rug and yield to the children's pleas for lunch, even though it's too early. I hunt for little bags of food amongst the Ray Mears accoutrements, and we sit ('Why are you sat in the mud? The rug, the rug, the rug') to eat ('Can you *please* sit still?'). Everything is wolfed down; tomatoes explode, cucumber pieces are devoured as fast as Mickey Mouse eats sweetcorn, sandwiches are pushed in a fistful at a time. When there's nothing left, it's time to play. 'Why don't you go for a paddle?' I suggest, as I swap their shoes for wellies.

'Isn't it too soon after eating?' jokes Andy, but the kids look as if they are about to cry, so I shoo them in the right direction.

I lean back on the picnic rug, but my pout peddles pessimism. 'Not far. Not too deep. Stay upright. Don't lean over. Just at the edge.' The kids stomp gently in an inch of water, giggling as it splashes up around their boots. But something arrives to spoil the moment.

A stranger appears at the water, stalking my children. I sit up and read his fear, which makes me nervous. I don't recognise this man. He hovers over my kids and I want him to back away, to give them space, but he haunts them, fear exuding from his pores like garlic the night after a curry.

He looks like Andy and talks like Andy, but this is no Andy I know.

He's on edge. Nervous.

Andy has always epitomised calm, even in the face of the most bizarre and upsetting scrapes I've ever experienced — and that mysteriously happen every time we go on holiday abroad.

In Florida, he drives our low-slung Mustang over a concrete hump in a car park, stranding it; we can't drive off (yes, we tried reverse). We've just had lunch in a deserted one-shop town on a Saturday, and we have to either find a way to lift the car clear or leave it here and hoof it back to the airport or we'll miss our flight home and have to pay hundreds for a new flight or for someone to rescue this stupid car and we're running out of time and nothing he can do is having any impact and why did we have to eat in this tiny backwater town in the middle of chuffing nowhere and why on earth did they put this hump here in the first place and it's really fricking hot and I need some water and shade and . . . breathe, Emma. Andy doesn't see the problem. Andy? Worried? Nope. He takes it all in his massive stride, and the waitress rings a tow truck to lift us clear for sixty dollars.

In Greece, we get quite-a-lot lost, taking a few wrong turns around a site of historic interest, and are soon walking haphazardly over long spiky grass that sticks into our feet like needles and it's now midday so boiling hot and neither of us brought any water for this quick look-see and the path we're following disappears and we're stuck with a choice of either retracing our steps (which will take another hour at least) or finding a way over brambles and spiky grass and rocks and treacherous footing down a steep hill with no path or sign that a human has ever travelled this route (oh look, a tortoise that's stuck) and I am far too hot and thirsty and I'm only in my sandals which are not made for this kind of scrambling, and I can feel the skin on my neck burning as we speak except I can't speak because my mouth is so dehydrated and actually I am not quite as panicked as this prose would have you believe but I am far from happy and quite unsure and a little bit anxious. Andy just shrugs and burrows ahead. We make it down with a shoe full of needles and a story.

In Bangkok, a few days into our honeymoon, Andy realises that he left our passports in the toilets at the airport over an hour ago. We're just about to start the Cambodia leg of our trip; Andy is unfazed. We go to the main desk and they ask over the tannoy if anyone has found them and can they please hand them in, and we wait for a while as I hop from foot to foot and the ladies on the desk look embarrassed on our behalf and a tourist stops me to ask me if I will take his photo and I nearly cut his head off (photographically) and the passports don't magically appear and we go to wait at the check-in desk to discuss our options with our flight reps and I start to hyperventilate because our honeymoon is in jeopardy and someone is now using our stolen passports to traffic humans or drugs or guns in our name to foreign countries and how could this happen? Andy sits there totally unruffled telling me it will all work out whilst I panic and fret. It works out.

But two toddlers and an inch of water and Andy is a bag of nerves. Who knew?

After all the pondering about what we'd be like as parents, I'm constantly amazed at how few of my predictions came true (just call me Mystic Emma). I'd never have envisaged that Andy, who's been a steadfast rock of exterior and interior serenity, would turn into a twitchy, agitated hawk with the simple combination of toddlers and a splash of water. I sit on the picnic mat and take photos as he tails the children, never letting them wander out of reach of his long arms.

'It'll be fine,' I implore, for his nerves grate against my dream.

'What if they fall in?' he moans.

'I have adventure sandals on,' I say. 'I'll just jump in and pick them up. The worst is that they get wet.'

This is evidently not the thing he wants to hear. I shrug his fears off a little, wanting to pick holes in their absurdity, but stop myself ruining this slice of paradise. It's only when they toddle up the beach and away from the water that the Andy I know and love returns. I close my eyes and savour this moment. The sun turns my lids deep red.

Today has been an extra-large muffin of chocolate-chipped joy.

36. We Need More Sleep

I love the baby monitor. It's cute and purple; its glowing balloon shape is soft and comforting. The gentle LEDs light up as our children emit tiny audible signs of life, a magical reminder of what's going on above our heads as they nap. It gives me that warm hug of reassurance that they're okay and I can put my feet up for a moment. Even though they're unable to escape their slatted cells (we've tested their Houdini capabilities and they're too weak), there's always that little nagging doubt: 'Are they still breathing?' Hearing them move, hearing her gentle whistling breaths, we know that they're okay.

And the baby monitor gives us a secret window into their world in the morning. Andy and I cuddle up together next door, clandestinely listening in on their whispers, grinning and winking at their hilarious mischief.

'Nibbles, Nibbles, Nibbles,' Bubbles urges in a high-pitched whisper, until her brother responds.

'Call for Daddy. Shout "Daddy", Nibbles.'

He loves his sister, so of course he shouts 'Dadda' at her command. We smirk at her deception. If Nibbles wakes first, he lies in bed singing or nattering to himself — a nonsensical burble peppered with words. It's like listening to Welsh people chatting incomprehensibly and then recognising 'carrier bag' or 'taxi' or the delightful 'popty ping'. His babbles are playful and joyful, but as soon as someone enters the room, it ceases (boo).

The baby monitor is the key to the secret garden of their lives when no one's watching.

How could I not love it?

I hate the baby monitor. Every sneeze, every toss and turn, every cough or splutter or dummy dropped from his cot wakes me up and leaves me wide-eyed and fretful, unable to return to sleep until my adrenalin dies down hours later. I'm robbed of sleep until just before the alarm goes off.

Tonight, Bubbles wakes us from the dark silence of the night, whimpering. A disturbing sound. Andy goes into the room to calm her down and opens Schrödinger's box. Sometimes he's lucky and a stroke of her hair will calm her back to dreamland; tonight is not one of those nights. Within minutes she's a jackknifing banshee, fighting him and sleep and the thoughts that inhabit her fears. We've tried hugging her, but that makes things worse. Sometimes the only thing to do is to take her out of bed, stand her up and watch with bleary but concerned eyes beyond the windmill of her arms as she burns through the maelstrom.

I'm weary from this alertness, ready to leap into action. I want to sleep like Andy — impervious to his own snoring, to loud crashes, to screams and cries and even my first round of pokes. The monitor never wakes him; it wakes me and I then wake him. At least he can get up, sort things out and be asleep again before his bottom touches the mattress. I toss and turn for hours. I turn down the monitor's sensitivity, but it still wakes me a dozen times a night. I don't want to hear every stupid rustle of their sheets and sigh of their mattresses. It's like sleeping next to a supersensitive microphone placed in the lawn; I wake as each blade grows.

I mute all but the loudest of noises and am genuinely staggered by just how often the monitor nudges me awake for a cough or a sneeze that I. Do. Not. Need. To. Hear.

Finally, I unplug it. They're only next door; if they cry loudly enough I'll hear it. With a celebratory jig, I put it away and snuggle back under the duvet.

And a new quality appears in my sleep, not as deep as BC but a definite improvement. I feel almost human some mornings. Then the warm weather appears and we tip open the window to let in the fresh night breeze and I'm assaulted by a barrage of noises that sound *exactly* like children crying. Just when one savage interrupter of my slumber has been banished from our sanctuary of rest(lessness), a horde arrives.

179

BC, my brain filtered out this stuff as irrelevant. Now, every stupid cat in the neighbourhood seems hell-bent on ruining my sleep. And don't get me started on owls. Twit-flipping-off. Then there are other people's children: our next-to-next-door neighbour's child seems to cry all the time, especially when ours are sound asleep. My brain learns to distinguish between wildlife and children quite quickly but takes far longer to work out whether it's a neighbour's child or one of my own. A few nights' jerking awake as a cat or owl screeches and I'm in danger of throwing a bucket of water out the window (except I can't as my *Mission: Impossible* brain has turned to Angel Delight so I have no chance of getting the correct sequence to open this darn thing in the dark, when I'm half asleep, otherwise I would become a safe breaker) or yelling obscenities until someone calls the cops.

I just want to sleep. Is that too much to ask? One solid night of great sleep. Please?

Turns out I'm not the only one who is sleep deprived.

It is Tantrum City today, with an extra dollop of hysterics on top. I've lost count of how many times I've frowned in a cocktail of surprise and despair. Bubbles has morphed from a cute little girl full of hugs and kisses into a biting, punching ball of a monster. What's going on? Andy and I turn to each other with looks that say 'what the?' It's not long since snack, so she's not hungry; we're playing with her, so she's not bored; her nappy is clean and dry, so that's not it either.

She snatches a toy from her brother.

'Please don't do that,' we suggest politely.

Her bottom lip pouts, she frowns at us in a devil-child look and returns his toy by hitting him in the face with it.

'In our house, that's not how we behave.'

We've been trained to not put adopted children in time-out (it reinforces issues of separation and rejection) but to use a time-in sat beside them. When Bubbles hits her brother, I tell her to come and sit next to me; she pouts and fidgets for the entire two minutes and then behaves as badly as ever.

She yells and then pinches him, and earns herself a stern time-in. She spends it stroking my arm and talking to me as I try to ignore her ('Stop it!'). This is not working. She pushes him over, so I sit her on the floor away from me.

Then I go to change Nibbles' nappy and when I get back, her legs are akimbo and she's snoring.

Oh.

I look at my watch.

Uh-oh.

She can't sleep now; it's too near bedtime.

It's 3.30 p.m. and bedtime is 7 p.m. and one of the ten commandments states that 'Thou must ensure thou's children hath four or more hours of daylight or gadding about before they retireth to that slumber thou wishes were deep and unbroken, but is frequently not'. I get the unenviable job of waking her up. I nudge her. No response. I shake her a little. Nothing. So I pick her up and struggle to cuddle a writhing mass of unhappiness. To say it went badly is an understatement. I might as well have told her that the colour pink had disappeared off the face of the earth.

Bubbles' behaviour leaves a lot to be desired the following afternoon as well, and I begin to rub my chinny chin chin (I've read that book so much I want to punch those stupid pigs — a house of straw? On what planet will that pass building regs? Frankly, they deserve to get eaten). She snatches a toy from Nibbles and I give her a time-in while I read to Nibbles on the other side of the room. And a strange silence descends two pages in. I look over and she's sparko. This anomaly is starting to look a lot less anomalous. And joy of joys, I get to be the Anti-Santa and wake her up again.

On day three, she stops moving for a millisecond and falls fast asleep. I don't need to draw a chart to conclude that she needs an afternoon nap.

We read some books (online books called the Internet) and the experts/webwriters all agree that if a child has just one nap a day, it should be in the afternoon. So why is Nibbles' nap in the morning? Andy and I have a parenting powwow. If Bubbles' nap is in the afternoon and Nibbles' is in the morning, then we'll be under house arrest all day. And how are we going to get Little Miss Hyper to nap at all? She's out of the habit and this is going to be a big change to her routine. They can't nap together — she'll natter him sleepless. What shall we do? We consult more books that unanimously advise us to gradually change his naptime by fifteen minutes a day. *Fifteen minutes. That's four days to move it an hour, and we need to move it two hours.* And we don't have that much patience in our parenting account so we scrub that advice and decide to just do it. Tomorrow.

The next day, we keep Nibbles awake when he's normally set-tling down to sleep, have an early lunch followed by *Shaun the Sheep*[8] because TV induces hypnotic calm. Then we take them upstairs to sleep — separately.

Bubbles is led into the spare room, into a single bed that's big, new and annoyingly exciting when we want her to sleep. I tuck her in, kiss her forehead and tell her to go to sleep, and then sit on the floor across from the bed. It's a strategy we're using at night too, because otherwise they giggle, chat and get overtired and then cry, scream and are a nightmare the next day. So we choose the lesser of two evils and sit in their room at bedtime. They pretend to be quiet and asleep, and eventually, because they can't pretend for long, they fall asleep and we creep out tentatively on all fours. Although the other day, Andy came up, thinking, 'They must be asleep by now', and 'Where's Emma?' to find them whispering to each other from their cells as I snored and drooled on the carpet.

She hasn't slept in a bed before, and whilst I worry she might fall out, I'm more concerned that she'll leave teeth marks in Nibbles' arm if she doesn't nap. I sit with my back against the radiator (which is surprisingly uncomfortable so I hope this doesn't take long) and wait. To my surprise and delight, she falls asleep in minutes. As I slink out, I high five Andy, who is leaving a sleeping Nibbles. Day One of joint afternoon naps and they're both asleep.

---

[8] **Shaun the Sheep:** God bless you, Aardman, for creating kids' TV that doesn't make me want to stab pins in my eyes. If I watch another episode of that bleeding fire-fighting animation and that knobhead Norman who's the very definition of a youth offender, setting fires and nearly annihilating AndyPandy every episode (their insurance premiums must be sky-high) and instead of being locked up or timed out, gets nothing more than a 'diddums, my poor lamb' from his WalkOver Mum, I'll take a baseball bat to my own TV.

Bubbles and Nibbles get naps (they start sleeping better in the evenings too), we avoid a crabby Gremlin mid-afternoon, and even better, Mummy gets ninety precious minutes every afternoon. A heavenly slice of me-time when I'm awake enough to appreciate it. I can dance, sing, frolic, eat chocolate without having to share, read *Fifty Shades* and contemplate where my libido has gone, close the curtains and watch TV that needs a PIN because it's packed with swearing, sniff a glass of wine (but not swallow) or . . .

Snuggle down into my mohair cushion on the sofa and close my eyes for a nap.

The next weekend, we're out for a walk again and off like a rocket. Well, if the rocket is strapped to a mobility scooter. Whose battery is running low. And that's overloaded with cut-price canned food. Going up a really steep hill. Against a gale-force wind. With a parachute billowing out behind it just in case it reaches the dizzying speed of half a mile per hour.

Despite her ability to put one foot in front of the other, Bubbles is not that fast. It's a sunny Sunday and we're at one of our favourite BC walks — a circular one (no shortcuts). We've been building up their distance (with the bribe of the park at the end) by taking more circuitous routes that pass anything vaguely interesting, which for a toddler is a leaf, a flower, a cat, a stone, a lamp post or a garden gnome.

We arrive and think, *This car park's empty!* And then realise that we're here hours before most sane people (and us, BC) are even up. We set off (like a rocket) and everything seems to be going well, even if we'd have finished by now if we were on our own. Through a gate and then up a slope that's a tangle of tree roots. We clamber over them with ease, but Bubbles trips and falls and scuffs her confidence.

'I want to go back now,' she says. We expected this.

'We are going back,' we both say, and point directly ahead. 'It's that way.' We are out in the fresh air. We need this walk. So unless either one of them needs to go to A&E, we're not turning back. We turn a corner and see the water.

'That's a nice pond,' remarks Bubbles. We laugh at how cute the comment is, which she takes badly (note to self — laugh on the inside).

'It's called a reservoir, sweetie. Can you say reservoir? Res. Sev. Wah.'

'Reje?' she attempts, and wins a smile.

'Reservoir. Res. Sev. Wah.'

'Rebeboir,' she says.

'Well done,' we praise, because it's close enough.

Nibbles and Andy are getting on brilliantly. Andy ducks under trees and makes a big fuss about knocking Nibbles out on this branch or that leaf to lots of giggling. In fact, there's far more giggling and laughter than there ever was when it was just the two of us. There is also far more mud, far more splashing in puddles, far more interest in leaves, sticks, bugs. There's even a quickly refused request to swim in the rebeboir.

'I want to go back now,' Bubbles recaps.

'We are, sweetie, it's that way,' we repeat, in the traditional parental volley.

'I want to go back now.'

'Look, a birdie.'

'I want to go back now.'

'Yes, I hear you.' (Subtext: even if I have no intention of acting on your idea.)

'I want to go back now.'

'Andy, did you see that programme on polar bears who eat children who ask to "go back now" too often? It was really good.' We resort to ignoring her pleas in a 'we're not listening any more' rudeness that was something we promised we'd *never* do when we were parents. Like answering the question, 'What's for tea?' with 'Wait and see'. Or ending an endless string of 'Why?' questions with 'Because I said so' or 'Just because' since I'm not an encyclopaedia and am fed up with asking Siri.

We find a bench and sit down for a gulp of water and a small snack. After a short rest, we get up and continue walking back to the car (with exaggerated emphasis on the last four words for Bubbles). We walk, point, toddle, splash then have another rest. The mobility scooter named Bubbles slowly drains of electricity before giving up for good, her recent banana intake having no observable effect on her battery. Mostly we encourage and cajole her, at times

I carry her or give her a shoulder ride, all the time reiterating that we're nearly back. And eventually we are.

We arrive at the car and I'm not sure who is happier — Bubbles because it's over or Andy and I because we finally *high five!* made it.

I look at my watch.

And after a short delay (normal brain service has yet to be resumed), I work out that it took us two hours to do that walk. Two hours? Will I ever get used to how long everything takes? It used to take Andy and me thirty minutes. My step counter astonishes me even more: how can it possibly take two hours to do just over four thousand steps? Clearly I should be using Nibbles' thumb for my estimating, as my rule of thumb is the wrong size.

But it's a start. A real achievement in what's felt like a very tricky first month. We didn't give up when she wanted to turn back. We kept going all the way around the rebeboir, no one is bleeding or crying and none of us stepped in dog doo. Woo hoo!

We went for a walk.

And reached the summit.

Today I climbed my Everest.

37. A Love-Scream Relationship

This is Andy's last day before he goes back to work (and those words crayon a foreboding black snarling mess in my stomach that is surprisingly difficult to remove). Instead of spending the day in blissful family harmony, I'm plugging numbers into a spreadsheet to submit my tax and VAT returns for my company, which keeps nagging, 'Pay attention to me', and Andy is at Stay and Play with the kids.

Earlier this week, SWN2, who will not be named in this chapter as I'm still cross with her, made me practise looking after the kids on my own. It's bad enough that Andy is going back to work, but he got to saunter off for an afternoon's bike ride whilst I got to experience just how hard it was going to be without him, hissing under my breath about SWN2 and the unfairness of it all. He came back beaming; he hadn't been for a ride in ages. I folded my arms, frowned and pouted as he effervesced about how lovely his afternoon had been. I'd played and read with the kids. I chaperoned them up the stairs, opened the gate, changed their nappies, threw the dirty ones in the — d'oh, I left it downstairs type rigmaroles. But that's no reason to *(a)* not be cross with SWN2; and *(b)* be complacent about what tomorrow will bring.

I submit my returns (rebate on the way, *kerching!*) just as the front door opens and they fall into the hall, an eruption of feet and words breathlessly fighting to tell me what happened.

'How'd it go?' I ask with undisguised curiosity.

'We had a lovely time,' says Andy, giving me the Reduced-Shakespeare summary of playing in the sandpit, bashing some instruments and cooking in the home corner. 'Although when they passed the fruit around, he grabbed half a kiwi fruit,' Andy continues, 'and he ate it all before I could stop him.'

'Even the skin?' I say. My face wrinkles and I shudder at the testicular hairiness of it.

'He ate the skin, Mummy,' explains Bubbles. She and I share an UGH face. 'Daddy upset Nibbles,' she adds in mild disgust.

'How so?' I inquire.

'(mumble) hand puppet,' he admits, sheepishly, and I look at him, agog.

'You didn't?' My eyes twinkle at the hint of story within. Nibbles is obsessed with hand puppets. He digs the lion puppet out of the toy box all giddy and excited then begs you with his big dark eyes and soft voice, 'Make it talk.' I gently refuse, but his sweet insistence has me yielding despite the precedents. His eyes are ablaze as the puppet slides over my hand and I try and wiggle my fingers into the right bits, but I only have five fingers; the puppet's designed for six. Nibbles bounces from leg to leg, and as the lion's head slowly comes up and the mouth opens, he stops and blanches. His eyes fill with fright. And as the first syllable leaves the puppet's mouth, Nibbles is shouting and screaming, 'Take it off!' and blaming you for this entire sorry affair. A definite love-scream relationship.

At Stay and Play, Andy picked up a puppet and cradled it to his shoulder. It wasn't a small hand puppet but an armful of one — like the grumpy old men off *The Muppet Show*. The minute the puppet looked at Nibbles ('I hadn't even opened its mouth,' argues Andy), he ran away screaming, earning Andy disgusted glances from parents who don't believe that scaring the bejesus out of your children is part of the parenting job description.

As amusing as this snippet is, and as glad as I am that I've finally submitted my tax return, these rays of light cannot burn the dread from the pit of my belly.

With each passing hour, tomorrow's getting inexorably closer. *How will I cope?*

'Please, please don't leave,' I plead, trying to keep jest in my tone, despite the lack inside. 'No, I mean it, please don't leave,' I continue. Andy shrugs it off.

'It'll be okay.'

'How do you know that? How can you be sure?' I know I'm being absurd and yet the thought of being alone with these two children for a whole day makes unadulterated terror rise in my chest, as though my life's about to tip into a dark, scary abyss from which I may not be able to claw my way out. Andy goes off to make a cup of tea, which is his answer to everything.

I can barely do this with Andy here; there isn't enough time in the day even with two of us. It's a full-time job just changing nappies, and what with laundry, meals, snacks, sweeping dust and a mountain of toys under the rug, when will I find the time to cram it all into a single day? There is no way.

Breathe . . . Breathe . . . Breathe.

You can do this, Emma. You're a bright, intelligent, creative woman with a raft of skills and experience and a house bursting with toys and books. And if the worst comes to the worst, remember Monday's plan and plonk them in front of the tele in their PJs.

My control freak comes out of hiding and decides to take charge by making another plan. Studiously ignoring the fantasy timetable that I created for Pam (I am too focused on my own fear to stay cross with her for a whole chapter) all those months ago, I carve my scary day into less-scary chunks.

06.30	get kids up, change nappies, wrangle them into random clothing, breakfast, teeth
07.30	say goodbye to Andy (try not to cry)
07.45	restore kitchen and bathroom to BC levels of cleanliness (as if)
10.00	snack time (five minutes of peace, longer if they chew)
12.00	lunchtime
13.00	naptime (sixty to ninety minutes of peace, on a good day, with a following wind)
15.00	wake after nap (aw or ugh)
15.15	snack time
17.00	tea time
18.00	bath time
18.05	Andy comes home, so who cares what happens next?
18.06	open wine/gin

19.00   kids are in bed

19.01   stare blankly at the TV and tell myself this is quality time together

19.23   give up the pretence, hug Andy and go to bed

With the day sliced this way, there's only one piece that's too big to eat in one go, from 07.45 till 12.00. The big kahuna. That solid, immovable, ten-tonne slab of four hours seems never-ending, even with a mid-morning snack. The afternoons should pretty much look after themselves — a trip to the park or some stories at home and they're sorted. If I can work out what to do for five mornings each week (or maybe four, with one for TV in PJs whilst Mum sniffs the wine vinegar), then I might *just* manage.

Maybe I can do this, I think optimistically.

How hard can it be?

Not content with something as hard as aligning the Hadron Collider, Andy and I ramped up the difficulty of parenting on my own by adding potty training into the smorgasbord of stuff to do.

I blame the paddling pool. Oh Jezebel.

The weekend before last, we put the paddling pool out, and as Bubbles poked her toe into the freezing cold water, her bladder went 'Woah'.

'I want a wee,' she said, hopping about. I dashed inside and grabbed a potty, she sat down, and as my face broke into a beaming smile of pride, she had a wee, on the potty, just like that.

#result

And based on that single event, we pressed Go (like parenting imbeciles) on potty training. She doesn't have a clue when she is wet or pooing into her nappy, but what's a sign like that between overeager parents with no experience whatsoever? We rashly decided that we might as well give it a go, because now was as good a time as any. It was not. It turns out that one can over-extrapolate from a single data point.

A week later, it's been a disaster of unhygienic and potentially dysenteric proportions. The poolside triumph was her only success.

On Day Two of potty training, she wet eleven pairs of pants and I had to make (read: send Andy on) an emergency dash to the shops to buy more knickers and a gallon of gin. Mostly we're not potty training her at all. She is using her pants like they're nappies and I am running around like a hysterical parent bleaching everything that doesn't breathe.

And then there's the poo.

Since meeting the children, I've gradually gone from arm's-length, nose-clip-wearing rejection of it (treating it like spillage of radioactive waste) to not-quite-finger-licking complacency. I'm no longer surprised by the variations in shape, size, viscosity and volume that arrive with bewildering frequency in their nappies. We haven't said, 'You should have seen that one — it was incredible!' for yonks. I wouldn't say that I welcome these nappy-wrapped gifts, but it comes with the territory, so I breathe through my mouth and work on doing the job as swiftly and precisely as I can, with a nonchalance born of repetition.

Yet the minute that poo leaves the confines of a nappy, I become hysterical. I'm not proud of this, but somehow poo in her underpants makes me freak as I shout, 'Do not move!' with an urgency that harks back to a present Bubbles delivered a few days ago.

I was distracted (aka thumbing through FB) when I glanced up and noticed muddy footprints in the lounge.

'What's that?' I inquired calmly. (Yeah right.) I'd already inhaled enough of their pungent odour to know exactly what those 'muddy' footprints were, so I was as far from calm as Brexit was an overwhelmingly majority and conclusive vote by the people to leave Europe.

'STAY EXACTLY WHERE YOU ARE!' I screamed. I continued somewhat more concisely: 'DON'T MOVE.' I donned my metaphorical deerstalker and launched into Poo Detective mode, quickly tracing the footprints back to their origin.

There it was lying on the floor like a brown toy car. And unbelievably (I'm still new enough to this parenting caper to be shocked), they have both, yes BOTH, stepped into it, not once thinking, 'That's an odd sensation on my bare foot.' Oh no, they've trod in it and then spread it liberally around the lounge like muddy footprint stickers that guide you along a nature trail in the forest.

We'd relocated our precious rug (100% wool, 100% huge, 100% over budget, 125% and growing on our credit cards) on Day One of this misguided attempt at potty training. If they'd trodden it into the rug . . . I'd . . . I'd . . . I'd. Thank God they didn't, that's all. My screams drew my husband into the fray and between us and a bath full of Dettol, we disinfected our children and our lovely oak floor.

This past week tested both our resolve and ingenuity in devising reward systems.

Plan One (Day Two) was a star chart; she earned twelve stars for liquid and three stars for solids. But the puddles the next day proved that stars were *so* yesterday *don't you know*. Plan Two exploited the ignore/praise double whammy; we showered her with extravagant praise if she even mentioned the word 'potty', and silently reached for more wipes and clean slippers without catching her eye. This cocktail lasted two days, but that soon fell out of fashion too. Plan Three was based on stories but failed outside the house (sorry, Sainsbury's, for the puddle). Plans Four to Umpty-One included variations on ignoring, praising, going berserk, watching her like a hawk, unceremoniously dumping her on the potty at the slightest hop and asking her to go every ten minutes, along with other brilliant ideas that were as short-lived as shrink-to-fit jeans (have you ever sat in a bath in jeans? — it's weird).

We don't want to go back to nappies, but tomorrow I lose my decontamination partner and my sanity in one go.

Please, don't leave.

Pretty please?

I'll buy you beer?

38. And Then There Were Three

Andy goes back to work today. Back to ironing a shirt, riding his motorbike, drinking coffee before it goes cold, savouring sandwiches that are more than white bread wrapped around white cheese, having conversations that don't end with 'That's enough!' and solving complex IT stuff (I have no idea what he does at work and should probably listen when he tells me about it but then his voice sounds like an adult's on *Charlie Brown* and all I hear is *wah wah wah*).

Why can't he be a stay-at-home dad? bleats my emotional brain. *Apart from the fact we can't afford it?* responds the other side. And I'm like, 'Who invited Spock and his impeccable logic to this pity party?'

Time to try another tack: '*I* want to go to work,' I say with a pout. Well when I say work, I mean I want to leave the house and let someone else look after the kids for a while, for that sounds like a hunk of black forest gateau right now. I'm hoping to simply get through the day without a trip to hospital or more than a bucket of bleach until Andy gets back and I open a jeroboam of champers.

We've been preparing the kids for this day for a few days. We're all up, dressed (ish) and breakfasted as Andy pulls on his motorbike gear. I'm being quiet but I look him in the eye and implant a hypnotic command.

'Ride carefully,' I say, because whilst I've been blasé about his motorbiking, now we have children to think of. 'Because I can't do this without you,' I continue, and I mean it. The idea of being a single parent scares the pants off me. I don't want him crushed under a bus. Bubbles stands in one of his boots and Nibbles wants to have the helmet on, until it is, when he really, really doesn't.

I lift the children onto the kitchen counter and we wave Union Jack flags through the window and it's all Proms in the kitchen as

I hear the faint strains of 'Land of Hope and Glory'. I hold on to them for dear life as they sway with their frantic semaphore.

'I miss Daddy, I miss Daddy, I miss Daddy,' laments Bubbles as the door slams and Andy's shiny head catches the light in the garden outside. 'I'm still here,' I rejoin sarcastically.

'Miss, miss, miss,' adds Nibbles, in round-robin lament. I have a stoic and painful expression plastered over my face, yet inside I'm joining in. All my fears come to the surface, and I hope the children can't smell fear the way they unerringly detect peanut butter on my breath when I sneak in a teaspoon (okay, a heaped tablespoon) during naptime.

I telepathically plead: 'Come back.' And I don't just mean come home safely later. I mean right now. Please be my knight in shining armour and rescue me. He turns one last time and I think he's heard my pleas and changed his mind. He waves and drives off and dashes my hopes on the reality of a mortgage and earning money to pay for all the nappies, baby wipes and bleach we're consuming at an alarming rate. He is teaching me to stand on my own two feet. And I hate him for it.

This is a defining moment: I have to 'mummy-up' and go it alone. I look at the clock and wonder just how I'm going to get through the next ten hours. *Ten hours? WTF?*

I revert to my kitchen comfort zone and get tea ready. A mite early, but if I get it ready now, I can stick it in the oven and we can go to the park after nap. There's a relaxing simplicity about cooking; it's restful, normal and I feel at home here. I put the radio on to drown out the silence of Andy's absence whilst pretending to be Jamie Oliver as I narrate the recipe down an invisible camera to an audience of none. (I monologue a surprising amount of the time, although when Andy's in the room I call it conversation.)

The kids are playing quietly in the lounge — the onions are sweating and a hunch has me casting an eye in their direction. I catch a glimpse and smile at their merry antics. But something's not quite right, and it's something about the way that Bubbles is wobbling. She puts her hand down the back of her pants and pulls it out; she looks at her hand, cocks her head and her face creases in confusion. Surprisingly accurate Mystic Emma tells me she's thinking, 'What's this?' as she investigates her hand for clues.

'What is it, sweetie?' I ask. My voice quivers in the false bravado of falsetto. I'm praying she says something like glue or Barbie.

'Poo,' she replies, all doe-eyed and in a tone that says 'I have absolutely no idea how that got in my knickers'. A resigned feeling washes over me; instant exhaustion.

I force air out of my mouth in an exasperated chuff. It's clear she didn't notice a wet sausage leaving her bottom — she couldn't look more surprised if she'd found a pink puppy in her pants (although I would've been infinitely more delighted).

Without a second's hesitation (except to chuff), I rush over and carry her away from the soft furnishings of the lounge into the more poo-proof kitchen. Then I wriggle her pants down, trying not to smear as I go. Is it okay to wash poo off in the kitchen sink? I'm sure Jamie O doesn't before he rinses his peppery rocket. Have I just sent a chocolate slug down the wrong pipe, such that a few hours later a little boy splashing near the outflow on some beach will get E. coli?

I text Andy the sordid details and finish with the hashtag #PooGate. I am frightened, frustrated and the day has barely begun. How on earth am I going to cope at home on my own, never mind with a child hell-bent on covering every single surface in special sausages?

I need you, Andy.

I'm going out of my mind.

Today's Friday, Andy's second day at work. Just one more day until he's back for the weekend.

happy dance

#PooGate was the lowlight of yesterday, and I got through the rest mostly unscathed.

Andy and I had an intense parenting powwow about potty training last night. We couldn't decide if Bubbles is simply not bothered, if we started too soon (the paddling pool is shouldering a lot of blame) or if we're just class-A idiots without a clue what we're doing. Or all of the above. We concluded that if things don't change by Sunday then we'll put her back into nappies. And with that get-out clause in the diary, I get a renewed sense of determination to try just one more idea.

Plan Umpty-Two. As the children wave Andy off to work, I whisper to Bubbles that if she has a poo on the potty, she'll get . . . a Jelly Tot.

A teeny tiny sugary pyramid.

I've barely said 'tot' when she asks for a potty. Her desire to wave Daddy off evaporates faster than their 'I'm starving, Mummy' declarations when they see cauliflower. I let go of her and her brother — both are on the counter doing the Proms thing (please don't fall) — dash to the lounge, grab a potty and slide it under her. And there she sits, on a potty next to the kitchen sink as Nibbles stands and waves goodbye and I hold on to him tightly.

What have I done? This is ludicrous. I can't possibly hold them both, and there is a fall of about two feet onto a solid flagstone floor, which means they're a wobble away from death by dangerous pottying. 'Is this even remotely hygienic?' demands my control freak. Before the thrum of Andy's motorbike has died away, Bubbles is beside herself with excitement and deservedly so — one poo in the potty in record time. I subversively (if the online experts whose pages we have trawled through nightly over the last fortnight are to be believed) reward her with a Jelly Tot. Her brother gets one too, for fairness, even though he has contributed nothing to this endeavour other than not falling off the countertop.

She is delighted. I dance a smug little jig and grin madly. I clean the potty out and put it back in the lounge. I praise Bubbles, but let's not gush too soon, for Plans One to Umpty-One all started well and then failed within hours. A few minutes later, I glance into the lounge and am surprised to see Bubbles sat on the potty again.

'What are you doing?' I ask in a mixture of astonishment and delight that's clearly a rhetorical question.

'Trying for another poo,' she says. *Bless,* I think, expecting her to bounce off when she realises you can't make poo magically appear. Twenty minutes later and she's still there, squeezing her face purple to get a tiny nugget out to exchange for a Jelly Tot, despite the obvious discomfort of the plastic seat and her brother's urging her to come and play. I point out the potty mark on her bum and tell her repeatedly that she can go back on the potty any time she wants, as often as she wants; she finally relents and gets off to divest the toy box of all its toys.

This first day she earns the grand total of three Jelly Tots.

Three tiny sweets that transform my house from the disaster formerly known as #PooGate into a sanitary haven. Call yourself an expert? I could've saved myself two maddening weeks of diabolically unhygienic potty training if I hadn't bowed to your expert wisdom. The only thing that made even the smallest dint in her behaviour is a tiny sugarcoated sweet in the shape of a pyramid. Ignoring you created a transformation of butterfly proportions.

Today has been a great day, an awesome day, a day to carve on the tablets of history, to pass down through the generations (and to laugh about whenever we go into a sweet shop).

All hail the power of the Jelly Tot.

39. A Bear Steals My Thunder

My heart melts, a smile spreads across my weary face and I know we must be doing something right.

A few days ago Bubbles went up to her daddy, gave him a massive hug (like a mouse hugging a gorilla) and declared in her high voice, 'You're my best friend.'

Aw, how cute, I thought, confidently expecting that she would then turn, flutter her eyelashes at me and give me a hug with the duplicate Hallmark sentiment. I smiled in anticipation, but she walked away and into the lounge.

What about me?

Has she no inkling of the etiquette of these moments of bold declaration? One cannot simply tell one person that one loves them and believes them to be a friend of the highest esteem if there is another similar person within hearing distance. For in doing so, one would instantly create a battleground for favouritism leading in later life to decades of therapeutic intervention by the most exclusive and expensive Harley Street psychologists, during which one opens up one's childhood to intense scrutiny to discover the basis of irrational beliefs that have held sway over one's life since one's formative years, and have stopped one from reaching one's true potential.

I stifled the urge to flap my hands wildly in the air and whine, 'What about me?' Or a more realistic, 'What am I? Chopped liver?' The latter would no doubt have had her retorting (for I have a smart Alexa for a child), 'You're not chopped liver — you're my mummy.'

I wanted to praise her for being so nice, yet the praise stuck in my throat. 'Best friend' is an invisible rosette pinned proudly on Andy's chest and I hanker after one for myself. I'm jealous. That innocent phrase began an unintentional rivalry. Well, not on Andy's part. He was too busy crowing over the fact that she'd bestowed that honour on him.

I'm waiting.

It starts to matter. I begin to notice just what it is that he does with the children that might explain her besotted state. And I can't compete with his smug, dashing, come-in-at-bedtime-and-whisk-them-off-their-feet attitude because I have to do all the tricky 'we have to leave NOW or we will be late' stuff as well as the 'please, just eat it', 'for heaven's sake put some clothes on' and the 'not like that, like this' just to get through each day. I'm going to have to up my game to win her heart.

I start to be deliberately nicer, courting her attention and love in the hope of being awarded the BFF rosette that I covet. Her recognition is even more desirable because of the scarcity factor. This item is genuinely unique. But am I willing to cast this phrase's uniqueness aside by getting one of my own? Let me think. Yes, yes I am. I've been working at least as hard as Andy at this parenting lark (for lark, read: struggle, challenge, exhaustingly mundane dumbing down of my life), and for many more hours a day, so yes, I bloody do want it. *sulky face*

I'm waiting.

Why won't she tell me that I'm her best friend too?

Not that I'm counting (I am), but it's been five days and I'm tired of this waiting game. I've been sneaking in extra treats — offering a few sprinkles on their yoghurt, tickling them, reading stories, making a big play of adding raisins to their cereal, even letting them eat biscuits, and what do I get in return?

Nothing.

Until . . .

This morning, without any intervention on my behalf (excluding the list above, so perhaps more accurately, 'without any specific prompting') I hear it: 'You are my bestest friend, Mummy.'

It's music to my ears.

For once, I don't even dash in to correct her. I am special. I am her best friend.

A symphony plays in my head, and I rush (though in the film, of course, it's a slow-motion version to the *Chariots of Fire* soundtrack) to her side and smother her in an enveloping hug, biting my tongue that really, really wants to point out that the word is 'best' not 'bestest' and that 'best' is a superlative and therefore should not be awarded to all and sundry. To be precise, there can be only one best friend at a time, but I'm not about to spoil this moment by asking her to choose between us — because I'm pretty sure that I'll lose in a contest with the will-o'-the-wisp that is her father.

Andy's already left for work (#gutted) so there's no independent corroboration of this award. I text him and then make the entire world my witness by posting it gloatingly on Facebook.

I do a little jig while singing 'I've got the rosette' and other childish nonsense. I want a badge, a pin, something with which to honour this moment and the accolade that I've received. I hear the cacophonous applause at a glittering award ceremony televised to millions of viewers. I bow and do a Gwyneth Paltrow as I sob over my thank yous.

Whilst the value has decreased (duplication making it no longer unique), shares in 'best friend' are still riding high. A warm glow suffuses my body, and I waft through the morning on an emotional high (either that or the lack of sleep is starting to have irreversible effects on my mental state).

We all go out to the blissful sunshine in the garden (within the maximum security of our four-foot fence) in a buoyant mood, and I respond positively to their endless requests for toys, the pop-up house and the tunnel. Then I put away the tunnel, help them on the slide, get the tunnel out again and hook it up to the house, get the trampoline, then put the slide onto the trampoline . . .

I wake up from my daze and say no to that one.

My garden is a post-nap haven in the sunshine that seems uncharacteristic of a British summer and is giving me a boost beyond vitamin D. There's something calming about sitting in the dappled shade, smiling at the cute tiny clothes billowing on the washing line. If only I could get over wanting sand to stay in the sandpit, and if the children had two of everything so never fought over whatever toy was boring a second ago until their sibling jumped on it, and if only I didn't need to initiate peace talks at just the right moment to avert war and could hold back on refereeing games to which I don't know the rules. But the sun bursts through all these trivialities, and I sit and let it warm my skin as I listen to birds chirping.

I flick through a magazine hoping to magically absorb its content. BC I would've read a book, but now I can't seem to understand prose. After spending a few nights rereading one paragraph of a book that I was halfway through when the children arrived, I realised that my brain is now simply unable to cope with plot, or characterisation, or complex structures. Neither can I cope with anything that is sad, despondent, or that puts me through an emotional wrangle (pretty much everything right now). I can only cope with light, happy books with simple, chronological plotlines aimed at readers over three years of age, so I'm rereading the Discworld series — apologies to Pratchett fans, but even my mummy brain can cope with *Mort*.

I'm listening as the children create imaginary worlds in the pop-up tent. There's a simple delight in their fantasies. They carry in pies (sand in an upturned something) for a picnic. As my troubles blow away on the breeze, there's no hint that my world is about to collapse. Lyrical tones waft on the wind.

'You are my best friend.'

My ears prick up.

Did she just say what I thought she said? Aw.

Hang on, is she talking to me? There is no head poking out the door, so definitely not me. Is she talking to her brother? No. Odd. Nibbles is playing in the sandpit. Well, mostly he is steadily disgorging the sand in fistfuls onto the grass (whilst I take deep breaths and hope that at least it might kill the moss).

'Who are you talking to?' I ask her gently.

'My bear,' she replies.

Pffft. (I deflate.)

Her best friend is an imaginary bear!

All this time, waiting, hankering for her to bestow this precious honour on to me, and now it's totally devalued. She's tarting those words around like Essex girls slapping on fake tan.

The market slumps.

Mummy slumps.

I wish I hadn't been so quick to tell the world about it on Facebook.

Bubbles has burst my bubble.

There's never any time to sulk in this world; one moment you're a BFF amongst many, the next you're rolling around the floor in laughter.

I'm drying myself off in the bathroom after a shower when Nibbles comes in (I locked the door once and spent more time bouncing out of the shower to open the door than I spent under the shower, so gave up any semblance of privacy) and looks around. His eyes widen in surprise, and then he points accusingly and remarks, in a tone that adults reserve for UFOs, 'Mummy has a bottom.' I howl as I bend over and swaddle my derrière in a towel. Then as I pee, things take a stickier turn.

'I don't have one like that,' says Nibbles. He's watching me on the toilet, pointing at my . . .

'No, you don't,' I say, as I grasp at verbal straws. 'You have a tail.' It pops out because I overheard a mum telling her son to 'tuck his tail in' at playgroup yesterday, and as her son exited the loo, I surreptitiously checked his back searching for his spikey tail, imagining that he'd fully committed to dressing up as a dragon that morning with a 'will not take it off' stance both stubbornly admirable and impossible to strap into a car seat.

Later that evening, Nibbles converses confidently about his tail with Andy, who is confused, surprised and then indignant.

'We're *not* calling it that!' he says in no uncertain terms the minute they're in bed.

'Fine with me. I'd like to see you come up with something better in a hurry,' I say, clicking Start on the stopwatch on my phone. 'Ten, nine, eight.' I count to fill the silence and add some pressure and urgency. Andy comes up with . . .

Nothing. Nada. Zilch. Zilcheroony.

'No rush,' I add smugly. And we crash into this whole truth/lies/tooth-fairy conundrum. Neither of us wants to call it a tail, but we're not sure that Nibbles is ready for 'penis'. We cringe at the thought of his shouting it at ear-splitting volume across the park and then singing, 'I've got a penis, a penis, a penis.' I don't want to plaster lies on top of dishonesty on top of fibs like mattresses over a pea, and yet there's something about the thought of certain words on their innocent tongues that makes me wince.

This isn't the first phrase that Andy has vetoed, nor the first time I've invented an unbearable if retrospectively hilarious alternative when put on the spot. For example:

'What's that?' Bubbles asks.

'It's a tampon.' *That's that question answered, go me!* I think.

'What's a tampon?'

'It's to soak up my blood.' A solid answer.

'Why are you bleeding? Have you cut yourself? Why don't you use the white cream?' Bubbles is referring to Sudocrem, which we use for everything from nappy rash to cuts and pretty much nothing in between.

'No, I haven't cut myself. This is a different type of blood.' I really want this discussion to be over so am desperately trying to get my tampon in place and launch myself off the toilet and away from this conversational dead end.

'Where does the tampon go?' Bum. This is not going to plan. 'Does it go up your bottom?' Titters all round.

'No, it goes . . .' (I'm feeling backed into a corner — literally and verbally — as I struggle to contort to the right angle given the overcrowding in this toilet, and my brain veers dangerously off-piste) '. . . up my baby hole.'

What? Fuck fuckity fuck. What have I said?

I'm an actor who's just ad-libbed outrageously in a Broadway theatre and whose fellow thespians are standing around in shocked outrage as they work out how to rescue their play from going off-Broadway on opening week.

I can't believe that popped out of my mouth. I gag and want to do that hands-over-hands-scraping-tongue to cleanse my mouth. With any luck, they weren't paying attention.

'Your baby hole? What's that?'

'It's where babies come out,' I say, and before you can say 'baby hole' I'm washing my hands and getting the heck out of Dodge.

Maybe they won't remember what I said, maybe they'll forget the phrase, maybe I can get away with it and pretend this whole sorry conversation was just a nightmare.

At bath time, Bubbles tells Daddy that she saw me putting a tampon up my baby hole. His face sours as though he were sucking on a lime without the tequila after shot. If he hated 'tail', he finds 'baby hole' loathsome. I concur meekly, my tail (except I don't have one, tee hee) between my legs, and after the kids are in bed, we try to find words we're happy to use. There should be a special parenting thesaurus for this sort of thing — turns out there is, and it's called the Internet. We find pages of food-based euphemisms such as fairy cake, Mr Sausage, broccoli and cookie (not only do we hate these, what happens when we want them to eat sausages and broccoli?), and weird ones like lady garden, dinky, lady moo moo and monkey. There's so much head shaking we look like octogenarians who have stubbornly resisted the march of progress trying to fathom out the point of Twitter.

In the end, the name happens by accident: they're washing themselves with sponges and it pops out of Andy's mouth.

'Did you wash your bits?' he asks.

Ooo. Bits. It's simple, and easy for the kids to pronounce. (She can't say the *K* yet, so it's all 'Can I take my Hello Titty bag?' We try to correct her without sniggering.)

'Is there something wrong with your bits? No? Then leave them alone.'

'One more wipe, Nibbles, there's more poo on your bits.'

And my personal favourite: 'Hold still, there are bits of glitter/cornflakes/Lego in your bits.'

Bits becomes shorthand for all fou-fou stuff. Occasionally I even ask Andy mischievously if he would like to put his bits in mine, and we laugh and shrug and say, 'Maybe tomorrow.' How anyone gets pregnant after having a child, I've no idea. We're so utterly exhausted just keeping up with our little ones that our libidos took umbrage and went on an extended vacation; we're waiting for a postcard to let us know when they'll be back.

Bits works. It's a non-sexual word that our children can innocently shout across a crowded café without our having to hide from the glares of Joanna Public. And we subdivide the new genus of bits into male bits and female bits, called Mr Tinkle and Mrs Sprinkles respectively, if not respectfully.

And we never talk about my baby hole ever again.

40. My Invisibility Cloak

Andy's home.

Late.

He arrives, as expected, just after six o'clock, but I ran out of steam three hours ago, at the precise moment that I woke my children and they bounded back into my day, smashing through my afternoon like hyperactive rascals. Those three hours from nap to Andy's getting home stretch like an interminable exam you know you're going to flunk before you even read the paper; you have three solid hours of bullshit to scribble before you can leave.

Hearing his keys in the door, they leave me mid-syllable. They bombard him with love, enthusiasm and the monkeys-on-espresso version of kids. He barges through the toddler barricade, takes his coat off, sweeps them into a hug and they end up in a ball of limbs and giggles on the sofa. Honestly . . . I look after them all day, yet the minute Daddy comes home, it's all 'who?'

In these post-Daddy-coming-home minutes, I become entirely irrelevant. I could dance the fandango, carve a melon into a scene from *Shaun the Sheep*, balance a herd of glittering zebras on my head and the only thing that would interrupt their devoted idol-ising of the revered Daddy would be the fridge light coming on ('What are you eating, Mummy? Can I have some?'). The first few nights I took the hump at his celebrity status — waved off with flags in the morning and welcomed back with fanfare at night. Daddy has the scarcity factor; I'm cheddar to his caviar.

But I've learnt to go with the flow, to savour their inattention. I sneak off to the toilet without having to answer twenty questions about colour and quantity. I sink into the softness of my duvet and daydream about my old life, or watch the clouds scud by, or pick up a book and open it and ponder how I ever used to make sense of all these words. And I don't have to wonder what mischief they might be making whilst my back is turned.

He asks them what they have been up to and is rewarded with chaotic jumbles of gobbledegook. When he's had enough of being clambered on and slobbered over and is drowning in the waterfall of their attention, he sends them off to find Mummy, ostensibly needing help decoding their 'enigmatic' ramblings peppered with the ubiquitous 'don't memba' and 'nufink' phrases that drive us both to distraction.

As he plays with them before bed, I potter downstairs to write a blog for my business, filled with confidence that since the kids are okay, I will magically be able to create some wondrous wisdom to let my clients know that I am still alive. I sit, rub my brain cells together, type, stop, shrug, delete, type, realise there is no spark in my brain, think about all the ways I was a rubbish mum today, shake my head, and by the time the kids are ready for bed sixty minutes later, my word count is zilch — I don't even have a title. And this is on a day I've had enough sleep. My creative business brain is on stand-by mode. There's a tiny red LED to let me know it's there, but I can't find the On button.

BC, I was madly and passionately in love with my business, but now I begrudge and resent it as yet another child. It demands my time and energy, of which there's precious little to go around. I feel guilty all the time — if I spend time thinking about it when I'm with the kids then I'm not giving them my undivided attention, and when I'm trying to write a newsletter during naptime, I wonder why I'm not having a rest so that I'll be a better mum when they wake up. It's like juggling an affair, with neither my kids nor my business getting the required attention. The thing that I created, that I love, that is built to be a perfect reflection of me, my skills, my personality, is sucking the fun out of being a mum. It's a haystack of extra straws on a back bent double.

Andy and I discuss it and agree to put the business on hold, in the hope that taking that extra load off will make things easier. It does and it doesn't. Being a mum to two new children carries far more responsibility than I ever had when I was running my business, and there are still a lot of straws on my back, lightened only when Andy finally gets back from work. When I get a text saying he's busy and running late, I become one certifiable momma.

Sometimes after Andy comes home, I do things that are impossible to do with two toddlers in tow, like thinking, or creating a perpetual motion machine, or popping to the corner shop. Tonight, we're out of milk, so I poke my head around the door of the lounge and tell them I am off to the shop and think nothing more of it, for my invisibility cloak is fully operational. As I drive off, Nibbles is waving from the window, and Bubbles too — except her waves are forlorn and I notice tears pouring down her face and sobs heaving through her chest. *What's that about?* I ponder. Maybe she's had a bump. About ten minutes later I'm back with milk, and as I walk up the path, she's still stood in the window, her hands on the glass, distraught, tears running down her blotchy face. *Uh-oh.* This is no bump. She has a look of fear on her face that shocks me. I dash in, stride over to her, wrap her in my arms and ask what's wrong.

Andy tells me that she didn't think I would come back. 'Mummy's gone,' she kept saying, and however much Andy reassured her that I was just going out for milk, she would not be calmed, she would not believe him. *Thank goodness I didn't go for a bit of a drive!* I think. I wrap her in my arms and try to hug away her fears, reiterating, 'I'm back now, sweetie,' but I don't think she can quite believe it. Lots of hugs and the evidence before her eyes are krill compared to the whale of her fear.

Tonight, when all is quiet, Andy and I talk about her fear of my not coming back and where it might stem from. We wonder if this is normal for adopted children; we get tangled up with the ease of writing off every unexpected thing as 'because they are adopted'. It's a convenient scapegoat for everything from the potty-training fiasco to her fussy eating. There's a lot we don't know about their time with their birth family, so it's tempting to always tip the blame into that black hole. After a few pointless evenings of playing an adoption matching game, where we pair everything we didn't like to her birth family and all the good stuff to us (conveniently forgetting Ken and Mary), we vow never to use the 'because they are adopted' excuse again.

We're responsible for them now, and we have to man- and woman-up and deal with the kids we chose. All of it: their lemon-faced tantrums, their snot, their hugs and their love.

41. A Bootful of Loneliness

Since Handover, five long weeks ago, it's been just Andy and me. And lately, with Andy back at work, it's just me. Not another soul has crossed our paths except the ubiquitous social workers.

As adoptive parents, we can't introduce our children to family and friends as birth parents can. During Intensive Training, we were informed that it could be *months* before they'd meet our family. I've been wanting to show them off like a glittering engagement ring to anyone foolish enough to come within gloating distance. So today marks a new milestone. Although quite honestly, given the number of milestones we have ticked off, this might be just another pebble on a long stretch of pebbly beach that is tricky to walk on and not as much fun as the term 'beach' might suggest.

Today, we get to introduce our children to some of our family. Pam shocked me when she said the kids were ready — because they've 'settled in so well'. I'd expected to wait longer. The rules: a short visit in neutral territory. We selected a big country park with a café and swings; but whom should they meet first? Who should be the Chosen Ones? We dithered a little and then I played my twin card (beat that!), thus drawing all discussions to a close. We print out photographs of Sarah's family and point them out to the kids, testing them on who's who. They quickly get to grips with this tiny slice of their family, even if Brian is always 'Aunty Brian', despite our persistent and somewhat sniggering attempts to dissuade them.

The picnic is packed. The location is set. We fill the car with the emergency kit (How to Survive the Jungle with Just a Boiled Egg meets The Potty Whisperer), refresh the emergency snacks (which Andy keeps snaffling whenever he takes the car to work) and pile in the picnic and a blanket. But it's my fears that fill the boot too full.

I'm afraid that Sarah and her kids might not love my children as much as I do.

I'm afraid that my children will not love Sarah as much as I do.

I'm afraid of being judged when I am badly acting my mummy role.

What if my children are tired and turn into screaming, tantrumming monsters today, so that even I fall a little bit out of love with them? I wish I could see this moment as a pebble, not a milestone; I'm bent double under the weight of expectation.

We arrive at the car park and wait. Impatiently. They are surprisingly late, yet they text to say they're here. *Where?* Brian's as tall as Andy, so he's easy to spot in a car park, crowd, gig, shop or even an arboretum. After some confusing texts and a phone call punctuated with *a-ha*s, it turns out they're in the *other* car park (who knew there were two?). There's a brief intermission to check nappies, fuss about the picnic and try to squeeze my fears back into the boot, and then they arrive like fans for an away game.

Five faces eager to finally meet our new children. Five new names for our children's family tree.

Brian hoists Nibbles onto his shoulder, and he looks like a hobbit riding a tree (I know they're not called trees in *The Lord of the Rings*, but the fan overlap between Tolkien and this book is likely to be slim). He giggles as Brian tells him jokes. I can barely see to take a photo and there isn't a single camera on this planet that could capture just how emotional I am. Bubbles is holding hands with her youngest cousin, who loves the fact that he is no longer the youngest and is swelling with responsibility; he walks her into some tree roots and she falls over. Everyone is getting along just fine, ignoring the blithering idiot who is Mummy. I hold my sister's hand too tightly, and the look she gives me tells me she knows exactly how wobbly I am today.

The next few hours I float on air. The sun shines, the wind blows and Nibbles picks up so many sticks that they overflow from his hands. Bubbles laughs and has everyone giggling and wrapped around her tiny beautiful finger. I watch as my closest family share in these wonderful gifts, and note the smiles my children leave on the faces of others. I see how small they look from a distance, how they toddle in a seemingly drunken way, how they get whatever they want because I don't want to spoil this moment with a no. We go to the playground, which my sister's teenager declares is the 'best adventure playground ever'. We point out cows, sheep, pigs, goats and ferrets running mazes. We swing and slide and jump and dance. We eat a picnic, sharing the most delectable foods on the planet (cheese and ham wraps *again*).

I am grateful, content and in a state of bliss normally associated with a wheelbarrow of gin and a splash of tonic. A magical day, for I'm sharing these precious lives with the people I love the most. These pots of gold at the end of our rainbow.

I don't want this moment to end, but naptime beckons and we promised our social worker that we'd keep this first meeting short. It's too soon, but we have to go. There is a complex set of hugs and kisses to get through as we say goodbye and tears come.

I don't want to leave.

I don't want to go home.

Today I realised just how lonely I am. I've spent many decades in my own company, especially during school (when I was bullied and ostracised). I left my career to set up in business and become a solopreneur; I'm used to spending hours thinking, writing, creating, walking on my own. Yet this is a loneliness unlike any other, like trudging through an inhospitable Arctic day after day, pulling a heavy sledge with no one to talk to and nothing but snow from horizon to horizon. I'm shipwrecked, cast adrift on a sea of nappies, spoons and baby wipes. I'm desperate for company. Desperate for a helping hand. Desperate for someone to share this load.

We strap the kids in.

I yearn for conversations about the meaning of life, for tricky problems to get my brain stuck into, for anything that isn't 'pee' or 'pea'.

I don't want to be alone any more. This snippet of company has opened up a wound and revealed the loneliness of being a mum.

'We'll see you soon' are my final words (more a plea) before Andy drives off and my silent tears fall. I grieve for my old life, for company, for freedom. Andy's so caught up in the children that our relationship seems like a distant memory. We're two adults trying to become parents and we're too caught up in it all and in feeling tired to think about each other. I want to be with my sister because being with her feels like home.

When we tell Pam how well today went, she gives the go-ahead for us to meet more family, so our next few weekends are spent adding grandparents into the mix. Nibbles takes to Grandpa John immediately because he's an older version of Andy. We go to parks and pile leaves on hands and toddle around stately grounds and have pretend picnics in tents and they become part of more lives, delighting everyone with their giggles and energy.

And I keep busy to avoid feeling the dark loneliness inside.

42. A Foreign Land

My social worker wants me to make some new friends — I guess it's par for the course (since I haven't admitted to feeling lonely). She suggests I do so at the local Sure Start centre, where we attend Stay and Play sessions.

Every week she asks me if I've met anyone to befriend; she sounds like my sisters after my divorce urging me to go on dates and find Mr Right. I keep shaking my head and pulling that face that conveys 'not sure but I am trying'. Despite my loneliness, so far I have asked only one mum for coffee (she had to rush off for lunch, so declined) and I am struggling to find someone else. To be honest, I'm not convinced that the mums at Stay and Play are my sort of people (words replete with pomposity — I admit it, I'm a snob).

There's Teen Mum, all false eyelashes as long as butterfly wings and badly applied fake tan, neon cropped tops and jeggings (I hate that bilious word). As a mum in my mid-forties, I have no idea what to say to her. She is Radio 1 and I am Radio 2 and Radio 4 when Vine comes on to ruin my day by drip-feeding me fear and worry about cancer or the cost of university. Her mum drops her off at the centre, and she looks as hopelessly out of her depth as I do (though for very different reasons), but I haven't said a word to her in weeks.

Then there's WalkOver Mum, all simply 'oh dear' even when her child's behaviour is appalling. How can I invite her over if her child will wreck my house without a single stern reprimand or time-out in sight? I roll my eyes at WalkOver Mum's sweet tone, frown at the lack of consequences and wonder just how her child will turn out in a 'been a parent for weeks, now I'm an expert' righteousness that I should just park with the buggies on my way in.

And I can't bear to be in the same room as Gloating Mum, who spends the entire time boasting about how well her child sleeps, or asking when my children started to walk (how on earth would I know?) simply so she can tell me that her precious is smarter than mine, or show me the bee he drew yesterday (he's only just twenty-one months, he's soooo talented) until I want to scream, 'Nibbles did the most enormous poo last night then signed his initials in the excrement in his cot,' just to shut her up and watch her sidle off with disgust whilst shooing her child away with a 'come on, darling, let's do some Mondrian-esque painting'.

I do and I don't want friends. What I want is my old life back. I used to be friends with career women, entrepreneurs, small business owners. The sort who are already back at work with their children in nursery, not hanging out at the Sure Start centre. There are a few mums I want to befriend, but I never get past the mundane, 'How old is she? Oh, it's a boy. It's just with that shock of blond curls . . .'

I'm too tired to walk the Adoption Tightrope, to pretend that my family fits the default setting until I know the person enough to confess that I 'got' my children rather than 'had' them. I am teetering on the edge of coping. Some of the children are a bit of a handful, and given that my hands are already full to bursting, inviting a handful for a play date at my house just to spend time chatting with another mum seems like a recipe for drinking a mug of tequila sunrise at 10 a.m. My energy and patience are running on the limit of my overdraft, and the thought of getting to know someone seems simply like too much effort, yet I am lonely, frustrated and bored. My life doesn't fit me, or I don't fit my life and I haven't yet worked out how to be me in this new situation.

But there's one person who saves me.

Bev. (Thank God for Bev.)

Bev is my saviour. My slice of sanity. A fellow adopter from our training course.

Because of her, there is now one element of my fictional timetable that's intact: a weekly play date. I jumped at the chance to meet up with Bev when she rang up after a few months of going stir crazy at home on her own. *Yay, Pam can stop bugging me now*, I think. Bev's my kind of person. She brooks no nonsense and is taking a year

213

off her high-powered job in finance to devote herself to being an adoptive mum.

Once a week, Bev and I meet up with our kids at a park or a play gym — not at the homes we're dying to get away from. This date is not about helping our children make friends. This play date is for us, for me.

In a couple of hours we share our thoughts, our frustrations, how tired we are, how fussy our children are, how much they nap and poop and how much we need wine to get through it all. We talk about what it's like suddenly being a mum, about how our partners drive us bonkers and parent differently to us, about how to juggle chores (she irons during naptime; I never iron at all), about our social workers, the foster families, our hopes and fears. We bond over what makes us different to other mums. We attend a paediatric first aid course together and practise CPR on dummy babies whilst I try not to faint and pray that I never have to do any of the stuff that involves blood or bones poking through skin.

The summertime is best, for we can walk around the park and chat as the three children hold hands and play together. And in the two hours that Bev and I potter around the park, we barely scratch the surface of what's really going on in our lives and our families. In the winter, we're stuck inside in a play gym, where there is so much happening, so much noise and distraction, and the kids are fighting or snatching or crying or whining. We hover like meer-kats, constantly checking where they are and whether or not it's one of our children who is screaming, crying, stuck or hurt. Bev's coffee will go cold, my diet Coke will go flat and we might snatch only five minutes of uninterrupted conversation. Five precious minutes when we sit and talk to each other, face-to-face, without being interrupted by the kids' needing us. Those five minutes, those precious five minutes, are worth their weight in gold.

I am not alone. I don't have to do all this on my own.

My deepest thanks to whoever suggested this play date idea, and to Pam for bugging me about it.

43. Caught Speeding

'Doesn't she look like you?'

Having a pram or a child with you is apparently an open invitation for total strangers to engage you in random conversation. I'm struggling to get used to these intrusions, during which I must also struggle to stop my children from running into the road. These innocent chats quickly dive into deep and troubled waters. Strangers ask me questions that I don't know the answers to and then peer at me suspiciously when I shrug and mumble vaguely. I'm asked when they first spoke, walked, ate a whole Weetabix; what their first word was; if they've ever had chicken pox, been on a train, wished on a shooting star — and I haven't memorised their backstory enough to be able to answer. Who knew strangers would turn a simple chat into the ominous black chair of *Mastermind*?

I used to sigh with relief when people would ask me how old they were (I can do this one): 'One and two.' But it became clear from their frowns that I'd got even this simple question wrong. It turns out that my answer was not sufficiently precise; at their age, the answer should be in months, so they aren't one and two years old but seventeen and thirty-one months — hang on, no, that's not right. What month is it? Oh. Okay, that means that he is eighteen, no, seventeen, no, sixteen months (jeez louise) and she is . . . wait . . . hang on . . . it's now mid-month so she is older by another month and he isn't, so . . . wait . . . and I'm frowning and looking like someone who has problems finding the right coins in a shop . . . 'You have to go? Your bus is here? Okay, bye.'

I even forget their birth dates, and that really confuses people — for what mum could forget the moment that her precious bundle finally entered the world? I'm sure the day and its antics are ingrained in birth mums' memories for life, but I've no idea what I was doing the day my children were born. Sleeping in, probably.

But people ask one question more than anything. It happened in a check-out queue the first time.

'Are they twins?' a lady asks politely.

'No,' I respond, shaking my head, not having a clue that I've just stepped into a minefield of judgement.

'How close are they then?' she inquires in a tone that drips with gossip.

'Fifteen months,' I say not realising that I might as well have said that I let my kids play with guns and machetes because then they'll learn to treat them with respect, or answered the question 'Why does alcohol make people do weird things, Mummy?' with 'Let's find out shall we? Who wants a double bourbon straight up?' loudly, in public.

'That was quick!' she responds. Her tone and expression imply that I've been caught speeding, way over the limit. I had no idea that a national speed limit for birthing even existed. A few days later, a mum at Stay and Play gets the same answer from me and responds in hushed conspiracy, 'It's because our husbands can't keep their hands off us, darling.' A frisson of ugh shudders down my spine. I don't like her 'tarts together' stance any more than the 'how quick? how could you?' version. A fellow adopter of three children under five had similar experiences. One lady, who inquired if the adopter's brood were triplets, on hearing the ages of this adoptive set, responded caustically, 'You need to get a TV!' And my mum, as she lugged four children under five around, had strangers ask with astonishment, 'Are they *all* yours?' After forty years of equality, nothing has changed.

I wish I'd deliberately shocked these busybodies by saying, 'Eight months,' adding, 'One was premature. But not the one you think.' I had no idea that women would criticise the speed at which my children were born. It happens again and again, and it gets my goat. Not once has anyone said, 'How fabulous. I bet they're really close and play well.' I want to show them the love and affection they have for each other; the times when he's been upset and just one hug from his sister and her saying 'there, there' in a tone that belies her years has made him smile again. I want to tell them about the time when he was upset in the car and she said, 'Hold my hand,' and reached across to him; their fingertips touched, and she held on with a tiny grasp on his hand and huge grasp on his heart and gave him his smile back. But those words never seem to come out when someone accuses me of speeding.

Why does it matter how quickly or slowly another woman has her children? Have women (and enlightened men) not fought for over a century for women to be treated with the same respect as men, to be given the right to vote and have a say in democracy, to be paid the same for the same work, to be allowed to follow their own paths and create their own opportunities? Why then do women judge and shame other women for the way they look or dress, their size or hairstyle, their career or business acumen, for wanting to have kids, for wanting *not* to have kids (there are days where I can *so* see your point), for having one child (how much easier?), for having an army of them (I don't know how you do it; you're incredible), for being emotionally literate enough to cry at the mewl of a kitten, or for any other choices they make? It's someone else's life for heaven's sake, and the choices *she* makes in *her* life do not in any way impede *my* ability to make *my* own choices. If you want to blend in or stand out, good on you. If you want to be rich and blow it all on champagne, speedboats and sexy crew with six-packs, go for it. If you want to curl under your duvet and eat crisps whilst watching *Bridget Jones*, go get 'em tigress. It's not my personal plan, but who am I to judge anyone else when I'm clearly someone who eats too much, drinks too often, is a snob and a wuss, wanted to be part of Europe and sulked when the vote didn't go my way, has a PhD gathering dust, pretends she's not incredibly bright to fit in, watches naff crime drama on TV, is addicted to notebooks and pens, cries at everything, loves a declutter — oh, and sometimes makes her kids cry. I am riddled with enough self-doubt. Adding to it is entirely unnecessary. I don't want to be judged for choosing to have a family, and I won't judge someone else for choosing not to. And I am royally fed up with having women I've never met cast aspersions on me for daring to adopt children who were born at the wrong speed.

May this chapter stop you dead in your tracks if you ever even think of saying 'that was quick' in judgement of another woman. Shame on you.

One evening at a family party, I took umbrage at the 'that was quick' comment and bit back. 'It wasn't *me*,' I countered. She looked confused, and as I turned to leave I hissed quietly, 'I adopted my children,' and let her work the rest out for herself. I swanned off with my head held high but then stumbled over a chair, having drunk rather more wine than is conducive to balance or good manners. *Get her and the horse she rode in on, being so judgemental, so superior*, I thought. I wasn't exactly proud of myself, but I'd grown tired of being shamed for speeding when I didn't even have a driving licence.

I confided in Bev. She was surprised. Not by what the woman had said but by the fact that I was getting all stressed about it.

'Why do you say anything at all?' she asked. And it suddenly hit me that I didn't need to.

And I stopped defending it or even diluting it with 'when it happens . . .'

If someone is rude or ignorant enough to say 'that was quick', I now simply agree.

'Yes it was.' Spoken in a tone that says 'stick that in your pipe and smoke it'.

44. A Huge Slice of Happy

I am sat on a chair in my daughter's bedroom. The floor is awash with bedding (I clench my fists and tell myself I can tidy in a minute), and the two of them are jumping on the mattress — bouncing around, bouncing off the bed (the *thud* as they land has my buttocks clenching), bouncing into each other (close your eyes, Emma, and only open them if they scream). They sing and giggle and yell and giggle.

I. Do. Nothing.

For minutes.

In a row.

And I gradually shoo my fear downstairs to wash the dishes or do something more useful than ruin this moment. I relax and soak in their fun. I video them, to remind myself when they are driving me bonkers how lovely they can be and to show Andy that we have fun, despite the moaning diatribe he hears every evening.

Fuff, fuff, fuff goes the mattress as their tiny feet and bodies move up and down.

'Ow!' *Fuff, fuff, fuff.*

'Yew!' *Fuff, fuff.*

'Bouncy, bouncy!' *Fuff, fuff, fuff, fuff.*

Her bunches dance to the rhythm of the mattress, flying madly through the air, punctuating her changes in direction; windmill arms try to control her movements. She bounces onto her bottom and laughs. He copies her. Two jumping beans with broad grins on their faces, which sometimes crumple with concentration as their bodies fight the random springiness of the mattress. When they lose, they end up in a heap, arms wrapped around each other, breathlessly giggly, their faces alight with laughter and love.

I hug this moment, giving myself an A plus (for doing nothing?) in parenting, which makes a refreshing change from my usual C minus, and I wonder why I haven't let myself do this more often. And as I sink into the relaxation I realise that I want to bounce with them.

Why aren't there play gyms where parents can play too? Where we fit on the slides and the castles are strong enough to take our weight and the cars are big enough for mummies and children to drive together? I enjoy having a quiet sip of me-time knowing they're safe, but what about playing together, teaching them that grown-ups can have fun and play too? BC, when I ran workshops on creative thinking, I wondered why there weren't adult ball pools and bouncy castles, places that gave us permission to let our imaginations run riot, to be silly and let go. If you've ever crouched, folded like an origami parent in a playhouse with a toddler, you'll know that if these structures were a bit bigger, you might've stayed and been an assistant in your child's ice-cream parlour or baked invisible cookies (whilst flinching when they said, 'How dare you,' or 'I'm very disappointed in you,' and resolving to bandy those stock phrases around a touch less often).

I want to bounce on that bed.

I'm happy and want to giggle and let go and have fun. Nothing needs to be added or taken away from this moment; it's perfect just as it i —

Is *that* the time?

'Snack time, kiddies. Tidy up. Time for snacks.'

I call time on perfect, letting schedules and fear of hangry children rule my day.

Being a mum is the hardest job in the world — it places utterly relentless emotional and physical demands on my time, my energy, my soul, just everything. And yet more and more, within the mountain of tiny things that expands to make my day feel constantly too short and too long at the same time, I experience snippets of joy.

A few days later, the sun is shining through the trees casting dappled delight onto the grass and the path. Two warm and grasping hands have finally released my fingers, and my arms swing pounds lighter by my sides. Two adorable children who have changed my life forever are running down the path (please don't fall *wince* please don't trip) to the Little Park, racing to see who will get there first. Nibbles is going to be last, but for once he does not mind.

I smile.

I capture this moment of peace in a memory snapshot. I swing them gladly for a glorious hour without a shred of tiredness. I take photos as they wriggle and make strange, giggling gurgles; we chase and play and balance and roar and scream and are the happy family that I imagined. Until guilt seeps in — today's special is flavoured with an Andy-being-at-work-while-I-am-out-enjoying-myself ripple. I shrug off the guilt, but I miss Andy. I want to share these wondrous moments with him, hold his hand and giggle with him at the children's silly voices. It doesn't seem fair that he's missing out on this, or that he misses out on all the hard-as-dried-on-Weetabix stuff too (uh-oh, time to stop before I start an *it's not fair* rant).

I shoo my thoughts away as though they're pigeons pecking at the seeds of my joy.

It's time to savour the glorious giddy happiness of well-slept children grappling with imaginary giants in the sunbeams. I delete the piles of washing that naggle my brain.

Today I am going to enjoy my children.

And in doing so, I cut myself a huge slice of happy.

Bubbles is soaking wet after her bath, which is a mixture of splashing, water play and begging for inappropriate toys (like electricity). She's stood waiting for help getting out, and I bend down to pick her up with a grip that isn't tight enough and discover just how darned slippery wet children can be. I lift her a few inches, but she bulges over my grip like a fistful of jelly and slips back into the bath head first. *Thud.* I quickly lock her tight to my body, lift her out and wrap her in a towel, but the look on her crunched-up face says she doesn't know if she can trust me anymore. She wails.

I revert to being a Secret Service parent again, suspicious of strangers, shadows, slipperiness, stairs and stuff, to the days just after we brought them home, when I couldn't let them out of my sight for five seconds, fearing that some mythical monster would swoop down and snatch them away.

But then the days tick by, memories fade and complacency comes to bite me again.

I'm chaperoning the children down the stairs. Bubbles slips ahead of me and she's too fast, so I shout at her to slow down. She sits on the step where the stairs turn, her back parallel to the wall, looking at me and Nibbles. To her right is the wall, to her left, a steep descent of stairs. She stops and looks at me. *Phew!*

Bubbles reaches out her left arm and my eyes widen.

'No!' I shout as she leans left, expecting to find a wall or step to hold on to. Her body tips as her arm finds . . .

Fresh air.

Nothing.

When she's just a few degrees from vertical, gravity takes over and her body follows her arm down the stairs like a slinky spring. She tumbles relentlessly as I scream, which turns out to be not that helpful. I run after her with Nibbles in my arms and am only halfway down when I hear it.

Crukkk.

Her head hits the open metal stairgate.

The bone-on-metal crunch silences my screams.

She carries on rolling as she hits the wooden floor below and stops in a crumpled heap. I bound down to the mess that is my daughter at the bottom of the stairs. Fear wells up. I feel sick.

Oh God.

Bubbles is not moving.

Please let her be okay. Please not a broken bone.

She's not even making any noise — *Please don't let her be dead.*

'WAHHHHH!'

Bubbles is crying.

Thank goodness for *M*A*S*H*, which taught me that during a triage situation it's not the ones who are screaming you need to worry about — it's the ones who aren't making any noise at all. That said, I'm deathly pale, worried out of my appetite and usefully replaying the incident in my head. I scan her quickly for blood or bones and then cradle her tightly, in the hope of squeezing the dread out of me as my brain continues rewinding: she was sitting on the top step and looked sideways at me, then her arm went out and down into thin air and before I could react, she tumbled. I wonder just how fast I could have moved, and whether I could have saved her before she hit the stairgate, and just how much extra damage that stupid stairgate caused when her head hit it, and . . .

I am awash with emotions that have no outlet. I want to lash out, yet as I turn to rampage on whoever is responsible, the image I see is my own. *I* was in charge. It is *my* fault. I need to confess my sins, to purge myself; I text my husband and tell him what a bad parent I am, but it doesn't make me feel better. I don't feel clean, refreshed, as if I can just shrug it off and let it go.

And I cut myself a huge slice of guilt.

45. The Promise of a Gift

It's a sunny day. A gloriously sunny day. And as we drive past the rolling hills and incredible landscape of this green and pleasant land, Andy and I wistfully ponder the changes of the last few months. Andy misses going out on his bike in the summer evenings. And me?

I miss the days just before we met them. Days of promise, of expectation, like a pile of presents waiting to be opened, waiting excitedly to reveal the wonders within. As a child, at Christmas I would often reflect that the promise of the presents was better than the gifts themselves; I felt let down by what was beneath the paper and bows. Being a parent feels like that today. For six years, I dreamt so often of being a mum, and after Panel I was full of hope, excitement and suspense. My life-to-be was a gift wrapped in glittering paper and sumptuous ribbon. I was full of optimism, hope and expectations of wondrous delights. But the reality has been somewhat different.

I stare longingly out at the sun on the hills and secretly wish I were out there walking, soaking in the landscape, swinging my arms and singing without a care in the world. I miss being me, I miss feeling light and fun and being able to think. I don't know when I might find me again. Andy feels it too, because I can see it written on his face, yet his thoughts run darker than I could ever have imagined.

One evening, as we're sat in extra-grumpy silence after the kids have gone to bed, I resolve to tackle the weird, sullen elephant in the room. Something isn't right and it's more than just the 'isn't it exhausting?' and 'they drive me bonkers' standard evening fare. I think that if I find out, we can sort it out and be slightly less cantankerous for the rest of the night.

'What's wrong, Andy?' I ask, my tone as stuffed with concern as a bowl at a help-yourself salad bar.

Andy doesn't answer straight away and that worries me. In the silence, I realise that there is no simple answer coming, but I'm not expecting what comes next.

'I don't love them.'

. . .

(speechless)

What?

As the shock wears off, my mind jumps around.

You don't love them? What does that mean? How can he say that? But they're our kids.

I can't even look at him, afraid of what else I might see. I start to shake a little, a tiny rumble vibrating in my bones.

He's frightened; I can hear his fear reverberate through those four words. He doesn't know what to do, or how to get through this, or what will happen if things don't change.

Tears run down my cheeks. He is my rock, my lifeline and . . . *What's going to happen now?*

I'm scared.

I'm stood in a room that's blacker than night without a single speck of very-dark-blue-but-not-quite-black to give it size, shape or context. My eyes dart around but there's literally nothing to see. I don't know where I am or what is in here with me. My skin crawls; goosebumps rise on my arms. I dare not even move in case the ground beneath my feet opens like a trap door and I fall down, down, down. I'm trembling, alone, afraid.

I'm also filled with compassion. I feel a surge of kindness for this man who has coped with so much in these last few months. I've grown to love him not just as my husband and friend, but also as Daddy to my children. I've watched him be patient, scoop mush into their mouths, save Nibbles from choking, cradle them when they're upset, read stories to them until we all know all the words, cuddle them, play horsey with them and work extra hard to keep money coming in as I play mummy. How can I not admire his honesty, when this is clearly not an easy thing to admit?

'It feels like I am babysitting someone else's children,' he continues, 'doing the agency's job for them.' He looks defeated. *My poor Andy*, I think. I've rarely spared a thought for how he is coping, presuming naïvely that he got the long straw of this parenting bargain. He works a full-time job, parents from the moment he gets home, washes up, deals with their nightmares and more. No wonder he's finding it hard. There is a deep resignation in his voice, an emptiness I have never heard before, even when Claire's mental illness took us to the edge of reason and sanity.

'If Pam came to us right now and told us there had been a mistake and we had to give them back, I would,' he says.

I discover an even deeper, blacker state of shock.

Black. Unending, unyielding, uncomfortable, infinite black, reaching into every corner of our lives. This conversation has taken a turn into a very dark and scary cul-de-sac and I have no idea how to get out. I have run breathlessly into a dead end with high brick walls. I turn around frantically searching for a way out; the scary thing I've been running from thunders behind me, closer and closer; the hairs on my neck prick in anticipation of certain death. I just want to wake up from this horror. And I realise in a way that chills me to my skeleton that I am already awake.

And the shock wave ebbs a little.

I'm angry.

'It's a bit too effing late to be having second thoughts!' I want to shout. I want to unleash the fear that's shattered my everything-will-be-okay illusion. That splinter of anger exhausts me instantly, until I want to hold him and stroke his head and sort something out.

I'm doubting myself.

Have I succumbed to busy-ness to avoid brooding on 'do I love my kids?' What if *I* feel that way too — what would that mean for our family? I close my eyes for a moment to block out the thoughts that circle my head like vultures. Am I too deep into the dream to wake up and look around and see that this is not the dream I wanted?

If we give these wonderful children back, if the adoption breaks down, then our last and final chance to be parents is gone.

All of this for nothing? I can't give them up. That would break me. I won't do it. But I can't do this alone. I need Andy to do it with me.

I cry for the life I used to have.

I cry for Andy and our children.

I cry with exhaustion.

And when the tears stop, I ask myself again: Do I love them?

I often tell them I love them: they are so cute and helpless and thoughtful and Bubbles just wants to be loved. When I shivered with fever and Bubbles brought me a blanket and read me a story, I loved her then. When she bought swings with her kisses, I loved her then. I know that something powerful and inescapable happens when my son cries — it's like my soul is crying too. When he makes those pitiful sounds, something profound resonates inside of me, like he's part of me and his despair is mine as well. I need to wrap my arms around him and comfort him until his crying stops. Is that love? It doesn't feel like any other love I have known: it feels primal, ancient, rooted in the soul of the earth. I feel the milk I do not have would run at his crying.

I want to run away from this evening, from this nightmare conversation, into the fresh air, but the children sleeping upstairs bind me to this house more effectively than any tracking device ever could.

'It's far harder than I thought it would be,' he admits, and I nod my head in silent agreement. If I could trust myself to speak, I'd agree. Despite all the 'how braves' and the warnings from the social workers, becoming parents overnight to two children has been take-us-to-the-edge-if-not-over-it challenging.

What does this mean? I don't want to know what this means, yet I cannot leave it like this; I cannot sleep with this uncertainty. I ask the unaskable question because I have to know.

'What are we going to do?' I ask quietly and hesitantly.

I can't even breathe.

This gap is killing me.

A million *what ifs* flutter through my uneasy stomach.

'There is no question of giving them back,' he says.

Puh-uhhhhh.

I gulp down one big shock of air and cry tears of sheer relief. I'm not going to lose my children. We're staying together. Woo (I'm too spent to hoo).

We agree to keep going, to keep putting one wobbly foot in front of the other.

We hug in relief, concurring that this is so hard, so so hard.

Tonight, in this moment of brutal honesty, we're united into a new family. We will learn to love each other and find our way in a rickety AC world. and. and. and. I am so happy and sad all and. and. and. at once and that's okay, because both of those feelings come with tears, so I just cry and. and. and. let my tears sort it out amongst themselves.

I hug his words to me: 'There is no question of giving them back.'

Praise be. It's a delicate strand of hope gluing tomorrow back together.

46. Living the Dream

I've been waiting for this day for a lifetime. The sand tickles my toes and the wind rustles my hair. I'm standing in the dream that gave me faith through the gloom and disappointments that lie behind me.

We set off in a buzz of contagious excitement which is heady and fragile and gone before we reach the motorway. It's been a long drive, with an eczema of 'Are we there yet?' and 'I want to go home' (repeat until you want to turn the car around), but we're nearly there. I wind the window down and inhale the salty tang of freedom. We park and climb up the steep sand dune that separates us from the beach. I'm weighed down with bags, the picnic, a blanket, towels, a potty and two children as I wrestle for a foothold on the slippery sand. We're making slow progress and I probably should've made two trips and it's not quite the unencumbered mummy-and-daughter dream, but close enough.

Then we crest the hill and I nearly sink to my knees in a hallelujah as the sea comes into view. Angels sing in my head. The glorious expanse of it washes away all my aches and exhaustion. I could just float away. Instant refreshment in a view.

I stand with my little girl's hand in mine. She has billowing curly hair, a cute tee shirt and shorts on, and eyes like pools of water that illuminate her expressions. After all these years, she has a name, a face, a voice, a personality and so much more. However vivid my dream, it has nothing on this moment. I never felt the warmth seep into my finger from her tight grip, or the sound of her excitement as she asks if she can paddle, or the tug on my arm as she races down the dune. I never knew how much my heart would dance just watching her. The way her face lights up when she sees the beach, and its huge play area is a tuning fork reminding me of the happiness in my soul. And in my other hand (empty in the dream) is her brother's. He is equally delighted, straining to play, a tiny toddler full of mischief, love and giggles. Contentment seeps like marrow into my bones. In my mind, the dream shimmers, adds my little boy and then is blown away like sand until it disappears, replaced by this moment here on the beach with my two children: my dream come true.

The tide's out and the beach stretches forever, a huge expanse of golden rippled sand. I unpack the rug and lay claim to a square within this gigantic sandy playground, where the only danger is a puddle and there's no stalking stranger to unsettle my nerves. All the watchful vigilance of the last few months melts away like chocolate in a toddler's hand (but without the mess). I close my eyes and savour the waves, the salty breeze, the warm sand beneath me, the chatter of seagulls, the sun on my skin and the sounds of happy children. I want to cry with relief, to finally wash all the fears that we might never be parents into the sea and have the tide take them away from me forever, like a message in a bottle.

There's a tug on my arm and I'm sweet-talked into making sandcastles with Nibbles. I teach him how to bash the sand tight and turn it quickly until we have a string of mummy-made fortresses that we decorate with seaweed and broken shells. And as I sit back to admire my work, Nibbles destroys it with a well-aimed jump. I build another village of sand castles and before I'm even finished, like a giant in a story book, he crashes into the scene and destroys it in a fit of giggles and noise.

I couldn't have done this without my friend Jane, who's brilliant. We all spend a fabulous few hours splashing in puddles of crisp, clear water, waging war on sandcastles, chasing wagtails, digging a boat out of the sand for a trip with the owl and the pussycat and eating a rather sandy picnic ('I dropped it, Mummy'). I slather suntan lotion on their bodies as thick as the foundation of a lady at the make-up counter and pull hats and sunglasses tight on their heads only for them to whisk them off moments later. The sun shines, there is plenty of food, no one needs a poo and my world feels like it has been turned upright again.

After lunch we head home. I am on a high. Not only have I been to the beach, but my children have been too and they loved it and I love that they loved it and it was all one heady day of sand and sun and playing and having fun. Bubbles is chatty and giddy and I think that she'll tire herself out soon and nap. Except she doesn't. Nibbles is sleeping silently, mouth wide open, head tilted back, fist clenched around a shell, and she starts a head-spinning, howling impression of a girl possessed by the devil. She is throwing herself all over the place, straining at her straps, and nothing that Jane and I do seems to quieten her. We try singing, soothing, stories, stroking her leg (not me, I'm driving). In the end, I lose my rag and pull over at a service station. I get her out of her seat, stand her next to the car and tell her that her tantrum is not welcome. When she's calmed a little by the simple act of standing still, I give her a long hug and strap her back in. Before we're even on the motorway, she is snoring.

I kick myself for not doing that forty miles ago.

But even her fiendish outburst cannot wipe the smile off my face that lingers almost as long as we keep finding sand in the house and the car and the *how did sand get here?*

I walked hand in hand with my little girl *and* little boy along a beach.

Living my dream.

47. Bunnies, Badgers and Key Stage What?

Time flies when you're exhausted. It's mid-June and I need to get my skates on, as Pam keeps reminding me. If I'd have given birth, I might have put my children's names down for the best preschool when they were just a few cells wreaking havoc in my body, for all the my-darling's-going-to-be-president mums know that their children must be precociously gifted by age two (where's that Baby Einstein CD?) if they're to be welcomed into the powerful elite of this world. Otherwise, they'll be chucked on the scrapheap of mediocrity and endure the ignominy of a string of minimum-wage jobs. Good grief, the pressure's on and Bubbles isn't even three.

Having finally mastered the impenetrable jargon of adoption, I'm now confronted with the equally incomprehensible world of school. Once Bubbles is three she's entitled to fifteen hours of nursery a week, and when she goes to school full-time next year, she'll start in Year One.

No?

Waddayamean no? Why isn't the first year of school Year One? Too obvious? So it's Year Zero? Nope. It's called Reception. Of course it is. Unless it's Foundation Year. Which may or may not be the same. Then there are Early Years, Key Stages 1 and 2, nursery, infant, primary, secondary and a whole lot of other stuff that has changed quite a lot since I was at school in the LIII (lower third form).

To make all these terms child friendly, schools and nurseries name these classes after animals or flowers, which will lead to conversations like this (in a year or so):

'Which class is Bubbles in again? Is it Dragons?'

'No, she's in Bunnies, except if she goes to the nursery after-school club, when it's Tigers.'

'So what's that stuff in the newsletter about Magpies all about?'

'Magpies is the group where she's with the outdoors come-home-covered-in-mud group, which is not the same group as the one where she does her guided reading, which might be Owls or Dandelions, I'm not sure.'

'What about Nibbles — what's his class called again?'

'Well, when he's at nursery-attached-to-school, it's Dinosaurs, but in the afternoons, at the nursery-not-attached-to-school it's called Brambles.'

'Oh, FFS!'

But before we can have such worthy and pass-the-gin-style discussions, Bubbles needs a nursery place for September and the end of the term is approaching as fast as the next laundry load.

I start with the school near the Stay and Play because it's familiar and seems like a logical starting point. The children and I have a guided tour: it's new and modern, all glass and light and spacious and airy. There is lots of room to move and breathe and find a corner by yourself if you want, and I'm trying my best to listen to the teacher whilst keeping an eye on my two toddlers in a large roomful of other children. Part of me is thinking, *Just get something sorted*, but a bigger part feels a niggling sense that this place is not right.

Next I drag Andy to visit a playgroup in a room that looks a bit shabby, dark. There's a rusty swing for outdoor play on hard tarmac and an indoor space that's one scream away from bedlam. I may be straying into wrap-them-in-cotton-wool territory here, but neither of us feels that this is the right place. Or am I just not ready to let someone else look after her? Do we even know what we want? I expected to walk into a nursery and say yes (job done). But so far, nowhere has clicked — and there are only a few weeks left.

And then just as the last grain of sand falls through to empty the hourglass, I snatch victory from the jaws of the Shark of Illiteracy. The children and I visit a school at the end of our long road. It's in an old building and I can't find the entrance but am saved by the headmistress, who finds me wandering like a lost shepherdess with two sheep in the car park. She's warm and welcoming and everything I imagine in a teacher for my children. Compared to the new-build school, it's a compromise on space and light and walls and hence feels just like the schools of my youth (before they were demolished as unpractical and dated). She gives me a tour, and as we potter through the classrooms, the pupils come up to my daughter with real interest and ask her if she is joining the school; she has a friendly entourage of inquisitive kids surrounding her.

'Most of the places have already gone,' says the headmistress, and my heart sinks.

'Sorry I'm late,' I say. 'I adopted them.' Trotting out my excuse.

'How long have you had them?' she inquires.

'Just over two months,' I reply, and she nods, impressed.

'They seem so content, part of your family.' Tears well up in her eyes. My eyes echo her sentiment, and in this moment of soppy connection, my decision is made.

A few days later and her place is confirmed: from September, Bubbles will be going to nursery/preschool/Giddy Goats five mornings a week. I'm delighted and not ready and confused and I can't help but wonder how on earth I am going to get them both ready and changed and out of the house on time each morning.

Still, that's months away. Plenty of time.

48. Knitting Spaghetti

It's the summer, so we're off on a lovely, relaxing, get-away-from-it-all holiday, staying with relatives. Holidays are usually about adventure, exploring, walking, new experiences and having Andy abandon me or our passports on a mountain in the midday heat without a drop of water to drink. But right now, my life is packed with adventure and new experiences, so I am hoping for something restful, rejuvenating, simple.

To get to our holiday destination, we have a long drive with the extra complication of two restless kids in the back. Even a ten-minute 'pop' to the shops involves negotiating ceasefires over a toy, suggesting they stop kicking my seat twice and stop hitting each other five times, retrieving the toy they dropped six times and pulling over once to wipe an explosion of snot off the back of the passenger seat. Then there's the game of 'name that thing that Mummy didn't see' which lasts until I miraculously pluck the answer from a list of increasingly bizarre guesses or give up in sheer frustration. How are we going to cope with something involving three motorways, fourteen pit stops and an entire day behind the wheel (for Andy; I won't drive because he tuts and winces too often at my 'fifteen years and no claims so I can't be all that bad' driving)?

The sat nav says that it's a five-hour journey, but that's about as realistic as Swindon Town winning the Premiership. We brace ourselves for a seven-hour slog. Within an hour, the broken-record starts.

'Are we there yet?' We soon discover that there is no right answer to that.

No has them wailing about how awful and boring this is; 'It's not fair and I hate this and why can't we listen to Kipper again?' 'Because Daddy nearly had an accident bashing his head on the steering wheel it was so kill-me-now.'

Yes works the first time, but then they realise we're not and react far worse than if we'd just said no.

Nearly is a lie too but seems the least fraught of the three options.

Mostly we go for option four: 'Look, a yellow car. Cheese on wheels.' And before you know it, we're playing a milk-on-wheels, ketchup-on-wheels, night-on-wheels game that we wish we hadn't started.

'I want to go home.'

'I know, sweetie. I do too.' And by now, I want to be anywhere but trapped in this car for another . . . *how long?* I choke as I check the time. One hour down, six more to go. In a heady bout of unrealistic optimism, I eschewed the idea of buying DVD players for the car, saying, 'We never needed them when I was a child, and we had four of us in a car driving the length of the country.' But only because I'd forgotten all the arguments and slapped legs and sulky faces; I'd forgotten the heavy weight of boredom that made long car journeys turn into a powder keg of bad behaviour that would ignite at the slightest elbow poked into someone's ribs. At least we always got to hear the story about my mum making the picnic in a traffic jam (boot of the estate car open, searching for the right sandwiches in the cool box); the road opened up and Dad had to drive off, leaving Mum to run to catch up at the next point of stationary traffic. Now I remember that my car journeys as a child were as godforsakenly dire as this one.

We finally pull onto Aunty Sally's drive and I jump out. I need a large glass of red, but we have tea, bath and bed to get through first (never mind unpacking a bootful of stuff we don't need). Despite the bath and TV, the kids are far too excited to settle down, and after half an hour of pointless popping up every five minutes ('your turn') to implore 'go to sleep', I lie next to Nibbles' cot and let him grasp my finger as I shush him. Why won't he sleep? After a time frame equivalent to at least two glasses of wine, his grip loosens and his legs stop twitching and he's asleep.

The next day the sun shines and we set off on an adventure, packed as if our destination's Borneo. We walk along a nature trail, and Nibbles only huffs when I insist on slapping suntan lotion on him. 'Not the face' is his general attitude to bubble bath, soap, suntan lotion, baby wipes and anything that might make a clean spot, but not, of course, to spaghetti hoops, ice cream, yoghurt, cake, crumbs, ketchup, glitter, paint, crayons or glue. We eat lunch at a restaurant and realise a picnic would have been a gazillion times easier (try using cutlery that's bigger than your head whilst sitting underneath the table because the chair's too low and see how much food you get into your mouth) and would have come without the burden of having to take out an extra mortgage. If I'm going to pay that much for a meal, it'd better come with a bottle of wine.

'Nap?' I suggest afterwards, trying to point Andy in the direction of normality, but he shrugs me off with 'it'll be fine' as he mutters something about spoiling his holiday. *What about crabby children ruining it?* I think. I give in because I don't want to argue on the first day, but my control freak is running around a padded room bashing her head repeatedly against the wall whilst screaming, 'Stick to the routine! The routine, goddammit!' The kids struggle mid-afternoon ('I'm tired') and won't eat their tea, then behave in a way that would draw a crowd in public. I seethe and witter about telling him so, and our hosts are unfazed because it's what kids do.

The following day we are in a park with our hosts' grandchildren playing on swings and slides, walking around the lake and eating ice cream. There is a water area on one side, where plenty of half-dressed children and babies in nappies splash in the freezing water.

'Can we go in the water, please?' asks Bubbles.

'That's lovely asking,' I say, letting her down gently, 'but I haven't brought a towel or change of clothes.' I know they'll get cranky if they're wet and cold. They sulk off looking disappointed but that's the end of it.

Except it's not.

Ten minutes later I find them in the splash park, soaked to the skin, because they decided Andy would be an easier proposition and he said yes. Looks like they got their Divide and Conquer Badge today. I'm fighting in a tug of war between fun and naps, with everyone else on the fun side of the rope. So I shake my head, go with the flow and wonder why I'm always casting myself as the bad guy.

Over the week, we eat more ice cream, build sandcastles, get sand everywhere — I become a born-again worshipper of Talc (thank you, Sarah), charade-ing its praises to every parent within miming distance on the beach — paddle, build pebble castles, dry the children off, rescue Nibbles when his paddle turns into an unexpected swim as the beach slopes steeply and he reaches for a leaf, learn not to tell Bubbles that if she runs around the lake she can get more time on the swings because I've only got flip-flops on and she runs for nearly a mile non-stop while I huff, puff, trip and get a stitch. On a rainy day we go to the swimming baths (they splash, we hover), and when the 'wobbly sea' is replaced by a calm sea, we take a boat trip.

On the boat, I'm mesmerised by my children — the wind dances in their hair and they are entranced by the bluey-green expanse that stretches all the way to the horizon. They're surprised and delighted as waves splash over the edge and shower them with spray, they stumble as the boat pitches, and the other passengers forgive them for treading on their toes as they march off for a five-step walk. We disembark, walk to a bench for a picnic and then queue for the return trip. On the boat, Nibbles falls irretrievably asleep in my arms, which is glorious and touching and I love it until I realise just how heavy he is; by the time I need to carry him off the boat again, my arms have gone to sleep and my back aches and the cute factor has worn off and I nearly fall in the sea on the slippery harbour steps.

Then it's Thursday. The grandchildren come over and our kids play with their relations (some combination of 'cousins' and 'removed'). We all eat lunch at home and for the first time this holiday, Bubbles and Nibbles have an afternoon nap and I get a few minutes' rest. We drive to another beach for a few hours and I cram in a short swim, floating whilst constantly scanning the beach for strangers or dinosaurs or other dangers that I couldn't save them from anyway. And when we get back, for the first time this holiday they eat all of their tea without a single whine while I state, drenched in none-too-subtle undertones, that it's 'amazing what a decent nap can do'.

By the time we arrive home, replete with sixteen loads of laundry and sand deep behind the wax in our ears, I feel bruised, as if I've spent the week running up the down escalator. Routines and holidays are like Baileys and coke — not natural partners, and a combination that can, in fact, result in a curdled concoction that gets thrown down the sink. If I'd stayed at home and taken the children to a local play gym every morning (and for lunch) whilst I read some chick lit and drank fizzy pop, the whole week would have been much closer to the sort of holiday I actually needed. I've never wanted a holiday that is lying on the beach reading every book in *Cosmo*'s 'Summer Reads' before, but I've never been this dead on my feet before now either.

But no, we never take the easy route (two children at once? how brave), not when there is a Countdown Champion of Champions level as an alternative. Now I can confirm that taking two toddlers hundreds of miles away on holiday is about as easy as knitting cooked spaghetti.

49. Nothing to Talk About

Liz sends us a text out of the blue, saying, 'I am free on [whenever it was] to babysit.' Oo. As I roll this around my brain, I'm set upon by a midge swarm of *what ifs*: What if the children wake up and she can't calm them? What if Bubbles goes ballistic? What if . . .

Unhelpful buzzing and I'm all out of what-if repellent.

My social worker Pam is not. 'We hired you two for the strength of your relationship. It's your relationship that is the foundation of this family, and you need to have time off. So what if the children have a bad night's sleep? They will recover, but you two need time to be together just for you.' That's sorted then. Pam gives me permission to put my marriage before my kids for a night, and as soon as she leaves, I text Liz: 'Yes, please.'

Some days later, Liz arrives. The children are glued to the TV so don't even register her arrival. Andy reads them stories and puts them to bed while I try and remember where I stashed my make-up.

'I don't want you to go out,' Bubbles whines.

'We'll be back soon', 'we won't be long' and 'you'll be asleep anyway' are our responses. Extra hugs and kisses and she calms down, just as my lippy (found it) slides on. For the first time in months I am leaving the house with a tiny handbag, unburdened by nappies and baby wipes. Oh, and without the responsibility of my kids, too.

'They're in bed,' we tell Liz as we come downstairs.

'Is that it?' she asks, as if something extraordinary has taken place.

'Yep,' we say. We're almost out the door when our ears prick to crying upstairs. We sigh, go up to Bubbles' bedroom and calm her again. A few minutes later we extricate ourselves and get in the car before she sets off again. We're *out* out.

Despite all the time we had to organise a great night out, we dithered until I booked a GF Italian near home an hour before Liz arrived. We perch on our seats, exuding awkward, unsure about the etiquette of a night out without the kids, as we sip our drinks and peek at the menu. There is an uncomfortableness about our inter-action — as if we have forgotten how to be a couple. Mostly, we haven't a clue what to say, partly because I hinted on the way that it'd be nice to talk about something other than the kids. Except we can't think of something. It starts to feel like a first date.

'Shall we go on holiday next year?' I ask, sounding like a hair-dresser chatting with a new client.

Why on earth am I — the queen of conversation, the queen of extended telephone calls (my record is five hours with two loo breaks), a well-known chatterbox from a young age — stuck for something to say?

I catch his eye and smile at him. I am overwhelmed to have this lovely man in my life; looking at him still makes me want to wink shyly at him and flutter my eyelashes coquettishly to reel him in.

Finally, we admit that we're going to have to talk about the kids. It may be 'breaking the rules' but it breaks the ice. Words start to flow and for the first time in ages we spend time in each oth-er's company talking, sharing our thoughts and feelings about the strangest few months of our lives and the mass extinction event that happened when the meteors known as Bubbles and Nibbles arrived from out of space and laid waste to the lives we used to have. And by the end of the evening, I realise that I am not lost, not gone, just hidden beneath the toys and nappies and schedules of this new role.

And I learn that for all the time we spend in the same room or on the same walk, we've forgotten to be together. Being in some-one's vicinity is not the same as being someone's friend or lover or confidant or wife.

And maybe, when we aren't so tired, we might do this again, to scratch beneath the surface and reveal the people and relationship below.

50. Miss, Miss

Today is a Big Day. Another pebble on the beach. And yet that's downplaying it. I don't know if it's a Big Day or a pebble so I'm going to let you decide. Today I'll leave Bubbles with a stranger for three whole hours. I'm a bubbling fusion of excitement and anxiety.

Over the summer, I've been walking the kids along the school route, getting them ready for this daily walk, pointing out our visual stepping stones along the way in the shape of carved rabbits, a pond, a bird table, a cat (who's never in the same place so let's scrub that one), a gnome, some swings and then finally the school. By the end of the summer, we're waving at it ('Hello, school') and talking excitedly about her starting in just nine/eight/seven (you get the gist) days. I am determined that we'll all walk to school together.

She starts today.

Two days ago, we went to the school together for an hour. She ate a snack and I filled in a form. Yesterday she stayed for an hour and didn't need me to settle her in or stay (my brave girl). Today she'll stay all morning (three hours) without me, starting at 8.45. She's excited to wear her new clothes and carry her new book bag. I take a photo of her Big/Pebble Day. I am ready. And I am not. I am ready for my life to be simpler for a few hours every morning, and I'm not ready to let her go and have someone else look after her whilst I wonder what she's up to.

We walk to school chatting excitedly about all the fun she'll have and the friends she'll make and how wonderful it all is. It's slow-going but we get there eventually without any incidents. During the summer, the children protested against the torture of walking to school. They'd start with a 'too tired' whine, and if I didn't turn around and go home, they'd crumple on the pavement, tiny placard-less eco-warriors in front of a mummy-dozer. Then I'd be forced to wait, studiously ignoring them, until they felt their demonstration had made its point. I have five minutes' lie-down-protest leeway built into my school amble, and today I didn't need it so we get there early and wait for the door to open. I stand self-consciously in the playground, my mouth as dry as a martini.

Bubbles goes in, puts her coat on the peg and gives me a hug. 'Bye-bye, Mummy,' she says, and then hugs Nibbles and says bye-bye to him before turning her back on us and wandering excitedly into a whole new world of glitter, sand, paint, glue, bricks, scissors, toys and play ovens.

My ego wants her to need me, but I'm glad she's ready for this moment.

The Big Day has arrived with less fanfare and pomp than I expected. But not unnoticed.

'Miss, miss,' bleats Nibbles, lamenting the loss of his partner in mischief, or simply repeating what Bubbles says as Andy leaves every morning. I don't know what to say, so I say nothing and take his hand in mine and we toddle slowly home. I feel like a part of me is missing, like I've forgotten something or left the house in my slippers. The house feels odd, as if we've had a power cut and the fridge has stopped humming. I blow up some balloons and Nibbles and I play catch and he forgets to miss her.

In the coming months, I'll feel disconnected from my daughter, for suddenly, after an immersive experience of being with her 24/7, I'm cut off. When I ask her what she's done, she'll murmur about play, water, snack or something, and I'll feel short-changed.

One day, she greets me with a large drawing of her family: six circles with dots that vaguely resemble faces. Her teacher has written 'Mummy', 'Daddy', 'Bubbles' and 'Nibbles' over four of them.

'It's lovely,' I say, and put it on the wall. I wonder about the other two circles. 'Who are these people?' I ask.

'Ken and Mary,' she says. Part of me thinks, *How lovely, she thinks of them as part of her family*, and part of me aches at the realisation that there are people other than me who matter too. Somehow I think it should be easier to be part of an Adoption Square, but my heart reminds me it's not. Ken and Mary's love and influence are like sprinkles in our ice-cream family — they make it different.

'Mummy,' she continues, 'my teacher made me draw hair on Daddy. Daddy doesn't have any hair.' I console her whilst grinning from ear to ear — that's one to tell Andy when he comes home.

Life goes on but it's not the same. My life will become marked by the school run and the school holidays, a giant sundial marking out the terms and years as the winds of time recreate the landscape of our family.

51. The Calpol Calamity

Bubbles has been in preschool for a month and we've been giving our antibodies an Ironman-style workout ever since. (It will be four months of constant sniffs, coughs and colds until our immune systems catch up, but we don't know this yet.)

We're on our fourth bottle of Calpol, having used up the one Allan gave us at the party yonks ago. I laughed when Allan said that there would come a time when we'd panic to discover we'd run out. I'm not laughing now.

I know the fear.

It's worst at night. One of the children is coughing and coughing and you need both the paracetamol and ibuprofen versions to knock them out so you can all get a few hours' sleep. You pick up the bottle and it feels — uh-oh, light. You hold it up to the nearest lamp, tip it and a creeping horror shudders down your spine; there are only a few drops left. Your eyes widen and you search for someone to blame.

It only happened the once before I bought an Emergency Calpol Supply but even that proved to be inadequate.

'Andy, the Calpol has run out. Can you get me the Emergency Bottle, stat?'

Sounds of rummaging around and crashing then a long pause.

'Where is it?' he shouts.

'In the kitchen, of course, where it always is.'

Sounds of cupboards and drawers being opened and closed, most likely at random.

'It's not here,' he concludes.

'What do you mean, "it's not here"? It was the last time I looked, and I know *I* haven't used it.'

Long pause.

'Umm . . . Ah . . . I probably . . . I might . . . I may know what's happened. I think I used it.'

'You used it!' I shriek in disbelief. '*When* did you use it?' (As if that matters.)

'Ah. Could've been a few weeks, maybe a month ago?'

'And you didn't think to write it on the shopping list?'

'I thought you knew, or would have noticed or something.' My husband seems to think that I do a psychic stock check every night whilst he sleeps.

'Of course, how silly, how utterly irresponsible of me not to notice that you have used something,' I want to say, heavy with sarcasm. But I don't.

'How would I know? What's the pissing point of having an Emergency Supply if you then go and use it and don't replace it. Right. Dibs on not driving to the twenty-four-hour pharmacy to get some then.' I like this alternative rejoinder better, but I don't say it either.

This conversation also happened only once due to my years of experience with Andy's abuse of the Emergency Toilet Roll. We used to have a single spare roll in the bathroom. However, I soon noticed that this was not sufficiently robust. It was during one of those scary dash-to-the-hall-cupboard situations that I decided dictatorially that we needed an Ultra Emergency Toilet Roll. Within hours of the first and only time we ran the house dry of medicine (we switched to cheaper, non-branded versions when we began consuming it faster than wine), I secreted bottles of it around the house in places both visible (and thus easy for my husband to find) and less obvious (my Ultra Emergency Supply is secret and away from prying eyes — now where did I put it again?). I aim to keep at least three bottles of each medicine in the house because I'm never getting dressed in the middle of the night to go to an all-night pharmacy again. Well, when I say again . . . I didn't go, because I fluttered my eyelashes and asked my husband (who was at a disadvantage as he was dressed and I was in my PJs) to do it. But it *could* have happened.

Last week, Bubbles cried because it was time to get up ('I'm tired'), because it was time to go for a nap ('I'm NOT tired'), because it wasn't snack time ('I'm hungry'), because it was lunch ('I'm NOT hungry'), because she had to go to the toilet, because she had to wipe, because she had to wash her hands, because she was given a toy to play with, because she had a brother; pick a reason, any reason, she cried. After recognising that this level of tears was a significant deviation from even her most diva-esque *EastEnders* audition days, we concluded she had a virus.

So far, we've all been ill: sore throats, tummy bugs, coughs, tonsillitis and Bubbles even had glandular fever. But one morning, just as I'm getting out of the shower, I hear an unusual noise. A sort of strangled gurgle, and it reminds me of a cat being si —

I wrap my towel around me, dash out and find my husband comforting Nibbles. I grab a J-cloth to start clearing up the contents of Nibbles' stomach and then hand it over to my hubby as we swap jobs.

I take Nibbles to the bathroom, stand him in the bath ('It's cold') and get him out of his PJs, careful not to flick sick over me or the ceiling. He looks so sorrowful. *Poor little boy*, I think, and as he stands there naked and bemused, I reach over the bath and give him a gentle hug, to let him know that it's not his fault, that I love him; I'm rewarded with a return hug and some proper meaty hiccups followed swiftly by his throwing up all down my shower-fresh back and towel. I release an involuntary shudder. Over the months I have acclimatised to poo, but this smell brings a little bit of bile to my mouth in sympathy. *Bleurgh*. Good morning, Parenthood!

I unwrap my towel and climb into the bath with him. The shower rinses us off — and it's mid-soap that I remember just how like greased blancmange a wet child can be. Despite this, we're soon clean and I can't help wondering how long this feeling of being clean and not smelling of puke is going to last. Yesterday Bubbles was wriggling next to me on the sofa ('Are you sure you don't need a wee?') in her PJs watching TV and I thought, *My leg feels cold, how strange. What's th* —? I looked down and realised that she's (we're) sat in a puddle of her pee on the leather (argh) sofa. After I changed her jammies and swabbed my jeans, we had the 'what's more important, TV or going for a pee?' conversation (Bubbles had a non-speaking part and just nodded) for the hundredth time.

After a small, tentative breakfast (for nothing will stop Nibbles — or Bubbles — from eating, even if the last thing in his mouth was the contents of his stomach), Nibbles starts to hiccup again. These are no normal hiccups: they are loud, as regular as a metronome, and his stomach pumps convulsively beneath his tee shirt. It reminds me of that scene in *Alien*. I wise up to the warning signs and move him gingerly (to avoid hugging the puke out of him again) to the sink. I take the dirty cups out of the sink to avoid splashback. It's not ideal, but it's too far (and across way too much pale carpet) to the bathroom. I remove his slippers and socks, just in case. He sits on the counter, feet in the sink, looking rather out of sorts as the loud hiccups become mini-belches emanating from his poorly body. I stroke circles on his back and make soothing sounds.

'Can I get off now?' he asks in his lovely sweet voice.

'Just a little longer,' I suggest.

We wait for the hiccups to die down.

They don't.

The last time, there were only a few before the main show, and I'm beginning to wonder if I've been a tad hasty. We wait some more as he *huck . . . huck . . . huck . . .* huckcups. It must be nearly ten minutes now. He doesn't want to sit with his feet in the cold sink and starts to get upset. *Surely if he was going to be sick, it would have happened by now?* He's pleading with me to let him get down.

What should I do?

He seems fine, and Andy is just leaving for work (lucky sod), so I delicately carry him down and we toddle to the hallway to wave Andy off to work. I kneel down, filled with sympathy, and then turn to my son and smile as I give him a gentle touch. And he spews his breakfast all over me.

sigh

A deep, resonating sigh that comes with rolling eyes and shrugged shoulders.

Time for the third shower of the day and it's not yet seven thirty.

52. Blackberries That Cost Too Much

A few months ago, I was going through my email inbox. *Delete, delete, oh for Pete's sake, delete, delete, Viagra? I wish. Delete, unsubscribe, delete, delete, shoes? Hmm, who am I kidding? Delete, delete, your uncle in Namibia? Oh purlease, delete. Am I the descendant of who? . . . delete?*

What's this? *wakes up slightly from inbox-induced stupor* Wait. *reads on*

'Are you the descendant of Ernest Steele?' asks the email. I don't know. Could be. Maybe.

sigh

All right, I'll check. *rustles through her research folders* *Yes, yes I am.* I read further and it's the email signature that really snags my attention — it comes with an abbreviation that everyone knows. The BBC.

Now I am triple-espresso awake and my body is quivering. Years ago, I uploaded my family tree to various websites in the midst of a Sherlockian endeavour to discover the furthest reaches of my ancestry. The email says they are searching for the descendants of Ernest Steele. And I'm one of them. My giddyometer hits the danger zone, and I tell myself repeatedly to calm down. This has the same impact on me as it does when I say it to my kids (i.e., zero). My brain takes over and sceptically suggests that maybe this is a windup; the BBC's contacting liddle ol' me is about as likely as my being headhunted by an agency to oust Cindy Crawford (who also studied chemical engineering) from her supermodel perch. I plaster composure over my excitement and reply to the questions they've asked without getting all weird and star-struck (like the time I went up to the lead singer of the Stranglers in a nightclub then stood in front of him opening and closing my mouth like a guppy fish until Claire came and spoke for me, as though we were in a weird ventriloquist act).

The next day I have a phone chat with a producer from the BBC and I might as well be talking to the Queen I'm so polite and deferential and confused. She knows quite a bit about Ernest, so I conclude that she is either from the Beeb or is taking part in an elaborate and well-researched hoax — but since no one has rung since the kids touched down, a windup of this scale seems highly unlikely. The mysterious They want me to travel to London and France (!) at the end of May, just a few weeks away. I gasp in excitement. Then reality hits — how can I take part? I'm a mum with two kids to look after and it's too soon to give them to someone else and how can I just up and leave at this crucial time?

I talk it through with Andy and we agree that this is an opportunity of a lifetime and somehow we'll make it work. I ring back and say yes then frown at the logistics of it all and just as my brain aches, the presenter has to go to South Africa and the whole trip is postponed until September and I snatch success from the jaws of crushing defeat.

It's now late September and the plans are in place: one night in London then two in France. Three nights in a bed without having to fight over the duvet or prod him when he snores or poke him when the kids wake up. Three nights of sleep unbroken by toddlers. Stuff the filming. The BBC who? The idea of uninterrupted sleep and a lie-in: I can barely pack my bag quickly enough. This is going to be awesome.

Super exciting. And also surreal.

Since Andy's working and the Beeb are paying expenses, I've found someone to look after the kids. We've been a family for six months, and these will be my first days away. Bubbles will go to preschool in the morning and then will join Nibbles at Naomi's. Naomi is a lovely childminder whose daughter is in Bubbles' class. I see her daily at the playground — she is funky, edgy, cool and seems incongruous with a pram, but there's a softness in her eyes and manner that makes me feel woefully inadequate as a mum (how do people take all this stuff in their stride when it threatens to topple me daily?). Last week we went over to her house to play, to see if the children would like it and to reassure me that she wasn't going to go all Sweeney Todd on them. The house was spacious and light with a huge open-plan downstairs and plenty of toys that drew them in immediately such that neither of them wanted to leave. 'Would you like to come again?' I asked. Both nodded enthusiastically and Bubbles said, 'Yes please.' I'm comforted to know that Naomi has minded lots of children and raised a rugby-seven of her own so knows a truckload more about looking after kids than I do.

It's time for me to catch a train to London. I'm in the playground and my legs have stopped responding to signals from my brain: I don't want to leave. My arms are shaking, my eyes are blurry, my face is blotchy and I'm not holding it together one bit.

'I'm going to Naomi's today,' says Bubbles with a big grin. Then she sees my sad face and diplomatically adds, 'But I'll miss you, Mummy.' She gives me a long hug and skips into class.

One down, one to go.

I hand Nibbles over to Naomi and he starts crying. She lifts him up and cuddles him and starts to walk away and the tears and the blubbing start and I can't stop. I want to run after him and never let go. Naomi looks at me gently but sternly and mouths, 'Go.'

I turn to walk home, to start my adventure and my chest is tight with the pain of separation. I can hear his tears and cries as I turn my back and I feel overwhelming guilt for deserting him. Barely able to see, I wipe my tears crossly from my face as I stride away head down. I want to change my mind, to tell the BBC to shove it, to charge across the playground with *Matrix*-style cool, sweep Nibbles into my arms, kiss his tears away, hug him until he can barely breathe and tell him I will never, ever let him go.

But I keep my head down and carry on walking. Naomi texts me to let me know he's stopped crying (way before I do). After a train ride, I get to London and settle in. I am hoping for a brilliant sleep, but nerves and traffic — and a pillow that even after some serious Hong Kong Phooey is too lumpy or too tall or too hard or too something — leave me feeling less than refreshed (d'oh).

Then I'm in the middle of who knows where in London, with a camera and fluffy boom mic invading my personal space, being quizzed by Fergal Keane. Suddenly we're rolling and he says something then turns to me (he's looking at me? what did he say?) and I'm all confused.

'I don't know.'

He frowns and turns to have a huddle with the producer as my brain slowly comes online. I rewind and work out what the heck he's talking about. The filming is interrupted by traffic, sirens, pigeons, dogs, pedestrians, sirens again (I forget this is London) and planes. But after the shaky start, I mostly enjoy the rather strange experience of being driven to various locations and asked random questions. We do a first take and then repeat the dialogue (trying to act surprised and remember what faces we pulled) for different angles because we have only one cameraman.

I am kidnapped by the film crew. I can't take a break or wander off, I don't know where I am, where I'm going next, how long things will last or even when I might eat or drink or have a pee. We drive to the next location, searching for a particular house number. I spot it out of the window and say, 'Wow!' The chatter in the car turns to awkward silence, and their blunder is obvious. It is my ancestor's house, which I've never seen before, and they would've preferred to capture my reaction on camera. But there's no undoing it now.

I'm so caught up in this experience that I don't have time to fret about the children. In fact, I only think about them when Naomi sends me videos and texts to reiterate how fine they are without me.

I return home for the weekend, fly to France on Sunday and meet with the crew again on Monday morning after another less than blissful night of sleep (gah). We have coffee and juice in a tiny village café, and then Fergal and the crew drive off for some secret filming. The producer and I potter about, in and out of the car, around the tiny church, kicking our heels for hours with nothing much more to do than sip some bottled water. I wish I'd brought a book. Then everyone arrives back in a hustle, and I ask for the loo (which seems to surprise them, even though they plied us with drinks two hours ago and I've been seriously considering having a sneaky wee in the bushes for at least an hour). We meet the town mayor, which is rather splendid, and I'm given a lovely letter to thank me for coming to their village and honouring all the men who came from the UK to fight for their town's people.

It's all wait ... wait ... stand here ... filming ... wait ... wait ... (bored, nice view though) ... get in the car ... wait ... wait ... get out ... they go off in a huddle ... I'm going to ask you about this ... filming ... wait ... come here.

Late that afternoon I'm stood by the road next to a field of cut straw in the baking hot sunshine as Fergal explains how they'll use an app on his iPad to locate the exact position of the trenches. Then we're off, walking over the field, the straw making a *crunch, crunch, crunch* sound beneath my feet and I'm thinking, *Surely the microphones are going to hear that crunching?*

'It was the morning of September 18, 1918, when Ernest was shot by a sniper on this very spot and killed.'

What? I mean I knew he didn't survive the war, but that's a bit sudden dropping it on me like that.

Fergal slinks away and leaves me standing there alone.

I don't really know how to react.

Well, of course I know how I *should* react, how any normal feeling person would react to this news, and how they're probably hoping or expecting me to react, but it is all so bizarre that I can't seem to feel anything. The cameraman and sound guy circle me for the best angle on a tear that never falls. Given that I cry at the slightest thing, like the lovely homeliness of the Bisto advert or when celebrities get voted off *Strictly*, I'm surprised how emotionally constipated I am on camera. I visit Ernest's grave and put flowers on it, and again, nothing. I'm given a copy of his diaries and two buttons from the coat that he was wearing when he was killed, and whilst I'm moved by this treasure, the tears stay inside, right until the camera is off and I'm in the taxi back to the airport, when they flow like wine after the kids are in bed. On the journey to Paris, I'm moved by just how many graveyards pepper this land. Each headstone is a life lost to war, and they're more poignant and immediate than the letters engraved on crosses at home. It is the sheer scale and number of these graves that plays a melancholy tune in my soul and drives home what we lost when we won the war.

And before you know it, I'm home.

As I open the door, the children tumble over me, greeting me like a celebrity, saying how much they've missed me. The welcome is almost overpowering, until I tell them what I've been up to and they get bored and walk off. I'll tell Andy once they're in bed. The weather's glorious, a real Indian summer's day in September, so we all go out hunting for blackberries for tea. I'm rested, peaceful, brimming with things to say, content in the knowledge that come 7 p.m. I will have Andy's undivided attention as I recount my tales of TV stardom.

There are hundreds of ripe blackberries and we pick them carefully, avoiding the thorns. With more on the other side of the flattened wall, Andy jumps over, stumbles, and then falls.

he screams

Like a lion. Raw. Intense. Powerful.

A sound I've never heard him make before. And as I look, his face displays all the screams he's still holding inside. His face is as colourless as lard.

I gulp down the queasiness in my throat, put down my tub of blackberries and murmur 'it's okay' to the kids despite the fact that even they can work out it isn't.

Something's horribly wrong.

Andy tries to push himself off the ground, screams some more and wobbles because the pain is making him faint. I try to keep him upright but he weighs more than my arms can hold, so I snuggle behind his back to stop him keeling over and hitting his head on the wall, which isn't going to make things better. He tries to talk but it's all slurry nonsense. I think he's trying to say that he's fine, but the garbled noises and his inability to sit up on his own belie that line. The children stare with confusion. Bubbles wants to help, so she picks a blackberry and offers it to him.

'Go away,' he barks.

He doesn't want to fall on her and hurt her, but his words hurt her more. I try to comfort the kids but I'm not sure how convincing

I am. We wait a few minutes, until his wooziness clears and he can sit without causing himself another injury.

'Shall I call an ambulance?' I ask, though why I'm asking him I don't know.

'I'm fine.'

'You're not. You nearly fainted.'

'No, I didn't,' says the refusenik.

'Just stay put while I go and get the car. Promise me you won't move — promise?'

'I won't move.'

I go to walk away, but Nibbles doesn't want to leave Daddy and they both get upset and start to scream. Andy needs to get to hospital, he's my priority, so I drag them unceremoniously home to get the car. We drive back to the footpath and I dash out.

Andy has, of course, moved.

'I told you to wait,' I say, fuming. 'What if you'd fainted? That would have made things worse!' As you'll know by now, calmness in the face of calamity is not an attribute that you'll find on my résumé.

I drop him at A&E, take the kids home and do the whole teatime and bedtime routine whilst texting Andy to find out what the X-rays have revealed. His ankle is broken (apparently not for the first time, although that's news to him). He gets a lift home from a friend and limps in on crutches; his leg and ankle are in a plaster that will be on for at least six weeks. *Six weeks? Someone else to look after*, I think. My heart sinks with the extra burden of it all.

For the first time in months I have amazing headline news to share and it's not even about the kids. Life silences me and relegates me to page two. Andy has newsbombed me and grabbed the headlines for himself. A broken ankle trumps the BBC, and I can't help feeling that those blackberries cost too much.

53. Melting the Iceberg

Why me? What did I do to deserve this? Why did Andy have to go and break his ankle? Why is this so hard? I wish we'd never gone blackberry picking. Oh woe is me.

I'm one fed-up Emma coping with three toddlers as Andy hobbles around doing a credible impression of a newborn giraffe, all spindly and unstable. Instead of channelling Florence Nightingale, I'm huffing at all this extra bother. *He can't even pick the children up or put a plate in the dishwasher. What use is he?*

And I discover just why I couldn't (and can't) do it without him. This extra load is tipping me over the precipice. How do single parents manage? I barely (in other words, don't) have the patience to parent, never mind brew endless cups of tea for His Lordship and take over all his daddy duties (the late and night shifts). I know I'm sulking, but I just can't help it. My slice of sanity (i.e., our weekend walks), the one time the kids don't fight or argue, is a bust. And don't get me started about how much he spins and wriggles and knocks my ankle with his stupid cast as he tries to get comfy in bed. Less sleep is not helping my mood; it swings from fuming to frustrated and back.

The doctors have told him not to get the plaster wet, but there's only so much a flannel-wash can do, and the idea of a bath gets under his skin. When he starts to whiff like that brie we shoved to the back of the fridge and forgot about for months, I run him a bath and we wrap his leg in plastic carrier bags and duct tape — an improvised waterproof wellie. Hopping him into a full bath is not the most elegant thing we've ever done together, and I am not even slightly tempted to join him and his three weeks of sloughed-off skin.

At first he lounges on the sofa during the daytime as the children trip over his even-more-hazardous-than-usual leg, but within days the novelty of not ironing shirts for work wears off and he's had enough of watching News24. So he balances his laptop on his cast and taps away precariously at work whilst I try to give Nibbles something to do to stop the endless stream of 'what you doing?' that isn't raising Andy's spirits one iota.

'I'm off to get Bubbles,' I say one morning, as Nibbles and I coat up to leave.

'But I've only just got going.'

Welcome to my world. 'Goes quick, doesn't it?' I say, just to rub the lesson in.

After four months at work, he's at home 24/7, immersed against his will in family life, bound to the unyielding daytime routines of preschool and naps because I'm in charge. He wants sympathy for his poorly ankle (here: *diddums*), without ever offering me equal sympathy for the pain in the neck that is my husband on crutches. For those of you who gasped at my total lack of compassion, this is just further evidence that I should never be a nurse. Under normal circumstances (BC, with plenty of sleep) I might have had a day-or-more's empathy to shower on my beloved, but my empathy balance is in serious overdraft — no bank will touch the size of my debt.

But in a slow process of osmosis (no thanks to my PhD for that one; that's O-level biology), things start to change. He spends many, many more hours with the children. They badger him to read whilst sitting on his lap, beg him to play with them, involve him in their games and imagination, take him plate after plate of pretend meals, cover his cast in stickers and hang around him like teenagers outside a chippy. At first he wants to swat them away like midges that ruin the fun of sitting on your balcony on holiday, but eventually he realises that resistance is futile — the more he tries to ignore them or push them away, the more they adore him and try to win him over with attention and hugs and stroking his arm and telling him they love him. And it turns out, that barrage of attention is exactly what the doctor ordered. As his leg heals, his heart melts a microscopic amount. The distance between him and his children starts to close, like the movement of a glacier over many months; it's invisible to the naked eye, but over weeks, time-lapse photography reveals the flow of ice down the valley and the changing landscape. Andy starts to feel less like he is 'babysitting someone else's children', and more like their daddy. Maybe it's because he gets to have more fun with them and isn't caught up in just the breakfast and bedtime routines.

When I notice the thaw and ask what has changed, he says he doesn't really know. I'm not about to push it, so I simply thank my lucky stars. It is no overnight awakening, but during this enforced rest, he starts to fall in love with them, the way he did with the idea of them when they were just photos and video clips, before all the responsibilities and tiredness overwhelmed us. As his broken ankle mends, so our family is mended too. By the time his plaster is removed, our family feels strong and solid and in a single piece. We'll walk into our future together, all the big doubts and faltering steps behind us, singing, 'We Are Family'.

Welcome home, Daddy.

(I missed you.)

54. The Incredible Sulk

It's half-term. Life has settled into a term-time routine, such that it is weekends or school holidays where out-of-the-ordinary stories (and hence chapters for this book) arise. The newness of being parents has worn off. It's like buying a new car — the vehicle gradually stops surprising you and you can even ('Found it!') put the fog lights on *before* the fog clears. They are just our children and we get on with being parents without getting fazed by every single meltdown or vomit rainbow. Or by Nibbles' putting on every item of clothing he owns so he looks like a WWF wrestler and we're running late so we have to try and strap him in the car with all those layers on. Or by Bubbles' deciding to test our mettle by saying she's not hungry (aka doesn't want *this* for tea) and her look of outrage when we tell her to just drink her water or else get down and play (and then wailing because she's changed her mind).

It's incredible how quickly you can settle into a new normal — this is our first half-term, and it's a shock to look after both children full-time again. I've been researching activities for days out and rainy days in.

'I'm so excited,' says Bubbles, wriggling in her car seat. Her hands clench and unclench in Morse code, spelling out her excitement in case her fevered movements weren't obvious enough. When I asked the kids what animals they most wanted to see at the zoo, Nibbles said 'ogres'. He may be disappointed.

Today is not just a day out during half-term though. A trip to the zoo wasn't even on my list (Andy and I find them morally ambiguous), and we aren't certain that we're doing the right thing, but we said we would, and no one has categorically told us not to, so we are. It's six months since we adopted our children and we're going to meet up with their foster carers, Ken and Mary.

Bubbles really misses them and still talks about them, though not as often as she did when she first arrived. To help her talk about her feelings, we put up a photo of Ken and Mary in her bedroom and told her about how much they love her and wanted her to have a wonderful family. But there's no clear precedent. The cases for and against continued contact with their foster family are based on rumour and belief rather than hard evidence. We hope it will help with their life story work if they have memories of Ken and Mary, but will it? Bubbles and Nibbles each have a book that Mary spent hours creating; these books chart the time they spent with their foster family in photos and annotations, and we look at the books together every few months (I swot up on the things I don't know). Our social workers don't agree on whether it's good for the children (some say yes, some no). Could seeing Ken and Mary again harm them? We don't think so. I guess we're about to find out.

We're doing it partly to appease our guilt for the grief the foster family suffered on the day we took the kids home; it's a peace offering. We made a promise, and as empty as we all thought it was, it's one we're honouring today. I've sent photos and kept in touch by text, but the children haven't seen or heard from them since Handover. Bubbles remembers them and some of their experiences together (though she also remembers things that never happened, like breaking her leg), but Nibbles hasn't a clue and can't even tell us if they had a cat or a dog.

We're meeting them at a café, and as we approach, my heart pumps hard and I feel strangely lightheaded. The building is tall, light, all glass and wood. I push open the double doors to let my giddy daughter rush in. The children scan the empty tables before I point to the left, and they zoom in on Ken and Mary. Ken walks slowly over, wiping the tears from his eyes, says a manly 'hello' to us, and then his face breaks into a broad grin as he bends down to Nibbles. Mary's all sing-song, 'Who's this then? I've missed you,' as she swoops in on Bubbles and catches up on a thousand hugs. Something deep inside Nibbles recognises Ken's voice because his normal shyness around strangers is replaced by a willingness to be picked up and held.

We share hugs and hellos and aren't-you-looking-wells and then toddle into the zoo. Andy tags along but I feel somewhat superfluous.

Months ago, in those first exhausting days when Andy was still on parental leave, we went to a local wildlife sanctuary.

'Owl,' I said to Bubbles as I lifted her in my arms so she could see the owl at the top of the cage.

'Owl,' she responded, and I thought, *How clever.* Then I noticed she was pointing to the photo taped on the front of the cage.

'Owl,' I said more forcefully, pointing through the bars to the back of the cage, in the other direction.

'Owl,' she responded, again pointing to the photo. There began an exchange that lasted about ten rounds before I gave up and let her miss the point of going to an animal sanctuary; we could've just looked in a book. The animals here are more exotic, reflecting the exorbitant entrance fee. There are spectacled bears, rhinos, monkeys, zebras; Andy is in his element, contradicting the little I 'know' about animals with his Wikipedian knowledge based on three decades of relentlessly consuming (and remembering, which is where we differ) the entire back catalogue of David Attenborough.

As we walk, I turn into the Incredible Sulk.

I feel slighted by my children as they dote on Ken and Mary, who return the attention in spades (though I also feel a smidgen of pride at how lovely the children are acting in public). I am not good at playing third fiddle, fourth if you include their interest in the animals, and I wince when Ken and Mary carry the children (*They can walk!*), but since no one notices my sulking, I eventually give myself a talking to and get over myself. I gawp at the animals and hand over responsibility to everyone else; the day becomes quite relaxing.

We turn a corner and there is a huge pool with a large glass side wall. Bubbles rushes alongside it chasing her brother until some penguins swoop by underwater. Her body grinds to a sudden stop, her face swivels and her mouth drops open, instantly captivated.

'Mummy,' she cries (and I buff my nails on my top, for mine was the name she cried out). 'Look! They are soooo fast!' She watches transfixed as several penguins glide past again and again in a circuit. She runs along next to them, barging other spectators out of her way in her enthusiasm. I apologise bashfully to the parents of the children she knocks over as I steer her out of the way of a wheelchair. She is entranced and I can't help but smile.

It's the giraffes that steal Nibbles' heart. As we approach their tall house, he looks uninterested, unable to work out what there is to see. Then he looks up. His eyes widen in total shock, darting up and up and up to find their heads. A broad smile spreads slowly across his face and his eyes twinkle.

'Want one,' he declares earnestly.

'Which one do you want?' asks Andy, inquisitively.

'Tall one, Daddy.'

'Where would we keep it?' I ask, with a practicality that's not entirely necessary.

'In the garden, Mummy.' A bright and logical solution. 'Can we take one home, Daddy?' he asks, recognising that he's more likely to get a yes from Andy. He takes it well when Andy says no.

We have a meal at the restaurant and I grit my teeth as Ken and Mary cut up the children's food (*They can do it themselves!*). I focus on my food and breathe, breathe, breathe. We take a trip on the monorail and they sit on Ken's and Mary's knees until Bubbles notices my quivering bottom lip, comes over and sits on my lap, saying she doesn't want me to feel 'left out'. This cures my sulk by replacing it with the hollow feeling of petty vindictiveness. This is ludicrous. It's not a competition; we're not going to stand at either end of the zoo with the kids in the middle and then crouch over, patting our knees and whistling for them to come to us, like a divorcing couple fighting over their beloved pooch. Andy is characteristically chill and hasn't even noticed there's anything wrong (I'd need a neon sign to wrestle his attention from the rhinos).

And then it's time to leave. Ken and Mary buy them cuddly toys, and I take photos of them with the kids (and toys) in their arms as tears well up in Ken's eyes and Mary puts on her brave face.

As we drive back, I realise that I'm jealous of the time that my children spent with their foster family — Ken and Mary got to experience things I missed, like Nibbles' first steps and first words. Today I pranged myself on the corners of the Adoption Square, for

I'm not their only mum. They have birth parents and foster carers. I'm the third in a line of mums, and even though I'm their forever mum, today was a visceral experience of how I fit into their life.

Despite the pouting, I think we've done the right thing, both for our children and for their foster family. Ken and Mary are not just names; they're a living and breathing part of their lives, they love them a huge amount (a bit too much for my liking) and spoil them in a way that I can't afford to right now. They are people to whom I am eternally grateful.

For they turned my children into the two young lives I fell in love with all those months ago.

55. A Fountain Pen of Fantasy

I've just got a letter to write and then I can snuggle down in front of the tele for mummy-time.

Forty-five minutes later and my head bangs in frustration on my desk. My fingers are stained with ink. I sweep the sea of crumpled-paper balls off the desk in a rage and shake my head in disbelief. Except of course I don't, for I live in a digital age, so instead I have software pretending to be paper. Forty-five minutes and a word count of . . . wait for it . . . zero. Hundreds of words typed, read and then deleted in frustration.

I'm not writing a story, so it's not my imagination that's at fault. I used to (note the past tense — before my brain was addled by nappies, tiredness and Spot books) write blogs and articles all the time. I've even written a book or two. No, I'm writing a letter, and I've written hundreds of letters, for I grew up before email (in the olden days). I would write letters to my family and boyfriends when we were apart. And Sarah and I used to swap Jane-Austen-style pretentiousness — all '*My darling and most precious sister, how extraordinarily delighted I was to receive your latest missive*' and so forth — devoid of news but filled with Dickensian nonsense which made me snort with laughter. But this is no ordinary letter. It's a bit like a Christmas letter without the unnecessary boasting: '*Darling Bubbles is precociously talented at the harpsichord and just last week she composed her second concerto, whilst Nibbles, who hero-worships Edison, confidently expects to patent his pocket-sized pushchair in the next week or so, although I've helped him a little with spelling the trickier words in his submission.*'

I type most letters in a matter of minutes, following the rules and general layout that we all know and follow. But this letter fits none of the templates I can download online. I have to choose my words carefully to provide just the right level of intimacy and disclosure without saying much at all. There are guidelines of course: things we can and cannot say. We can't mention specific locations such as towns, holidays or schools; we can't include photos; and we can't include any personal information that might help their birth parents track them down.

This is Letterbox Contact: an annual letter sent via the adoption agency to my children's birth parents. It is the only sliver of connection that their birth family has with them, and the responsibility to get it right lies heavy on me; it stifles my words so the page remains an uninterrupted swathe of white. I picture the page being folded and stored in a wallet, carried everywhere as irreplaceable treasure, taken out and unfolded and read again; I imagine the recipient searching the words they've committed to heart until the page is as fragile as butterfly wings and as precious as a love letter from a soldier who never came home.

No pressure then.

I'd rather do that essay on nihilism and Nietzsche than this. Let's bash out an opening and then we can get on to the good stuff.

'*Hello.*' Is that too cheery from the person who stole your children?

'*Morning.*' What? That's what I say to my neighbours or a stranger on the street. Too weird.

'*Dear [Names].*' Now I'm writing to my bank.

'*To whom it may concern.*' That's like flicking the Vs at them, pretending we don't even know their names, which is rude, untrue and implies we haven't told their kids they even have birth parents.

'*All hail the Almighty.*' Now I am definitely taking the piss as I steadily lose the will to live.

Gah, I can't even start this flipping thing. Let's move on and come back to that later. Perhaps the end will be easier?

'*Yours sincerely.*' No, no, no, no, no.

'*Faithfully.*' Definitely not.

'*Best wishes.*' Why is this so difficult?

'*Love.*' Really? Talk about rubbing their noses in it.

FFS why isn't any of this easy? I write '*We read books every night*' and wince — it sounds like a middle-class boast: 'We can afford to buy books just for the heck of it.' I think about something totally harmless, like their favourite foods, and dither over another minefield. Whilst I know they love potato dauphinoise (who doesn't? it's glorious), writing about it would make me look like *(a)* I am bragging that I have the time and culinary expertise to slice potatoes and smother them with cream; *(b)* we're rich enough to drench the cheapest food known to man in something rather more luxurious; *(c)* I think plain old mash is too lowbrow for our little darlings; and *(d)* I am already teaching my kids French (I'm not, although I'm hoping to get away with *merde* a little longer). Yet if I honestly write that, like most kids, their favourite foods are pizza and ice cream then I look like the sort of mum who feeds her darlings chips through the school railings after Jamie Oliver balances the nutrition in school dinners. Every single phrase is censored and redacted until there's nothing of substance left.

I try and put myself in the birth family's shoes, thinking about how I'd feel to receive one of these letters. I'd want to devour every tiny detail about my children, to catch a glimpse into their lives like a child sneaking a look through a mysterious neighbour's letterbox to find clues in dusty sunbeams that shine onto secrets in a narrow hall. What would I want to read?

I search online for advice and, since I'm not the first person ever to write a contact letter, discover useful ideas for structure and content. I type and delete endless variations and am unhappy with all of them, so I go all factual: '*Here is a letter about Bubbles and Nibbles.*' It is awful, impersonal and I hate it, but I can't seem to think of anything else, for acting as if they are my friends feels fake too; it stays. I swing dangerously between two extremes — bland insincerity that makes me flinch and an electronic trail of breadcrumbs right to our front door. Why is this so hard?

I write, edit, rephrase, delete as I huff, undo the deletion, read it again, convince myself it is wrong, write something else and generally torture myself for another hour.

This letter eventually morphs into a part-fact, part-Facebook version of our lives: sanitised and overly positive. I end up with a 'skipping through a wild-flower meadow in the sunshine' version, studiously avoiding the rain, hay fever and dog poo. I tell them that the children went to the beach and loved jumping over the waves because it's vague. There is something levelling about the beach; it unites us all regardless of class, wealth, education or other. I write about reading and eating, about going to preschool and their love of the park, and whilst I try to inject these stale descriptions with the children's personalities by mentioning their favourite books and shows and things to do, there isn't a great deal to say about these two young lives. They toddle. They eat. They sleep. They cry. They poo. They scribble. They plead to go to the park in the midst of a hailstorm then insist on watching TV the minute the sun comes out. They inhale pizza in a single gulp but eat veggies one tiny *petit pois* at a time until I am banging my head on the table ('"*Petit pois*"? What's wrong with goddamn "peas"?' I hear you cry; how bourgeoisie). I don't mention PooGate or the Guilty Shoes or the Asda Meltdown. I end by promising to write next year and saying we hope to get a letter in return.

It takes me two hours to write a few hundred words and I am less than happy with the result; with the rich details removed, it feels like a letter written home from boarding school but without the mater and pater salutations. It's as full of holes as my knitting. I have an empty feeling inside me, nagging me that I haven't said enough, for if these were my children there would never be enough words. Before I lose all confidence, I post it off and draw a line under it. Maybe next year will be easier.

Whilst Andy and I wrote the letter as their parents (okay I wrote it, showed it to Andy and he mumbled 'fine' in a tone that said 'it's not great but I can't think of anything better'), we aren't actually their parents yet. We're just their carers. The legal adoption process began a few weeks ago, six months after Handover.

We write to them because it is the right thing to do — it's both the least and the most we can do. We write to them because one day, when our children are old enough to ask questions and get answers, we can show Bubbles and Nibbles the letters we wrote every single year to their birth parents, whether or not we get letters back; a yearly snapshot recording of how our family has changed over the years.

We write these letters so our children know that we did our best.

56. Balancing on the Tightrope

I'm walking back from preschool with Vicky, mum to Bubbles' best friend, who's expecting her second quite soon. She's sharing her hopes and fears, confident she's talking to someone who has the 'mum of two' tee shirt, and I'm fit to burst because I can't join in the conversation the way she expects me to. I'm about to fall off the Adoption Tightrope.

I haven't worked out when to drop the A-bomb into the friendships that blossom at the school gates by virtue of simply being in the same place with nothing to do, day in, day out.

'He might grow to be as tall as his dad,' the mums comment when conversation turns to my son, followed by an apocryphal story about a child who grew from a small bean into a one-hundred-foot beanstalk one night in his sleep.

'Yes, he might,' I respond with a smirk — because they mean Andy (the giant), and I mean his birth dad (not a giant). And I wonder now why I find this petty secret amusing. When am I going to grow up and get over myself? Not by the end of this book, that's for sure (I wrote 'fo sho' but decided I couldn't get away with it).

I quickly flounder in conversations about pregnancy, childbirth, breastfeeding, weaning, learning to walk, first words and a host of other things I've no idea about. When someone asked me, 'How was your pregnancy?' I nearly swallowed my tongue before hastily blurting out 'pretty normal', only to discover that no one on earth has ever described those nine months as normal. Everyone stared at me as if I'd said 'like an orangutan's'.

As Vicky and I waddle and talk, I start with a few 'uh-huhs' but we soon stray into foreign territory that has me squirming inside. I'm waiting for the right time to chuck in the A-bomb. She talks about the balancing act of looking after two, and finishes with this throwaway comment: 'You know how it is.'

This is my moment. My chance to shed the veil of duplicity that's damming the flow of conversation and giving me the sort of indigestion that is going to end with wind. I have to say something because she's expecting some wise words to let her know it'll be okay. Words I don't have.

'Vicky, to be honest, I don't know how it is.'

She stops mid-waddle.

I stop too.

She turns and looks at me, her face all 'is she pulling my leg?'

I answer her face: 'I've never *had* children, so no, I don't know how it is.' Is that clearer? Maybe not. Her mouth drops, and she seems to be struggling to say something. Lordy, why is this so difficult?

'But you have two kids . . .' she says, and I nod.

'I adopted my children, Vicky, so no, I don't really know what you're going through.' It's an admission of failure; I never managed to get pregnant. Mostly, she looks relieved. The shock and confusion glide off her expression, although she's still suspicious, as if I'm joking.

'But they look just like you,' she says, as if trying to convince me that I did indeed go through a birthing process (twice) and have simply mislaid that memory the way my husband loses his keys. As if what she sees with her eyes contradicts the facts. I nod and retain a friendly but stern expression so that she knows this is no joke.

She starts walking slowly, shaking her head slightly.

'I couldn't have kids,' I say, and for once, this confession doesn't matter one jot — she doesn't say sorry, or treat me like I have cancer. She just asks how old the children were when we adopted them. As we walk some more, we talk about our experiences and how different they are. The air is fresher between us and it feels good to come out from behind the blanket of half-truths and misdirection that I've hidden behind. It marks a change in our relationship: I've shared my not-secret-but-not-on-a-billboard-either truth with her and it deepens our friendship. I am their mum, they

269

are my children and the first few years when we were apart will matter less and less as they grow up with us.

The tightrope is lower now.

Less scary.

But I'm still not ready to wear an 'I adopted my kids' tee shirt.

57. Nibbles Ad Libs

Bubbles is at preschool, and Nibbles and I are reading together in the peace and simplicity of one adult with one child. I've reached a level of parenting skill where this kind of thing feels ordinary, and so I sometimes worry that I'm not fully present with my children. The days are now orders of magnitude less exhausting than those in the first whirlwind months. Mostly there isn't much to say about my days with Nibbles, which start to blend into each other like an amorphous mass of grey Play-Doh speckled with blobs of pink or yellow. We take Bubbles to preschool, wash up or do some laundry, read a bit, play catch with a balloon, Nibbles tells me to 'get it' because his car is lost under the kitchen table and I say that since he pushed it there he can go and get it, and before you know it, he's behind me, patting my bum and giving me a shove, sternly demanding I 'get it', and I laugh so hard I need a Tena and then we go and collect Bubbles.

But this day is about to become memorable.

I ask Nibbles to put on his coat and get his shoes so we can start the long process of getting to the playground to wait for the door to open at half past eleven. He ambles back into the kitchen, coat in hand, as I'm wiping up the glue splodges and glitter grenades that scarily reproduce faster than debt on a payday loan. Something stops me mid-wipe.

'Love Mummy,' he says.

I play the mannequin game then nearly keel over like a fainting goat.

Everything stops.

My heart is pounding in my chest. I want to rewind. I want to experience this heart-stopping moment again. All the frantic hurry-up of getting to school on time and removing all traces of glitter (because Andy is allergic to those sparkly squares of fun) evaporates. Tears well up in my eyes and my face softens.

In the months the children have been living with us, Nibbles' language has grown word by word, phrase by phrase. He's said these words before, but only as an echo, a predictable response in the well-rehearsed 'love you/love you too' script (which sometimes includes a competitive 'love you more' or 'love you high as the sky'). I grin when they say, 'I love you to the supermarket and back,' or 'I love you to the stars and back and then to Aunty Sally's.' These declarations are touching and sweet but they're part of a game and lack the impact of Nibbles' declaration. He has voluntarily expressed that feeling to me; he's ad-libbed.

I skip, dance, nearly sing with joy.

I am delighted, speechless.

But not without ego.

I go over to him and kneel down.

'What did you say?' I ask. *I want to make sure that I heard right,* I tell myself, but really, I ask the question because those two words were possibly the sweetest thing that has ever jumped from one person to another.

'Love you, Mummy,' he says again, his eyes shining bright with meaning.

I hug the breath out of him in a boa embrace as I imprint this exact moment on my soul. He hugs me back and we relish this clinch that I never want to sto —

He pulls away and puts his shoes on, oblivious to my happiness or his impact on his marshmallow mummy. During the Intensive Training I shared my fear that one day they would say 'you're not my mummy'; my counterpoint hope was to one day hear them say 'I love you, Mummy'.

Today I heard it and my soul vibrates with the love that binds us all.

I float to school impervious to drizzle or poo, hearing Katrina and her Waves in my ears.

58. How to Upstage a Magician

It's Christmas — a time of traditions and rituals and a Scrooge of a husband who hates Christmas and its rampant consumerism and would rather hibernate until it's all over. The kids are super excited about it and about their presents, even though Nibbles has asked for only sticks, leaves and stones. It's a time of goodwill to all man; wrapping up warm; toddler nativities that turn me to mush; stupidly expensive credit card bills; mountains of nasty plastic toys that take forever to untie from their packaging and break within seconds of being opened; stealing batteries out of the remote and then yelling 'Turn it off!' when *Corrie* comes on and you can't change the channel; untangling tree lights; and getting so bored you eat and drink so much that you can't wait for fresh air and a diet to reset your slovenly body.

The new leather of our family has stretched, yielding to the new additions, becoming suppler; we all feel more comfortable together. Andy and I look at our children now and see the mischievous, loving imps from the DVD that Ken shot all those months ago, and sometimes we even sigh with satisfaction and think to ourselves, 'We made it.' Seven months on and things are getting easier, calmer. I no longer feel scared of what the day or night might throw up (unless it's that, which doesn't faze me but still makes me gag). I feel like I've finally earned my stripes as their mummy. Although of course, the minute I feel as if I know what I'm doing, they move the goalposts and I have to learn a whole new skill, like how to manage the hyper-caffeinated version of my children that coincides with the annual influx of toys and stuff that has me hyperventilating into paper bags.

And the traditions of a childless couple at Christmas (champagne for breakfast and lazing in our PJs in front of a roaring fire) also need to stretch. I'm scrolling through the outside world on FB one day and notice someone's mischievous Elf on a Shelf; my brain sparks. That evening, I get a small toy Rudolph out of the loft — he's going to create fun, havoc and mischief every evening and tax my brain and Andy's as we try to invent new things to surprise the kids with in the morning. Rudolph decorates the tree with their tiny socks, flies across the lounge in a hot air balloon, builds a book house, races other Christmas decorations across the kitchen table, wraps up some presents, gets mummified with sticky notes, bakes a cake, gets stuck in a jam jar, steals cornflakes for an early breakfast and more. The first morning (cornflakes), the kids' eyes shoot to the ceiling in delight.

'Muuuuuuuuuuuuummy! He's got cornflakes!'

'Oy, that's my bowl. Naughty Rudolph.'

Massive grins and giddy excitement and the scene is set for a little bit of magic to offset the grumpy daddy. It's the start of a new Christmas tradition.

It's Twixtmas and we're gathered in a function room. The room is dark, packed with unsteady toddlers tripping over each other in the gloom, and we weave through and find a space to sit, searching the heady heights of adulthood for a glimpse of friends to nod to or air-kiss in recognition. Seats surround a dark and suspect carpet (the paisley design fails to hide the stains). One table hosts a buffet swaddled in cling film, another keeps a tottering tower of presents in check as new arrivals search for a space to set their offering.

We are at a children's party.

I squirm at these things, as out of place as a flamingo at a snooker tournament. I say things like 'Is she yours?' or 'How do you know Bev?' whilst pretending not to track our children like lions stalking wildebeest. At mealtime, I coo encouragingly about cucumber and fruit, hoping they'll choose a balanced diet amongst a table heaving with chips, crisps, pizza, cake, cheese, biscuits, lard and one tiny sacrificial tomato.

Children's parties are no longer the at-home events of my childhood, for parents have worked out that it's much easier to hand over responsibility to someone else and save themselves a morning of buttering sarnies and an evening of bleaching the floor. This party has a whole new vibe though — there's an entertainer.

The children sit in a poorly executed semicircle. If that boy on the right edged forward about four inches, and that poppet in the *Frozen* dress nudged to her left about a foot then the semicircle would be so much neater. I yearn to be on a lonely beach and breathe in the peace and solitude; this is the very antithesis of that moment, all chaos and noise, gloom and claustrophobia, so rearranging the semicircle gives me something to focus on that isn't how icky the carpet feels when I accidentally put my hand down on it; the bare flesh winces at the texture it's not expecting.

The entertainer is pulling things out of a hat with a flourish, losing the crowd. The parents roll their eyes. I've coughed up phlegm that's more exciting than this. Any minute he's going to pull some crappy flowers out of his sleeve . . . There he goes. Blimey. Time to play Which Child Is the Snottiest?, a game for all OCD parents to play (where's the hand sanitiser?). Just as I'm about to choose a winner, things get interesting.

'Would anyone like to come up?' The words are barely out of his mouth when my daughter jumps up, runs over, turns to the audience and grabs the mic, which I'm not even sure was offered, out of his hand. It surprises the heck out of me. *That's my little girl*, I think. I'm proud yet cautious. *What is she doing?* followed swiftly by *Please don't embarrass me.*

The 'magician' starts to talk to her about his act. 'Do you like magic?' he asks, enticing her into the routine.

'My name is Bubbles,' she announces loudly and proudly. I stare open-mouthed at her confidence and poise. The entertainer looks on with a kindly yet somewhat bemused expression. He gently moves her to the side and then tells a story whilst pulling some not-very-magic things out of a box and quickly loses her attention (which can be found only with a high-powered microscope at the best of times). Midway through the trick, she takes matters into her own hands. She brings the microphone to her lips (he didn't take it away from her — didn't think that through!) and decides to entertain her audience.

'That's my brother. He's called Nibbles. He is two,' she declares, pointing to her brother, who is just in front of her two somewhat baffled parents. *How sweet*, I think. *She wants to include him.*

The entertainer smiles at her and tries to recover the microphone. She holds on stubbornly; she hasn't finished.

'I am three.'

The audience laughs and I wink conspiratorially at my husband, wanting to point to her and mouth to everyone in eyeshot that she is my child, as she's making the audience laugh a whole lot more than the so-called entertainer. I love her guts, her bravado, her lack of fear. She is a little powerhouse packed with kindness and love. The sheer sense of pride and wonder I feel threatens to burst out as tears. The magician has that fixed smile that fails to reach the corners of his eyes and I wonder how long he'll endure the fact that all attention is on my daughter and he has lost centre stage. Best bit so far for me, of course.

Today I realise that at every nativity, at every prize giving, at every school play or summer games, I will be that mum: the one sobbing loudly.

Every single thing about them is incredible, these tiny little people who've changed my life.

Today my child blew me away.

Go, Bubbles.

Go, girl.

My incredible little girl.

59. Earth to Ikea

Hall. Eh. Loo. Yah. I'm free. Unshackled from the giggly chains of parenthood.

It's been four months since Bubbles started preschool, and today Nibbles starts nursery. Today started badly. He fell from a bench in the playground and cut his head open: cries from him, hugs from me and stares, glares and tuts from the other mums, who didn't see it wasn't my fault. We drop Bubbles off and then walk to his playgroup as I wonder if Nibbles will go as quietly as Bubbles did.

We go through the front door and hang up his coat and he seems okay, if a little quieter than usual. I give him a hug, nudge the door into his room ajar and he toddles through hesitantly, until: 'Toast, Nibbles?' With that, he runs away without so much as a backwards glance. As happy as I am to know that he's going to be fine, I'd like to think that I'm more important than toast. I'm not.

As I close the front door behind me, the enormity of the moment hits me. For the first time in eight months (bar the Beeb trip, where I was kind of busy), someone else will be looking after both my children. For so long they've been my whole world, my sole responsibility; now, I feel weirdly bereft without the heavy mantle of mummy-hood. Then I skip a little and walk home with a spring in my gait that says I'm over it.

I have three hours to do whatever I like.

What shall I do?

The options are endless. I could . . . umm . . . or even . . . errr. *What did I used to do? How did I spend my day?* I've forgotten who I am and what I like to do. *Work?* No. Hell no. *Walk?* I've just walked the kids (slowly) to school, so nope. My brain isn't doing a good job of coming up with something cool to do. It just shakes its head and says 'nu-uh'. Stupid mummy brain.

Finally it kicks out of neutral and churns out all manner of exciting things to do, like the cinema, a jaunt to the big town, coffee and cake, the beach, a bookshop to browse, or . . . and I can't cram this list of things that I've been yearning to do over the last eight months of house/park/shop arrest into the time left until pickup.

I choose to leave my orbit, which was put in a hot wash and shrunk the minute the kids arrived, reduced to a small ellipse of space bounded by my house, the supermarket and the school, no more than a mile in each direction. I grab my keys and handbag (having taken the nappies out) and get in my car. I put my foot to the floor and enter a galaxy far, far away. I go all the way to Ikea.

Ikea?

I just want to travel to another universe and hang out there for a while, with no kids, and feel like a grown-up again. I drive there singing to the radio without a single critique from the kids and then dash around the showroom at break-ankle speed without a single retrace-our-steps-to-go-to-the-toilet-yet-again or 'put it down' or thought about snacks. I leave with a bucketload of tea lights to add to the mountain of tea lights we already don't use given that children plus tea lights equals a burnt-down house. Content with this trivial yet symbolic purchase, I glance at my watch (phone) and drive back like the wind because I am in danger of being late.

As I drive, I wonder what they've been up to whilst I was investing in tea light futures. The narcissist in me wants to know they've missed me.

Get a grip, love; you're a grown woman and your self-esteem does not belong in the hands of two toddlers — for they tend to break and lose things. And then one day you'll ask them, 'What did you do with my self-esteem?' and the best they'll do is shrug, spin around once with their eyes closed and respond, 'Dunno, can't find it.'

Three hours of madness, but I made it.

I reached escape velocity and left my known universe and entered deep space: Ikea is at least ten miles from my house. In that journey, a banal drive across boring roads, I felt a freedom seep into my bones. A lightness, a heady pointlessness that I've missed since we brought our children home. I was free to do whatever I chose.

I smile.

Not at my children, not at my husband, not even at the TV or a book.

I smile at the glorious space in my head that was freed from thinking about my children every second of every day. Those two little people take up a huge amount of headspace. And the moment that responsibility was handed over to someone else, I found her again.

Boo.

There you are.

Me.

Hiding out in a tiny recess of my brain and then released to run wild around the jungles of Ikea.

60. One Second Is All It Takes

Spring is finally here; the sun is shining and Mum, Sarah and I are sitting outside at a café without needing to be wrapped up in tartan and foil like wrinklies-in-blankets-on-wheels. We've eaten lunch and are having a natter about something or other.

It's spring half-term, so I'm cramming the break with grandparents, cousins, aunties and more. My sisters' three boys are playing in a copse on a large grassy area, and over the way is a big playground; there are also some nature trails if we need to get away from whining about someone having a microsecond longer on the swing. I'm sipping my drink and luxuriating in the peace of the café before relaunching myself into the mayhem. Both my kids declared they couldn't eat another bite ('Unless there's ice cream?' Bubbles asked hopefully) and have wandered off to join the older ones, who have already wolfed-and-gone.

Eventually, I feel that I've shirked my mummy responsibilities long enough. *Best just check on the kids.* I drag myself reluctantly out of my chair, throw off the pretence of a chic café lifestyle and idle over to the field on the other side of the low café wall, to tick my two kids *Here.* I soon spy the three boys playing with Nibbles in the trees and relax. I glance around just to make sure the set is complete.

Huh! Bubbles is not immediately obvious, but she's easy to miss, so I duck beneath the branches to see if she's climbing out of sight. Not there either. Odd. I stop idling and start walking, feeling marginally ruffled.

'Have you seen Bubbles?' I ask the boys.

They shake their heads and shrug with a grunt. She's not with them then. Oh. My mouth goes a little dry and I ask them gently if they'll help me find her. They look a bit disgruntled but join in, if slouchingly half-heartedly.

'Bubbles,' I start, all sing-song and light.

I walk in ever-increasing circles from where the boys were playing, covering the whole grassy area in a systematic-ish manner.

'Bubbles, where are you?' I continue with slightly more urgency whilst trying to make it seem like a game of hide-and-seek where she's hidden really well (like she did on the fabled supermarket trip with Ken and Mary; she ran off and hid so effectively that they had to seal the doors in case she escaped).

Please come out, I pray.

As I stride around, my speed increasing with every Bubbles-less segment, panic rises and my voice becomes louder and more frantic. I jog down to the roadside, still no sign, then up towards the café again, my head searching like a lighthouse for a flash of pink. I scour the perimeter, calling for her, checking deep into bushes and trees in case she's sat singing to herself, oblivious to the search. And then I start to run and shout and despite it all, she does not appear.

'Bubbles, Bubbles!' I'm no longer hiding my concern, my voice a cocktail of desperation and hope. I shout and walk blindly in all directions. The boys join in wholeheartedly now; this is no game. When I'm certain she's not in the field, I return to the café, my heart pounding and all sorts of dire scenarios running helpfully through my head.

'Can you help me find Bubbles?' I ask my sister, treading a delicate tonal balance — I don't want my mother to panic, but this is serious. Sarah hears the words I do not say and immediately joins the search party. The grassy park is small enough that we cover it quickly and both conclude with concern that she is not here. The fact that Sarah can't find her either adds to my distress; I've not simply overlooked her. She is not here.

She.

Is.

Not.

Here.

My head spins, my stomach hollows and tears well up in my eyes. I can see myself on the news, a mum blubbing silently, too distraught to speak, my blotchy face speaking volumes as Andy pleads for her safe return. I see big photocopies of her cute smiling face plastered over trees and front pages and practise what I might say when I ring Andy to admit that in my laziness and inattention I've lost our little girl and I know that I shouldn't be so narcissistic but the blotchy-faced look is not the look I want to have on national TV and the shame of it and how will I ever walk down my street again with my head held high? He will go mental. Who would do something like this? Why does she have to be so cute? And none of this catastrophising is helping me think straight.

I want you back, Bubbles. I promise never to shout at you or deny you ice cream ever again.

Just please, please keep her safe and bring her back to me. I don't know who I'm asking, but I'm willing to convert to any faith if their deity will intervene on my behalf.

Breathe. (Breathe, and again.)

Rewind.

Think.

I replay what happened and the details are tellingly sketchy. If only I'd been paying attention to my child instead of a slice of grown-up conversation. Right . . . I was sat at the table with the grown-ups and Bubbles walked away (I definitely saw that). What was it she said? What were her exact words? Did she say she was going to play, or going to play with the boys, or something else? She went into the grassy park area. Oh. Actually . . . Well, did she? And I realise that I never saw where she went; I just presumed she was going to join the boys.

I think she said she was going to play . . .

We search the same small area a third time because I'm sure that she wouldn't have wandered off on her own. She's not here, so perhaps my belief in my own parenting is sorely misplaced.

Where can she be?

Let's review the facts. She is not in this area. We are confident of that. Therefore she *must* be somewhere else. But where? Let's be positive and imagine that she's somewhere within the boundaries of this extensive park, not stolen away like those horror headlines that whisper to and feed my fear and which aren't as likely as the newspapers would have you believe.

Tell me again why we picked a massive park with a trillion places to hide and get lost.

And then I ask myself a magic question, an incredible question, a question that wins Question of the Year in a ticker-tape ceremony. It instantly unblocks my brain.

If I were Bubbles, where would I go?

And it hits me, like a freight train of obviousness. I've barely even finished the question when my legs start moving beneath me and I want to slap myself for being so stupid and the tears start to come because I know . . . *Oh God, I know where she is. Thank you, thank you, thank you.*

What does my daughter love most?

Where would she choose to be in a park?

And it's all so clear to me now the fog of panic has cleared.

Where else but the swings?

Her heart belongs to the swings . . .

. . . which are in the other direction, on the other side of the café, across the road, and I'm almost flying as I walk really fast without breaking into a run that might spread the contagion of panic that lives on the skin of parents in a crammed playground. And as I turn the corner, my mouth is dry with anticipation, my heart is pounding and my eyes are searching for her pink clothes and big hair, and now I can let the fear inside me flow out because . . . I. CAN. SEE. HER.

There she is.

My gorgeous, amazing girl, lost in a sea of children. I've never been so happy to see anyone in my whole life.

My tiny little girl looks around, notices that she's alone, and her eyes widen with bewilderment and fear, which she almost shrugs off as she turns back to the swings and waits for her turn. But I know. I can see that she's scared and lost. And in one balletic movement, I sweep her up, swaddling her tight with a desire to never, ever, ever, ever let her go.

'I couldn't find you,' she says pitifully, as my tears dampen her curls. *My poor little girl.*

'I couldn't find you either,' I say, and we hug in happy reconciliation. I'm torn between the sheer delight of finding her and the stress of her being lost, so I end up both consoling her (and myself, *phew!* I don't have to tell my hubby that I lost her) and chiding her for going off without a grown-up. As some Italian friends once said, 'First a hug, then a kick.'

I want to tattoo my mobile number on her arm. I want to insert a GPS tracker beneath her skin (tonight I'll research these trackers when fear returns to haunt me).

I carry her back to the others; the boys shrug and carry on with their game, but I watch relief wash the fear from my sister's face when she sees Bubbles in my arms.

When my daughter and I are both calmer, I talk to her in great detail (as my hubby would say, 'tending to a monologue') about how she must always be with an adult and tell us where she is going and be within sight of someone she knows and never cross a road without a grown-up and not go off without asking and if she wants to go to the swings, to ask first and . . . time to stop; she didn't hear a word after 'be with an adult'.

But mostly I tell her that she must never, ever, ever do that again.

Knowing that what I'm really saying is that *I* must never, ever, ever do that again.

I scared me.

After the trauma of nearly losing Bubbles, I just want to keep my head down and get through these final weeks until the children are legally ours. The court date is in the diary. Soon we'll be their forever family.

This morning, after breakfast, I send Nibbles to the thinking step. He refuses, kicks up a fuss and says he doesn't want to go. I bite my tongue and avoid snapping, 'That's the bleeding point of it.' Instead I calmly go over, gently pick him up from his floor kicking and half-carry him to the step.

And that's my blunder.

I am carrying/walking him in a hunched stoop out of the kitchen and towards the thinking step just outside the kitchen door when my big toe smacks into the slight rise between the kitchen and the hallway. It's not a step, only two centimetres, and it's been there for over five years, since we did the kitchen up and discovered original flagstones under some ugly 1980s terracotta tiles. The blip was a small price to pay for an original feature, so we left it. For months afterwards, I frequently, swearingly stubbed my toe on it, as did the kids when they first arrived, but with more wailing and less cursing. Occasionally Andy and I ponder how to sort it out, and then forget about it and just carry on stepping over it.

Today Nibbles' body makes a bad window, so I don't see it. Instead of just stubbing my toe and *ow*-ing, I start to trip. Without Nibbles' weighing me down, I might have stumbled, caught my balance, righted myself with a 'ta-da!' then mopped my brow dramatically whilst praising my narrow escape. But my arms, the heart of the balancing trick, are lead weights and my centre of gravity is all messed up by the toddler between my legs.

I'm tempted to say that everything slowed down in that moment — that the horror spread across my face like ink in a bath. I'm tempted to say I shifted my weight and dramatically launched Nibbles out of the way, sacrificing my own nose in the bargain but winning his ever-lasting gratitude (until the next time I use my cross voice). But this didn't happen. Because it would imply that there was even a second where the destinies diverged. There wasn't. I barely register the pain in my stubbed toe before he's shrieking. My fall is broken by my son's face hitting the hallway wall.

He screams.

I scream in fear.

Ironically, I sit on the thinking step as I spin him around and check him out. His nose is bleeding and I grab a tissue and hold him tight and repeat an 'I am so sorry' chorus saturated with as much guilt as the tissue is with blood. Things don't look good and I dread what he's thinking.

Damn, blast and bugger it.

I unpeel him from my desperate grasp. Snot has joined the blood from his nose to create a cake of yuck on my shoulder — I'm going to have to change my top. But he's no longer bleeding, so that's a relief.

'Why did you hit me, Mummy?' he asks indignantly, disbelief and disgust writ deep in his furrowed brow. *He thinks it was deliberate?* I want to respond that it was the wall that hit him, but decide this might not be the right moment to get all pedantic on his sentence structure and blame apportionment.

I look deep into his eyes and tell him that I am deeply, deeply sorry for tripping over. I say this over and over again, to instil the truth in him — that I tripped and fell into the wall, I tripped and fell, I tripped and fell. It was an accident. But I am afraid. Because I know that Nibbles will open his mouth and share anything that seems interesting or unusual with the first person he sees, and then every other person after that, until they've all stopped listening.

He's going to talk about this and I want his words to come out right. I patch him up, change his top and mine and get ready for the school toddle. At nursery, I confess that he has a bloody nose because I tripped when I was carrying him and he fell face first into the wall. I say it because I want to forestall their phoning child protection. I say it to unburden myself. I say it and pray that they believe me, because even though it is the truth, in this world of suspicion, what proof do I have?

I am humbled and slightly scared. What if they don't believe me? We are still 'parents in the making' and this is the most scared I've been of having them taken away from me. Mostly I'm scared because I know deep down that I'm a fraud. I'm not the parent that I promised to be during all those meetings and conversations, in all those answers I typed. Even Andy, the original 'mild-mannered janitor type', has found that two toddlers stretch him beyond his ability to stay entirely composed. What if someone finds out? What if someone has been watching us? What if they all compare notes and join the dots and realise that 'she's not the mum she promised to be'?

I'm afraid that someone will tell on me, that I will tell on myself in a moment of panic, that I'll be found out to be a mummy who doesn't cope as well as she said she would, who gets tired and crabby with her kids, who lacks the patience to do the crafting and baking she promised she would do, who threw the timetable out shortly after they arrived and who feels like a poor imitation of the WonderMum that she invented in her head during the years she dreamt of having children.

I am an imposter.

I bow my head in supplication as I make my confession.

I hurt my child. I did not mean to. Yet he was in my arms when the accident happened and it was my actions that led to his bloody (but thankfully not broken) nose.

The nursery manager listens and nods and asks if Nibbles is okay.

When I pick him up at lunchtime, she says she's glad that I told them about the accident because Nibbles has spent the day telling them, 'Mummy smashed my face into the wall.' I fake a smile. And I wonder if secretly someone told on me anyway.

First Bubbles wanders off in a park, and now Nibbles is telling everyone that I beat him up. A few months ago I thought we were finally getting a handle on this parenting caper, that we'd reached a new level of competence and skill, and now (as if to prove me wrong and move the goalposts again), just as we're one flaming hoop away, we're (although Andy had no hand in either of these experiences) making horrendous mistakes that could ruin everything.

And I want to wrap myself and the children into a huge bundle of impenetrable Kevlar or . . .

I'll just hire the A-Team to keep them safe for a few months until the paperwork is signed, sealed and delivered.

61. The Stairgates Disappear

Drum roll please . . .

The social workers have left the building.

A judge has approved Bubbles' and Nibbles' formal adoption into our family. It is now a done legal deal (we get a phone call to confirm). After months of daily, then weekly, then fortnightly, then monthly visits, we've had our last visit from a social worker: SWN4. No, that's not a typo. A few months ago, we swapped SWN3 for SWN4 when SWN3 moved areas or quit or something (I wasn't listening too hard as Nibbles was tearing at books at the time). I wanted to scream and say 'just piss off' because I couldn't be bothered to start from scratch again and break in a new one. But now the visits are officially over. And I'm delighted, for whilst the visits supported us, especially in the winter of those first bleak months, latterly they just felt intrusive, as if we were being constantly watched and judged.

'Bye.'

I close the door on SWN4's final visit, take down the stairgates then do a happy dance as I sing 'Na Na Nee Na Na' whilst pointing at the carcasses on the floor. The children are more than used to going up and down the stairs on their own, and since Bubbles can open all the gates by herself, or for Nibbles, there's barely any point keeping them, especially given how often we trip over the darn things or get wedged with an armful of laundry and have to ask Bubbles to open it for us. To celebrate the fact that no one is going to be coming to our house and checking whether the children have pillows in their beds (I kid you not), I remove the symbols of oppression from our lives (but not those on the stairs to the cellar, not yet).

We then have a Celebration Day. Andy takes the day off and we drive to the big city to attend Family Court. It's not a legal day but a way of marking the adoption and meeting the judge who approved it. When do we arrive? Ridiculously early of course. We drink coffees and hot chocolates in a café over the road. As 10 a.m. approaches, we enter the court through the metal detectors and are en route to being perfectly on time when Bubbles suddenly starts hopping and announces she needs a wee (despite strenuously denying she needed one two minutes ago in the café). We trudge back downstairs to the toilet and turn up late to scowlingly whispered 'you're late' remonstrations from Pam.

I don't remember much of what the judge says. Pam's here because even though she's SWN2, she created this Match; she has led us through it and she has championed the joining of our families since she first set eyes on our photos. The clerk surprises the kids with some sweets and toys, and when proceedings get underway, I don't hear a word as I'm trying to get Bubbles and Nibbles to sit still and be quiet and to 'leave the sweets alone, will you? You can have them in a minute'. And by the time they settle down, it's over.

We take photos of the kids sitting on the judge's chair and then file out with some certificates and the knowledge that our children now have our surname and are legally ours. It is over in less time than it took to sip the hot drinks earlier and I feel odd. I'm not sure what level of fanfare and parade I was expecting, but I got a laminated certificate in a brown envelope and a strange ceremony in an oak-panelled room that I didn't even hear because I was too busy hissing at my kids.

We have a lovely celebratory lunch out together and I celebrate with a glass of fizz.

But I'm unmoved by the legal stamp on our family — it's not the adoption certificate and the new birth certificates, which will arrive in a month or so, that really matter (although try telling that to officials at the passport office). These things matter in a legal sense and give us genuine status in the lives of these children; they're a final part of the maze-like puzzle through which we have twisted and turned these last months. But these pieces of paper do not make me their mummy.

I earned that title (I couldn't be prouder if it were an OBE — although, Your Majesty, as your humble servant, I wouldn't turn one down for services to adoption, hint, hint) over the last ten months through blood, sweat, truckloads of Calpol and an Olympic-size swimming pool of wine.

I earned it from the teaspoons of snot, poo, vomit and pee I bleached from my favourite top, my fingers, toes and fringe; from falling asleep next to their cots as they squeezed the life from my pinkie; from comforting them after a nightmare when I really needed to sleep; from misting 'monster repellent' under their bed; from reading *We're Going on a Bear Hunt* a gazillion times until I knew every word and yet still gladly made all the *swish-swish, stumble-trip* noises to bring it to life; from sticking their drawings on my fridge and acting delighted to receive every page dripping with unbroken grey paint; from cutting up their green beans, spaghetti and anything of chokable size with scissors, cooking the life out of difficult-to-chew things and taking all the chilli, spice and excitement out of our meals; from receiving their gifts of leaves, sticks, stones and petals with 'how lovely' until my pockets and wellies were bursting with tiny presents then grumbling to myself when I found them after the wash; from patiently listening to the words that tumbled from their mouths while trying to work out which of the vowels and consonants might be right (Chibley? What's a chibley? Glibly? Fiddly? Tiddly? Piddly? Wobbly? Bobbly? Chimney? You have to be kidding me) even when it took twenty minutes; from watching him chase a pea around a dish with a tiny fork, finally stab it, and then drop it before it reached his mouth and almost never just picking the darn thing up and throwing it into his open mouth to get tea over with five minutes sooner; and from enforcing boundaries and pouncing on their misbehaviours, even when they wailed at me for teaching them lessons they did not want to learn in the middle of Lidl.

This legal certificate would be meaningless if I didn't love my children.

Sat in this glorious setting, looking out over (Ow, be careful, sweetie) patchwork fields, I gaze with undisguised awe at these two gorgeous (Sit still), wonderful and (Where are you going now?)

consuming creatures who (Put the salt down; it's not a toy) have turned my life (I said put it down!) upside down and then right sided it again. (Can I have another glass of fizz, please?)

Yes, I'm now legally your parent, but what matters is that you call me your mummy.

62. One Year and a Day

How can it be a year already?

Today we're celebrating with a One Year and a Day party. A party. Actual grown-ups (and their kids) coming over to our house during daylight hours when I have half a chance of being awake. A chance to hear stories about what's going on in the world beyond school and back. My friends can regale me with tales of derring-do and adventures in foreign lands outside my world and I can contribute to the hubbub with . . . Um. Ah.

I feel woefully unprepared, knowing that not everyone will want to hear the director's cut of my one-woman show on being a mum. You may be able to detect what I'm most excited about: seeing people after nearly a year in what has felt like solitary isolation. It's another full house of friends and family, although Claire, thankfully, declined. She's not entirely sober and to be honest, I don't want to deal with unpredictable madness exploding in the middle of this party.

It's the usual chaos in the morning, and Andy finds an ingenious way to stay out of my way — by rewiring a light switch that's been a bit dodgy for ten years but with which we have lived quite happily until 10 p.m. yesterday. Whilst I'm rushing around rearranging crudités into Tower Bridge, I have to dodge miles of curled cables and avoid whisking plaster dust into cakes and Florentines as Andy randomly turns off the electricity to save himself from electrocution. I kick myself for even mentioning that the light looked a bit odd yesterday.

I've been gripped by Year and a Day fever for several months. Andy gave his cautious 'uh-huh' assent, and before he came around from his tablet-induced coma and realised what he'd agreed to, I'd already designed and sent out invitations. It's a gluten-free party this time because there's more chance of finding a parking space outside Ikea during a sale than of toddlers keeping crumbs out of the margarine. I've kneaded, minced and baked the biggest GF pork pie known to man — think bottom tier of a wedding cake. It required an apprenticeship of eight pies and five months. And it turns out that a huge pork pie doesn't serve more people than a small one, as Ken takes about a quarter of it (the first slice), setting a generous (aka gluttonous) precedent that sees the whole thing disappear before ten people have helped themselves.

This is a family event, so I rope the kids into decorating and making games. I ask them if they'd like a theme but don't let them name the party in case it becomes Party McPoopy Face. *Frozen?* Bubbles nods, Nibbles frowns. Pirates? has the reverse effect. One of them vetoes dinosaurs, and then princesses, until we finally are left with a Minion theme. I duly research Minion-themed food (too much faff), fancy dress (I made some wigs) and then turn my focus to Minion-themed games. I crochet Minion goggles for a blindfold for Pin the Horn On the ('it's so pretty') Unicorn, paint blue-and-yellow paper cups for a ping-pong bouncing game, glue paper strips into a Minion piñata that proves surprisingly difficult to break (and requires a hefty swing that nearly smashes someone's face) and sew tiny Minion finger-puppet kits with sticky googly eyes for the (you guessed it) Minion party bags.

I also create a wall of fifty photos that chart the first year, from when we first met them (top left) to our family day in court when they became legally ours. And all this preparation is evidence that *(a)* it's not as hard as it was in the beginning; and *(b)* the kids are in day care for part of the week (which explains *(a)*).

As people arrive, I feel a real buzz running through me. I'm happy and excited — and not just to say hello to people I haven't seen for a year. I'm more relaxed than I was last year, when we were just about to crest a wave and ride it as it crashed onto the beach of our lives. I try to get the kids to eat healthily and stop glugging fizzy pop but give up and hope someone else will mop up the resulting puddle.

I'm content, surrounded by the people I love most in the world and who seem equally happy; I don't want this day to stop, but I know that people will peel off soon enough, so I call everyone into the lounge. Once they're assembled, I press Play on my big surprise. Look, I've made a film and . . . Oh. The film starts then stops and won't budge. *Darn it.*

Andy goes to sort it out whilst I shuffle the programme around and move on to some heartfelt thank yous.

First Liz, because she had our back this whole time; she was our lemon-drizzle and African-stew angel, and then she kicked Andy and me out of our house so we could spend time together. And I start to cry as I remember the cake. I dab my eyes and take some deep breaths because I haven't finished and it's too soon to let it all out. I give her a huge hug and a massive bunch of flowers and we share some teary kisses.

Then Ken and Mary. I thank them for looking after Bubbles and Nibbles before we even knew them, for guiding us through the daunting process of Introductions, for opening their hearts and homes to us and for taking the photos that made us fall in love with the children. More tears, another bouquet and a roomful of people either rolling their eyes at it all or quietly joining the tissue tribe.

A few days later I will write Liz and Ken and Mary thank-you cards to express more eloquently and completely all the things that I wanted to say but didn't because sheer emotion stuck them deep in my throat.

I will tell Ken and Mary the words that I should have said:

Thank you for . . .

The first words I ever heard from my daughter: 'Flowers for my mummy' — I will never forget that moment.

For helping Bubbles and Nibbles be so excited every morning.

For taking over and calming them during the confusion.

For helping me to believe that I was their mummy and would do a good job (you set the bar very high).

For loving them, caring for them and being fabulous carers during your time with them.

For the photos you took which made us fall in love with them and choose them over others.

For your bravery and courage in letting go and still being a part of their lives.

These words are not enough and they are all I have to give you.
With huge love,
Emma (and Andy) xx

Finally the not-as-surprising video is ready, a compilation of my favourite videos and photos that illustrate how the last twelve months have changed our lives and melded our two families into one, all set to two pieces of evocative music: Rob Thomas' 'Little Wonders' (which David sent me as we drove home the day we first met them and which I'll associate with my children for the rest of my life) and Emeli Sandé's 'Heaven', from an album we played all the time in the car on those journeys to and fro, until even the kids knew it off by heart. As I watch, tears pour silently down my face, and we pass tissues around the room. I cry at all the changes these children have wrought on our lives, for the beauty of it all, for the love that the film represents and for all the times that I was too exhausted, or frustrated, or annoyed to even notice the joy that had seeped into our lives.

And then it's over, and we break up and go out and wipe bottoms and get more food and drink and play party games with the kids in the family room. We destroy the piñata, hand out party bags and those guests with younger children say their goodbyes and wend their way home.

Then I tell Andy that the kids *have* to go to bed *now* and then convince the kids too as I wrestle them into their PJs, brush their teeth, read them stories, kiss them goodnight and turn out the lights.

Why is music rattling the kids' bedrooms and thumping out of the lounge? Have they no idea? I chase adults with their beers and loud music out into the garden.

A wave of exhaustion hits me as the tide of adrenalin drains out, and I resist the urge to lie on my bed for a moment, to listen to the party through my bedroom window, because if I do, I'll wake up in the morning, having missed the rest entirely. And part of me doesn't mind that idea, but I rouse myself and put on my party face and carry on, knowing that next time the invites will say 'until 6 p.m.' because just holding things together has worn me out and I've no party left in me.

I stay up almost late, and when everyone has gone I offer to help Andy tidy up, but he refuses my tipsy help, so I just watch him and give thanks that there won't be a kitchen bombsite to deal with in the morning. I reflect on how lucky I am to have Andy and the kids. And that I'm a lot less drunk than I was after the last party, which is a good thing, for if this year has taught me anything, it's that children don't know the meaning of a lie-in, that sleep is the most precious thing in my life, and that *Scooby-Doo* is even more intolerable at 6 a.m. with a thumping hangover.

As I go upstairs to flop into bed, I stop for a minute on the stairs, in the dead-of-the-night peace that swaddles my house, and soak up a feeling of contentment and joy.

Today we truly celebrated.

Today I had the party I wanted last year, but with one enormous difference — in those rooms at the front of the house lie two sleeping (and one snoring) beauties.

More and more often since Christmas, Andy and I have walked hand in hand, embraced in the kitchen, lain in bed in the morning at stupid o'clock or sat in the car and given thanks, sometimes silently and sometimes verbally, for the family we now have. We're grateful that we got through the difficult months when we didn't feel like their mummy and daddy, however often Bubbles told us we were (and we're glad to wave goodbye to that time). For all the tiredness and all the frustration of juggling jelly, there is so much more love and laughter in our house. They've filled our lives with magic and wonder; we marvel at their fresh innocence and their unbridled curiosity that asks questions about whether bees sleep and why stars twinkle (yay for the Internet).

We howl at how hilarious they are. We remember, for example, the time when Bubbles pretended to be a hairdresser, using a hammer, and then calmly asked, 'Now take your clothes off, Mummy.' 'Uh, that doesn't happen at the hairdresser,' I said nervously. 'It does at mine,' she replied quick as The Flash. And the time when he asked where oranges grow. 'Somewhere hot, a long way away,' I replied. 'Like Birmingham?' he asked. And the time when she asked what courgettes grow on (great question) and then what spaghetti hoops grow on (roll on the floor laughing).

We've discovered that standing on a dinosaur model is worse than an upturned plug; that a two-year-old can make serious dents in an oak table with a kiddy knife; and that children can produce snot-noodles measuring six inches that dangle from their noses the minute you've used all the tissues up (and you learn to improvise by using their scarf instead, and then learn that you shouldn't leave that scarf in your pocket and forget about it).

We've experienced the prideful high of seeing them finally master a new skill (catching a balloon, writing a credible O, tugging a sock onto their foot the right way around or using a potty instead of their pants), and we've seen the ocean's worth of patience it takes to build that skill. We've let them down gently when they've wanted to walk before they could run — when Bubbles asked to have her nose pierced like mine and I said she was too young, she said she'd do it herself by 'poking a hole with a screwdriver'!

We're far more confident as parents, and maybe because they no longer smell our fear, the children have settled down too. They have stopped shadowing our every move; they play together and leave us alone for, oh, minutes at a time; when we go for walks they run off and Andy and I get to hold hands and chat until they notice and decide they want to hold Daddy's hands too and I am booted off his team. Nibbles and Bubbles are now like the children we fell in love with on the video, the children they were at Ken and Mary's. They look at us with adoration, with unadulterated love that shines out of their faces, the way they looked at the cameraman.

It's easy to forget just how achingly tiring and hard this year has been, especially the first six months. It was far harder than we had imagined, not because they're adopted, but because overnight we had to upskill ourselves and become the parents of two toddling, talking, mischievous bundles who said they wanted to go back to Ken and Mary's. It was hard because they changed every single aspect of our lives; we landed on the alien planet called Parenthood with no time to catch our breath, on red-alert mode every single second of the day in case they fell, slipped, bit each other, ran into the road (it happened once when Nibbles was startled by a car revving its engine), choked on a conker or were stolen away beneath my nose. Extreme vigilance took its toll in ways I could never have imagined or understood.

When I dreamt of being a mum, did I really know what I was wishing for?

It's tempting to look back through the rose-tinted spectacles of hindsight and wish I'd done things differently, to wish for those months back so I could enjoy them more, rather than just put one heavy foot in front of the other and try to get through each day. And maybe all parents feel like this. I simply don't know. People used to ask me what it was like being a twin. 'I don't know,' I would say. 'What's it like not being one?' This is the same. What's it like being an adoptive mum? I don't know, because I don't know what it's like to be a birth mum. There's a time when you look back on it and forget the memories you deleted or the tiredness that had you on your knees and wonder just why you complained and shouted so much.

Nibbles and Bubbles have given me some of the most incredible experiences of my life, including an experience of softening — it's hard to believe I could be any more of an inner marshmallow, but my kids have barbecued that marshmallow into a Dali-esque melted shape — and a deep, blind love that took me by surprise. They've changed me and taught me more about myself in one year than everything that's gone before, and whilst some of those lessons have been painful (for not everything I saw of myself reflected in my children was a good thing), I'm a better person for learning them. And as the yoke of responsibility becomes lighter, and I grow more confident in my role as their mummy, I smile, laugh and just wallow in their gorgeousness.

They continue to amaze me every single day. When they walk hand in hand in front of me, giggling, making up a fantasy world about Spider-Man ('No, Spider-Girl'; 'No, Spider-Man!') or Elsa or whatever they've seen most recently, I wish my dad were here to meet them. As a mischievous trio of old and new, they would have had the world in stitches. They would have adored him, his tickly beard and his bad jokes, and he would have doted on their cute mischievousness. They have his twinkle, his creative spark, his undampened curiosity, and they've put a twinkle back in my life, and in our family's too.

They are my children.

Our children.

I am rich, truly and deeply blessed to have them in my life.

Still Four: Epilogue

A Thousand Cuts

For months, this July afternoon has been a shard in my soul — a sharp reminder of the inevitable, unstoppable changes ahead. Its razor edges urge me to make the most of the time we have left together, and cut me with memories of wasting these precious, dwindling hours when I should have been making memories to get me through the years ahead. I yearn to hold on a few months longer, to delay the inescapable *tick-tock*s that mark the children's growing from babes. One day he'll spurn my hand as we walk to school, so I hold tight whilst I still can.

Being a mum is death by a thousand cuts: when I fed him his last bottle at naptime, when she stopped holding my hand to cross the road, when he no longer wanted to bounce on my knee and giggle, when she started to read to herself, when they got too big to swing between our arms as we walked, when they no longer fell asleep in the gentle rocking of the car, when he stopped asking me to '*brum*' cars around the roads of his car mat. Every step they take forward feels like a step away from me, even though we're still walking side by side, sometimes hand in hand.

Every cut is also a tear that falls — a happy tear shed when pride, when love, when happiness overwhelms me and I cannot keep it inside any longer. My job is to make myself redundant by providing my children with the skills to do things on their own, by giving them independence.

I never knew before I had kids just what it takes to be a parent, and my own children won't know either until they have their own. Raising kids has multiplied my respect and admiration for my own parents hundreds of folds. I am astonished that my mother looked after four children under the age of five (the last two being twins) without a car, without central heating, without an automatic washing machine or disposable nappies or even much money. I can't count how many times I've asked myself how she coped, for there were times when two seemed too much, despite all the mod cons at my disposal.

I had no idea just how deeply the children and my love for them would burrow beneath my skin, how utterly besotted I would become with their smiles, their mischief, their love and spirit. I couldn't have imagined how torn I would feel between wanting to keep them safe and knowing there's nothing I can do to protect them from some of the suffering that they'll encounter in their young lives; or how intensely they'd react to a broken toy, a stubbed toe, a mean word, the wrong cup, a burst balloon or a tiny sprig of cauliflower.

Their experience of life is so full of spirit, raw and simple. They live on a knife's edge of emotion, swinging wildly in trees of joy, love, compassion and with one swift leap moving to pain, to lashing out and screaming with frustration at the challenges they face. As someone whose heart lives very close to the surface, who is touched constantly by deep tugs of emotion, riding the valleys and hills of their feelings has left me emotionally spent in ways I did not anticipate. When they wail, as she did a few days ago after a stick scratched her leg, a hug seems too little, too meagre a response. Yet I admire their emotional literacy, their ability to express what they feel without delay, apology or censor, for I have sometimes been appalled by my own softness. While working as an engineer, I was once told by a senior manager that I needed to stop wearing my heart on my sleeve. I left his office dumbfounded, for he might as well have asked me to cut off my breasts. How dare he ask me to be less of an emotionally sensitive and literate woman and more like the emotionally constipated men with whom I worked, uncomfortable with displays of passion or sentiment. That environment in which I worked for years made me wary of my sensitivity, scared that my own nature would frighten people away or ruin my career or somehow point out to my colleagues that I was indeed a female and not the tomboy that they'd come to expect. Would my tears one day betray me such that people would simply ignore my qualifications, my PhD, my intelligence, my creativity and brand me a 'silly woman'?

The emotions that have pained me, guided me and delighted me over the last three years are very much a part of who I am as a mother. At times I've wished to have an Off button, or at least a volume control knob so that I could turn down my feelings to concentrate on functioning, but I've yet to find it. As I write this, I struggle to express these feelings that blur the words in front of my watering eyes.

I don't want to write about this day because I did not want this day to come.

Nibbles and I are sat on the front step, the door wide open, the sun beaming down, having a lunch of crackers, ham, cheese, cucumber and cherry tomatoes. It is peaceful here. As he takes his tiny bites and lets a tomato explode in his cheeks, I marvel at the little ray of joy who sits beside me in his blue peaked cap (his impassioned choice), his checked blue shirt and shorts. As he put his cap on, he said, 'I am a farmer boy'; I nodded and grinned, thinking, *He's only missing some wellies.*

'Is this serrano?' he asks, and I think that a boy who has yet to start school but talks about serrano versus slippery ham and can identify potato dauphinoise is going to struggle to pretend to be working class if the mood takes him later in life. We let the sun warm our faces as we eat, watch the world go by, point out shapes in the clouds (a lot look like sheep to me and food to him) and just sit in silence and be, together. Yet my heart is weighed down knowing this is our last afternoon.

'I've got a new adventure planned,' I tell Nibbles.

'Where are we going?' he asks, and instead of answering, I give him a blue-and-yellow float to carry ('It's a Minion,' he declares). I grab a bag packed with swimsuits, goggles and towels, and we climb into the car. We're going to the Splash Pool — I've toyed with the idea of going but never got around to booking until last night. We park, walk up to reception and hand over our tickets. He's super excited, I'm super excited, and we rush off giggling until the receptionist shouts at us to stop because we've run right past the changing rooms. We struggle into our costumes and put everything into a locker, and then enter the pool area, which is heavenly and surprisingly quiet. We turn valves and watch the water jets ebb and flow, we dance through the showers and sprays, we float around the whirlpool, but mostly Nibbles spends his time going up and down a slide fifty-three times in rapid succession because hardly anyone else is on it. His face beams with joy, and as he grins, thoughts of the mortality of this experience with him shroud my soul. I sit and watch but melancholy threatens so I join in, going up and down the slide with him, laughing all the way. The lifeguard whistles and tells me off for going down face first, with some excuse about not wanting to have to pick my teeth out of the pool, and I shrug and wink at Nibbles in our rule-breaking conspiracy. And when I stop for a moment and listen to the music playing, which speaks of love and loss and missing you (and it's all Sad Café), tears join the bleachy splashes on my cheeks.

I kick myself for not coming sooner, for not making even more of the time we've had together. For even though I've enjoyed the walks and picnics, Nibbles is having the best afternoon of unfettered, seat-of-the-pants, hilarious fun. I tempt him out of the pool with the promise of cake at our favourite café. We snuggle into our usual seats, welcomed by the staff who recognise us from our weekly visits, yet as we eat, I know (too late) that even the sweet buttercream is nothing compared to the exhilaration of the water slide. And despite wanting to hold on to this moment, to stretch it out like pizza dough until it lasts forever, our time is up and we're walking to school to pick up his sister and I am trying really hard to keep the conversation flowing and talking about anything and everything because I know that if I stop for even one second . . .

'Tomorrow is going to be the hottest day of the year,' I say, reverting to that great British conversational nonentity: the weather.

'Will we frazzle like bacon?' Nibbles asks sincerely, and I stop, bend double and laugh. That is one to keep. We collect Bubbles, who talks about the swarmies of ants on the way home, and I just know that mix of 'armies' and 'swarms' will trip off my tongue for years to come.

We make it back home, and as they start to play, I sneak down to type these words, while the feelings are fresh and raw. And I have to trust my fingers for the tears come at last and I don't even want to stop them, for these tears tell me everything about my children.

About the joy they bring to my heart (except yesterday, when they were both whiney and awful), about how I feel when they are happy, about how much I want to make them happy (until they make me so frustrated I forget), about how they make me want to be a better person; when they say 'Mummy, you look beautiful', I see myself through their eyes and believe them.

I am going to miss these afternoons with my son so much. I'll miss the simple pleasure of lunch sat on our front step (I'd never once, in ten years, lunched in the sun on that doorstep until he suggested it). I'll miss our strange and hilarious chats about aliens, superheroes, cake, sunshine, a Spider-Man watch he wants for his birthday, the forthcoming summer holiday and whether bats dream. I'll miss the feeling of pride as we walk fingers in hand. I'll miss the feeling of connection travelling through some of my favourite spots with someone who has the wide-eyed innocence and raven-ous curiosity of a tourist in London.

It's over.

For next week, the summer holidays start, and in September he'll be in Year Zero (let's agree to call it that, shall we?) from nine till three. We have six weeks of the summer holidays first, with a spaghetti-knitting trip to the seaside and the new-improved-so-ber version of Aunty Claire coming to stay, but these mummy-son afternoons are . . . I struggle to type the word . . . *over*. It's been three incredible years since these two children arrived in our lives and turned it upside down and back to front, and these years have been deeper, richer than I could have ever imagined. In the early days, I would have given them back, if only for a break, for a few hours off to breathe, to sleep, to hold my husband in an embrace of coupledom, to put on some music and dance a little Ceroc (if we can remember the steps), for a magical lie-in until 8 a.m. one weekend morning. Yet now, all I want to write is that it is too soon. I am not ready.

I have never been ready for this experience; I am not ready for the places it will take me tomorrow or next year. And if I have learnt one thing from these incredible, enlightening years, it's this:

You will never be ready.

So don't wait.

Grasp life firmly with both hands and never let go. Create a life filled with adventures, with jaw-dropping experiences; a life packed to the brim with memories so that the book of your life is chapter after chapter of unforgettable events: funny, touching, strange, ordinary, extraordinary moments that take your breath away when you see them all jumbled together on the page (you'll later edit out half of them to make the book shorter than Tolstoy's masterpieces).

You can live your life in fear, afraid of being wrong, afraid of failing, afraid of everything. Or you can go out there, do your best, fall flat on your face, pick yourself up and keep on going. I've face-planted too many times to count in my quest to become their parent. Some incidents are here in this book, and many are not. Yet it is in the falling that we really discover what we're truly made of.

Sometimes we need to have the courage to take the first step. To admit to ourselves that our dreams are bigger than our fears, to pick up the phone and start the process. For that moment when I rang the agency to inquire about adoption — that moment changed everything.

Like nudging a domino over.

My son reminds me of the wondrous spirit within me, and it's time I let her out without needing him next to me, giving me permission to release the childlike wonder inside. I can be astonished by the world, kneel and stare at a ladybird. I can believe in magic and dragons. I can skip with joy, delight in an ice cream, picnic in the sunshine on my front step, ask questions about the world that only Google can answer. I can do all these things myself, if only I let me. Life does not become predictable; it's our jaded habits and thoughts that blind us to the magic of a flower's opening in spring, the patterns Jack Frost draws in a winter's puddle, the dew that hangs on spiders' webs like pearl necklaces; that blind us to the pride of creating something (no one's quite sure what) from cereal and egg boxes, something with a loo roll for a handle or nose, a creation with more glue, tape and glitter than a Disney parade; that blind us to the fact that a cake can never, ever, ever have too many sprinkles ('More, Mummy, more').

My children remind me to stay curious and innocent, and to explore this adventure called life (we don't get another turn).

They've taught me how to open my heart to a love as deep as the Mariana Trench — unfathomable and profound.

There is nothing you could offer me in exchange for the experiences I've had these three years. Loving my children and being loved in return has made me the richest woman alive, and I wouldn't swap it for all the Prosecco in Italy.

If it ever came winging this way, I know this for certain:
I would take a bullet for my children.

I am their mummy, they are my children, and we four quirky, flawed individuals are a family.

Now we are four.

Acknowledgements

To my family (I love you), thank you for giving me the time and space to creep away and write these words and feelings down before I forgot them.

To Nibbles and Bubbles, you gave me unconditional love and a purpose in life that was greater and more challenging than I'd ever dreamt it would be. It is the most incredible joy, the deepest frustration and the most fun I have ever had, and I can't wait to watch you change and grow as you keep pushing my parenting skills to the max. Thank you for completing our family, for bringing more laughter into this house, for waking Andy and me up to the simple pleasures in life (like a lie-in) and for your unwavering belief in us. I love you very much and I adore being your mummy.

To Andy, I couldn't have done this without you. This whole experience, from start to finish, has tested our relationship in ways we could not have imagined. I never knew what I was made of until we hit rock bottom, and I never knew how much easier it was to get up from that dark place if there was someone else there in the pit with you, holding out their hand and saying, 'Let's get up now. Tomorrow is another day.' Sometimes it was just a hug at the end of a difficult day, sometimes it was buying wine on the way home, sometimes it was simply reminding me that every single day brought joy as well as tears, frustration and more. Watching you change from my husband into a father has been an experience I will never forget — from the way you took my breath away at Panel as you explained how you felt about our children, to the casual ease with which you sat on the floor that first time we met them and let them crawl over you as I sat and wrestled with my emotions, to the honesty with which you told me that you didn't love them. And who knew you could be so impatient? That surprised the heck out of me. I love you very much, and I hope one day you find the time to read this book right to the very end (unlike the Big Report), or this paragraph will be a waste of ink.

To Mum, without your steadfast correction of my language as I grew up, I might never have mastered its use to the point of being able to write this book. May you forgive any typos or grammatical errors that you find and instead see the story beneath. I love you and I have no idea how you managed to raise four children who mostly turned out so normal.

To Sarah, as my first language teacher, you taught me the importance of communicating with others and sharing our experiences. You taught me from an early age that language is powerful, and how tiny tweaks to tone and pace can change a sentence and its impact. Thank you for blessing me with the ability to touch people's hearts and being an awesome Aunty.

To Claire, you gave me permission to see myself as an author, to follow my soft heart, to embrace my emotions and become the leader of the #tissuetribe. Thank you. I am so proud of you for getting and staying sober.

To Pamela Burrows, my superfan. For supporting me — starting with your review of the first chapter that inspired me to keep writing and finish this book. Thank you for being the first person to read the full book (when it was fifty thousand words longer) and for sharing how much it touched your heart and soul. Thank you for helping me to believe that this book was worth writing, finishing and publishing.

To everyone who kept my spirits high and made me want to get this book published rather than hide it away on my computer for the all-important-three to read, thank you.

To our social worker, SWN2 (called Pam in the book), for teasing us the very first time we met, for leading us with confidence through the Panels and for Matching us with our children. You are our fairy godmother and you made our dreams come true; you'll always have a special place in our hearts.

To Ken and Mary, for letting them go, for putting on a brave face, for keeping in touch, for loving them beyond limits and shaping them into the adorable children whom we fell in love with through your photos and video. And for many more reasons, most of them mentioned in this book. Mary, you helped me believe that I could be a mum, even when I sucked at it. Your faith in me is unwavering, and I try and remember that when I am too tired, or overwhelmed with screaming. May you continue to be a part of their story. Ken, your quiet tears showed me more than words could how very special these children were and how much they would steal my heart.

To my editor, Rachel Small, for helping me see which bits of the story I needed to let go of, which made you laugh, which sentences were powerful and more. Despite my pouting when you deleted my hard-typed prose, your changes made this book richer, funnier and more honest. You were right nearly all the time, and I bless you for your enthusiasm and dedication to helping my words have even more impact.

To Tanja, for taking my sketchy ideas and outline for the book cover and breathing freshness and life into my thoughts until I loved it so much I wanted it framed on my wall.

To Raina, my proofreader, who found the inconsistencies and commas that we'd missed and ensured that this book was the epitome of professional. For pointing out all the idioms that would trip up a non-UK audience. You had me when you quoted a Hart's Rule.

To my readers. If you read this far, then bless you. Get in touch and let me know what you thought, how you felt, what passages had you reaching for the tissues and which had you laughing out loud. Thank you for honouring me with a slice of your life and an opportunity to chat to you about my adventures.

To life, for being an incredible experience that is as simple as breathing yet as complex as knitting spaghetti. For the highs and lows, the tissues and the tiredness, the melting ice cream on a hot sunny day and the huddling around a fire as snow tickles the windows. May I continue to make the most of the days I have left and embrace your wondrousness. Here's to more stories, more adventures, more tissues, more love, more, more, more of everything please.

Delving Deeper — Q & A with the Author

1. **Why did you decide to write the book? Was it to help other people on a similar path as you and Andy or was it purely to tell the story? (Sarah Harding)**
   When I started writing things down — not knowing if I would ever finish something that might become a book — I just needed to write, to capture the stories, as I could feel them shimmering in my mind and escaping. I knew that they'd get forgotten under layers of new stories and experiences. As life became a little easier, I knew I'd forget how hard it was, and that the raw intensity would fade and be whitewashed by the present. I wanted to write our family's origin story so that one day my children could read about what it was like for me to become their mum.

   But as I wrote, I realised that it was also the book that I wished I could've read before and during this process — something to help me feel that I wasn't alone, to help me recognise the humour in the strange intensity of it all, to help me feel a connection with people who had been through this before and, most of all, to be reminded that there was light at the end of the tunnel. This book may give hope to people as they are struggling, making difficult choices and feeling tired beyond reason as new parents (adoptive or not). I found it was a struggle, and just knowing that it would all work out in the end, that there would be a happy ending, might have helped. If there was one thing that I wanted this book to be about (other than love), it was hope.

   And I want people to learn about the process of adoption, to see into a world that few understand and to help others understand it. Because however much we tried to explain what was going on to our family and friends, they didn't really get it. So this book might help those conversations flow (and stop people from asking the 'from abroad?' question). We met a few people who could not conceive but would not adopt; I have no idea if this book would change their minds, but I wanted to write something from the heart that might give them another perspective to consider. It isn't written to influence people to adopt, but it would be good if it helped more people to adopt two at a time (sibling groups are hard to place) or older children (the preference is for babies).

As I began to share the words with others, I realised that there were more reasons to keep going and get it published: so that the people in my family would understand our story better, and more people would understand infertility and adoption. These are still hidden worlds, secret worlds, to some extent, and confusing worlds, even when you're going through them. To write a book that was not too earnest, that trod lightly over intense subjects and spoke from the heart: that was my goal. May it start a million conversations about fertility, infertility, mental health, depression, alcoholism, sex, adoption and what it means to be a parent.

2. **What's different about your journey from that of other adoptive parents? (Sarah Fox)**

That's a tricky question. I'm sure that there are a huge number of things that happened to Andy and me that other adopters will recognise — the forms, meetings, training courses and paperwork — although the current process is different from the one people will read about in this book. I don't think that anything was particularly different about our journey; in fact, when we met other adopters, we felt that our infertility experience had been relatively easy, in that we hadn't miscarried or had IVF or other intervention that proved unsuccessful.

But every parent's journey is different, whether you're a birth parent easily, a birth parent after difficulties, a birth parent after intervention like IVF or an adoptive parent. Adoption accounts for a small percentage of parents in this country, and only a few adopt sibling groups, but I don't feel that we were particularly special in our experience. I think this book will show that we have more in common with other parents than we might suspect.

The longer you've been trying for children, or building up to the day that you finally become a parent, the more the dream can take hold, and our dreams of being parents were rather unrealistic: meadow-skipping rather than drowning in bottles and nappies and spoons. The more you want to become a mum (or dad) the more let down you might feel when the reality is so far removed from how you thought it would be. But having talked to other parents, it seems to me that wanting to give your children back for a moment because you are so tired and fed up with the responsibility is hardly unique to us.

3. **You write about other people's difficulties and struggles in trying to get pregnant, or to reach full term, or to understand their infertility. Yet you only heard about these things when you started trying yourselves. No one really ever educates you about how difficult it can be to get pregnant, only about how not to get pregnant when you don't want to. Why do you think infertility remains such a taboo subject? (Sarah Harding)**
It's not something I thought about a great deal at the time; I was too busy going through it and hoping there would be a nice, simple, wrapped-up-with-a-bow answer to our problems. I think the taboo stems from two other hush-hush topics: sex and failure, neither of which accompanies roast beef at Sunday dinner as a conversation topic. I was shocked when you told me that as many as one in six couples experience infertility, for at the time I felt like I was the only one.

It's hard to have conversations about infertility. We celebrate when women get pregnant the first time, as if it's a hole-in-one on the golf course, a real achievement. And when it takes a long time, or doesn't happen at all, it's a sign that our bodies don't work properly. As a society, we shy away from failure, we hush it up and sweep it under the carpet, and that makes it even harder for couples like us to feel that we can talk about it. So we don't, and a vicious cycle is created. As I mention in the book, when I told people I couldn't have children, they looked at me as if I'd said 'cancer'. They felt empathy and sympathy but also a powerlessness. I felt disabled by the stigma.

But I think it's also tied up with that very British approach to sex. How can we talk about fertility or infertility if we are not prepared to discuss sex in the first place? It's like the awkward conversation with our GP, where I wanted to shout 'Sex, sex, sex!' at him. This book is about infertility, about the choices we made and how, in the end, we created our family through adoption; and if it starts more discussions about infertility and the support that there is, or is not, in our society, if it helps more women to admit the challenges and struggles they've faced, if it has a few more people sharing the tragedies of their lives, then that will be a good thing. Because until we all start talking about it a little bit more, it will continue to be a hidden burden.

4. What help would you have liked in adopting but didn't get? (Sarah Fox)

Much of the Intensive Training course and discussions with our social workers focused on the children and how to parent them, particularly regarding their specific challenges and issues, such as attachment. Yet one of the areas we struggled with the most was grief for our old life, which wasn't mentioned during any of the training we received even though we wrote about it in our Big Report. I think that there could be a whole lot more done to prepare parents for the all-encompassing change that will happen when they have children, whether by birth or by adoption. Perhaps then there would be less post-natal and post-adoption depression.

No one prepared us for Andy's 'I don't love them' wobble, for the fact that we might experience a glowing honeymoon period that would fade and leave us with children that didn't feel part of our family. When I shared this experience with another adoptive mum, she said her husband had a similar 'don't love them' moment. If only we'd known that this was normal, expected even, then it might not have come as such a shock to me when Andy said it. We would have been a little more prepared.

As an adoptive mum who is also an entrepreneur (aka self-employed), I also wish there had been the same level of financial support for that first year of maternity that there is for people who are employed (giving birth or adopting), or self-employed and giving birth. It feels distinctly unfair that someone should adopt and be financially penalised because she or he is self-employed. The law should be changed so that all parents, adoptive or birth, whatever their employment history, receive maternity or adoption pay (and they should just call it maternity pay and get rid of the separate category for adoption pay, since we are all just parents).

5. **Is there anything in the process that you wish you had or had not done, or anything you think should be changed in the process you went through? (Sally Inkster)**

My experience with the fertility clinics was not what I wished for. There is a world of difference between giving a couple a leaflet about counselling for the fact that they can't have children and feeling listened to and treated as individuals. I would have loved to have a single person who saw us at every appointment, rather than a disjointed string of consultations with different specialists every time. I would have loved those specialists to be more than just qualified in their field; I would have loved them to show compassion and empathy, to look me in the eye and maybe even hold my hand as they told me that I wouldn't have children. I would choose someone with compassion and who connects with me in a heartbeat over someone with so many letters after her name that she forgets that I'm not a number but a woman who wants to have a family. I found that whole experience to be confusing, distant and mechanical. I wanted to have meaningful discussions with my doctor, to have things explained in simple terms when I was emotionally fragile and to feel like someone cared.

Is there anything I wish I had done differently? That's a tricky question. At the time I wish I had quit my job and taken Clomid the first time it was offered; we missed the boat on that option. But then I wouldn't be blessed with the incredible children that are in our lives now. Overall there is nothing I would change about what happened because I feel utterly blessed to have these young people in my life and completing my family.

6. How do you feel about your children tracing their past when they're old enough? (Pam Burrows)

After my father died, I spent a few years delving into the far corners of my own family history to get a sense of who I was and where I came from, so I could ask my mother questions before it was too late. So I think I would empathise with my children's desire to know who they are and where they came from.

Nibbles and Bubbles are part of two sets of families — they are my mother's grandchildren but are also the grandchildren of their birth parents' parents. One day, I hope to be able to show them their entire family tree, to show them all the people who have contributed to the people they are today.

I understand that they might wish to trace their birth parents to find out more about them, to get in touch with them, to learn about the people behind the names. I think I'd want to if I'd been adopted. I also know that I will support them whatever they choose because it is part of my role as an adoptive mum not to stand in their way or make it difficult. I feel that it might be an emotional journey, in the same way that sometimes I can feel a bit left out when they're with their foster family. My self-confidence gets a workout, but I know that their love for other people doesn't affect their love for me. I'll tell myself to grow up, to pull myself together, to woman-up and deal with the emotional tugs on my heartstrings that their journey to trace their birth parents might create in me.

If they choose to trace their birth parents, I don't know how that process will go for them, and how it might affect them emotionally. And I want to be by their side, if they want me to be, every step of the way. They might want to do it entirely on their own, to not include me at all, for this is a very personal journey for them. They might do it separately or together, in private or with full disclosure. I hope I can show them that it's okay for them to do that search while I'm still alive, and that they don't have to wait until I'm gone, as seems to happen so often on those 'find your family' type programmes. By the time they're allowed to start the process they'll be young adults, and hopefully I will have prepared them as best I can to deal with life and everything it throws at them, including making this choice whenever they feel ready to do so.

7. How can other parents prepare themselves for adoption? (Sarah Fox)

I would suggest that you get lots of practice looking after kids, especially the ones people call 'a handful'! The more skills you can get under your belt in terms of knowing how to respond to tantrums, or how to recognise when a child is tired, or even just how to talk to them at their level, the easier that transition will be. I thought as an involved aunty that I had quite a few skills, but the reality of parenting 24/7 was like the difference between driving a bumper car at the fairground and driving a forty-tonne truck with sixteen gears.

My most passionate recommendation would be to get physically fit. Being a parent is a physically demanding role — the younger you are, the stronger you are, the more your body is prepared for the marathon of looking after children and keeping up your energy, the better. If I had my time again, I would lose three stone, start going to the gym three times a week and be considerably more fit, flexible and strong in order to give myself a fighting chance of keeping up with the physical demands.

Unfortunately, we can't store sleep in a bank, because if I could, I would have. I also would have filled my freezer with several months' worth of home-cooked meals that needed little more than a defrost in the microwave, for we really struggled to find the time to feed ourselves in the evening, and better nutrition could only have helped.

8. Have you considered how your children may react if at some time in the future they read your book and it brings up old painful memories? (Dr Lynda Shaw)

I thought a great deal about how my children, and the other people mentioned in this book, would react when they read it, for this book is not just about me — it is about my husband, my children and many others. I made some conscious decisions about what to include and exclude from this book, such that it is *my own* journey to becoming my children's mummy. It isn't even Andy's story, because he remembers it differently. I asked permission, of those who could give it, to use their roles in my story as part of this book, and I was particularly concerned about the impact it might have on my husband and my children. Andy gave the book his blessing and at times adjusted the story when our memories diverged too much. I also asked my children, and whilst they both said yes it was okay that I write about them, they're too young to really answer that question.

I would hope that there is nothing in this book that they have not heard before, for over the last four years, we've talked about and reminded them of their entire life story, including what we know of the time before we met them. Ken and Mary provided excellent books packed with photos of the time they lived with them, and Nibbles and Bubbles still ask to read them and explore their past.

Life story work is very important for adopted children, so we use every opportunity to remind them of the whole of their story, even if they have no memory of it at all; they only remember the stories in this book because we keep them alive through photos and reminiscing. They will never remember being told they were adopted because it is something they have always known, even if they didn't understand what it meant when they first heard the words.

I guess it will be up to us to decide at what age they are ready, psychologically and emotionally, to read this book. I have deliberately not included their backstory in this book for reasons I have already explained.

Will it bring up painful memories? I don't think so, but I cannot be sure. I do wonder if my children will think differently about me, and about the adoption, as a result of reading this. I hope not. For there is nothing that I wouldn't do to protect my children.

Printed in Great Britain
by Amazon